From the Future

From the Future

Getting to Grips with Pannenberg's Thought

John McClean

First published 2013 by Paternoster
Paternoster is an imprint of Authentic Media Limited
PO Box 6326, Bletchley, Milton Keynes, MK1 9GG.
authenticmedia.co.uk

British Library Cataloguing in Publication Data

A catalogue record for this book is available from the British Library

ISBN 978-1-84227-756-0
978-1-78078-308-6 (e-book)

Cover Design by David Smart
Printed and bound by Lightning Source

Contents

Abbreviations

Each of Pannenberg's works receives a full reference when it first occurs. Thereafter each work is referred to by the abbreviation given below. Other works treated in the same way are also listed below.

ATP   *Anthropology in Theological Perspective* (trans. M.J. O'Connell; Edinburgh: T&T Clark, 1999)

BQT 1–3   *Basic Questions in Theology* (trans. G.H. Kehm, 3 vols; London: SCM, 1970–72)

BWE   *Beginning with the End: God, Science and Wolfhart Pannenberg* (ed. C.R. Albright and J. Haugen; Chicago: Open Court, 1997)

IST   *An Introduction to Systematic Theology* (Grand Rapids: Eerdmans, 1991)

JGM   *Jesus – God and Man* (trans. L.L. Wilkins and D.A. Priebe; Philadelphia: Westminster, 1977, 2nd English edn)

MIG   *Metaphysics and the Idea of God* (trans. Philip Clayton; Grand Rapids: Eerdmans, 1990)

RaH   *Revelation as History* (ed. W. Pannenberg; trans. D. Granskou; London: Macmillan, 1968)

ST 1–3   *Systematic Theology* (trans. Geoffrey Bromiley, 3 vols; Grand Rapids/Edinburgh: Eerdmans/ T&T Clark, 1991–7).

TKG   *Theology and the Kingdom of God* (ed. R.J. Neuhaus; Philadelphia: Westminster; 1969)

TPS   *Theology and the Philosophy of Science* (trans. F. McDonagh; London: Darton, Longman & Todd, 1976)

TTN	*Towards a Theology of Nature: Essays on Science and Faith [TTN]* (ed. Ted Peters; Louisville/Philadelphia: Westminster/John Knox, 1993).
TWP	*The Theology of Wolfhart Pannenberg* (ed. Carl Braaten and Philip Clayton; Minneapolis: Augsburg, 1988)
ABD	*Anchor Bible Dictionary* (6 vols; New York: Doubleday, 1992)
CD	K. Barth, *Church Dogmatics*
CDP	*Cambridge Dictionary of Philosophy* (ed. R. Audi; Cambridge: Cambridge University Press, 2nd edn, 1999)
Inst.	J. Calvin, *Institutes of Christian Religion*
NPNF	*Nicene and Post-Nicene Fathers*
Summa	Thomas Aquinas, *Summa Theologica*

Abbreviations of Journal Titles

AD	*Ars Disputandi*
AsTJ	*Asbury Theological Journal*
CC	*Christian Century*
CTJ	*Calvin Theological Journal*
CTQ	*Concordia Theological Quarterly*
CTR	*Criswell Theological Review*
CurTM	*Currents in Theology and Mission*
EvQ	*Evangelical Quarterly*
ExpTim	*Expository Times*
IJPS	*International Journal of Philosophical Studies*
IJST	*International Journal for Systematic Theology*
ISR	*Interdisciplinary Science Reviews*
JBS	*Journal of Biblical Studies*
JES	*Journal of Ecumenical Studies*
JETS	*Journal of the Evangelical Theological Society*
JR	*Journal of Religion*
JSHJ	*Journal for the Study of the Historical Jesus*
JTS	*Journal of Theological Studies*
NTS	*New Testament Studies*

NZSTR	Neue Zeitschrift für Systematische Theologie und Religionsphilosophie
PRSt	Perspectives in Religious Studies
RBL	Review of Biblical Literature
SBJT	Southern Baptist Journal of Theology
SJT	Scottish Journal of Theology
TrinJ	Trinity Journal
TS	Theological Studies
TSK	Theologische Studien und Kritiken
ThTo	Theology Today
TynBul	Tyndale Bulletin
WTJ	Westminster Theological Journal

Preface

As I finish writing this book I am very aware of the people who have shaped and helped my thinking, as well as those who have encouraged and supported me in the various steps along the way.

I began thinking about systematic theology and reading Wolfhart Pannenberg when I was a student at Moore College in the early 1990s. Peter Jensen, then Principal, particularly challenged us to give eschatology a place in systematic theology as a structural element and not simply as an isolated topic. That challenge continued to stimulate my thinking, especially as I understood how key eschatology is to the thought of the New Testament. Robert Doyle's teaching deepend my engagement with systematic theology and convinced me of the importance of historical theology. Soon after I graduated from Moore College I began work on a thesis for an MTh under the supervision of Robert Doyle. I decided that I would examine Wolfhart Pannenberg as a contemporary systematic theologian who had allowed eschatology to shape theology. I have valued the support and interest of Peter and Robert in the years since.

In 2003 I began to teach at the Presbyterian Theological Centre. At the time I thought that I had an almost complete MTh thesis, however Robert Doyle suggested that I should develop it as a doctoral thesis. After a few years finding my feet in teaching, I enrolled with the Melbourne College of Divinity (now MCD University of Divinity). Christiaan Mostert, my supervisor, showed great grace and patience and proved a reliable and inspiring guide into the thought of Wolfhart Pannenberg and a model of Christian scholarship. My colleagues at PTC were also a great encouragement. John Davies (Principal till 2009) and Ian Smith (Principal since 2010) supported my work on the thesis and the book. They also read both works and provided invaluable proofreading. Teaching at PTC is a great joy. I have learned so much from students as well as from my preparation. This book harvests some of those insights into theology and I have tried to write for theology students. One student, Sheryl Sarkoezy, read the manuscript and gave some very constructive comments as well as helping me find the confidence to finish.

Before I began to study theology formally God blessed me with a family in which I learned the Christian faith and saw it lived consistently. My mother, Marslaidh (1939–87), taught me the basics of study as well as the basics of the Christian life. Twenty-two years after her death, her absence remains a source of pain that will only be healed in the eschaton. I'm sure that my father, William, was the first person with whom I argued about theology and he has always been interested in and encouraging of my theological writing.

When I married Elizabeth she knew that she was getting a theologian. I cannot express how encouraging and supportive she has been of my work, study and writing. Like everything else in my life, this book is a product of our partnership and only achieved because of her love. Michael and Brianna have both grown up with me working on 'the thesis' and then 'the book'. It is wonderful to see them growing into impressive young adults. I pray they will grasp the hope of God's future, even if they never read this book.

There are many family members, friends, colleagues and students who have contributed to this book in innumerable ways. I have benefitted from stimulating conversations, supportive enquiries, searching questions, rich fellowship and loving prayers. I cannot hope to list everyone who has helped get this book written.

My prayer is that this book will help to introduce a great Christian theologian and will help readers think about why theology matters and how it may be done faithfully. I pray that this book will glorify God by helping God's people think deeply about him and understand more fully their life in him. Studying Pannenberg has helped me grasp more of the wonder of God's love in the work of creation, reconciliation, and consummation. My words fall far short of the God they seek to describe, but I pray that the Spirit may use them in the praise of the infinite, Triune God.

John McClean
August 2012

Introduction

I have written this book with two goals but for one main reason. I want to give you an orientation to the thought of Wolfhart Pannenberg, the great German theologian and I want to help you think about theology by having a conversation with him. Let me explain the reason and then return to the goals.

I am convinced that theology is such an important exercise for Christians that it is worth doing well. Theology is the study of God, Christian reflection on God and his ways, his word and his world. As I explain in Chapter 3, theology helps Christians to know God and to live for him. It provides a kind of map to help us understand what we know of God and to help us think about how we live in light of that knowledge. I hope this book will help you think about why theology is important and how it can be done well. Pannenberg is an interesting figure, but the reason to make the effort to understand his thought is because he helps us think well about God. All Christians have some kind of theology with which we navigate life. Engagement with Pannenberg can help us develop that theology in rich ways, making use of ancient Christian tradition and recent developments.

The conviction that Pannenberg can help us do theology well leads to the two goals of the book. First, this is an introduction to Pannenberg's theology which I hope will serve theology students, pastors and engaged Christians: people who are not specialist theologians but who want to understand an important modern Christian thinker. Pannenberg's theology is not easy. He thinks on an enormous scale, integrating ideas from a wide range of disciplines into a very sophisticated position. It takes some effort to discover how that integration is achieved. Moreover, for those of us who are English speakers and used to evangelical theology, his style of theology is quite unusual. So an introduction to his thought is justified. There are several good introductions to Pannenberg's thought, yet they all assume good knowledge of theology, its terms and history.[1] In this book I fill in some of the background information, explaining the thinkers with whom and the debates in which Pannenberg was engaged. I also dedicate a chapter to explaining Pannenberg's very distinctive idea of how reality operates (his 'metaphysic'). He claims that things are what they are because of what they will be in the end, that is, reality comes from the future. Our commonsense idea is usually that the past creates the future; Pannenberg claims the reverse. I have found that understanding why Pannenberg claims this and tracing how this 'metaphysic' works in his thought is a key to 'getting' him. I think you will find that following that track makes Pannenberg easier to understand.

My second goal is to help you think about theology using Pannenberg's theology as a starting point. Most of the chapters include a wider discussion that flows from reflection on his work. Theology is an art and the best way to learn about it is to look at the works of a master. Discussions about theological method risk being bland and thin because they are abstracted from any actual discussion. I find it far more satisfying to sit in the theology workshop and watch a great theologian work through an account of the faith. Pannenberg shows what theology can achieve and how to go about it. Like any master class we learn a great deal from the strengths of Pannenberg's works. At some points I disagree with him and argue that elements of his theology are not satisfactory. There is still much to learn in trying to clarify the problems and to think about what different approach could be used. He is very aware that theology requires ongoing critical discussion and reformulation of views, and I hope this book makes some small contribution to that discussion. I have not set out to be comprehensive in the discussion of Pannenberg or of theology. My aim is to help you engage with an impressive thinker and develop your own reflections on some areas of theology from that.

The book begins by introducing Pannenberg's career and some of the main themes in his work. Chapter 3 looks specifically at his systematic theology, especially his three-volume *Systematic Theology* and how he goes about developing his systematic account.

That chapter finishes with the first wider discussion, about what systematic theology is and what Pannenberg can teach about how to approach it. The following chapter considers Pannenberg's doctrine of revelation. This was a crucial issue in German theological discussion in the generations before Pannenberg and became key to his own project. The chapter finishes with some reflections on the strengths of his view and some suggestions about how it could be further strengthened. Chapter 5 is probably the key chapter in the book, since it outlines Pannenberg's metaphysical proposal and some of the responses to it. I finish that chapter with some suggestions about how we can assess the proposal.

Once Pannenberg's approach to theology and metaphysics is clear, I turn to his treatment of three important doctrines. Chapter 6 considers his Christology which is focused on the historical human Jesus and reformulates classical two-nature Christology. The chapter looks at how his theology compares to the classic approach and points out the relative strengths of both. It finishes by raising a concern about Pannenberg's Christology: that he cannot give an adequate account of how Jesus is truly divine and human. I suggest that the most important way to see if this is a genuine problem is by examining his doctrine of redemption. Chapter 7, therefore, is a study of this topic, showing how Pannenberg understands Jesus as the reconciling representative of sinners. This chapter helps to show that Christology and redemption are always closely connected and argues that the suspected weakness in Pannenberg's Christology emerges again in his doctrine of redemption. The final substantial chapter takes up Pannenberg's doctrine of God, the very heart of his theology. Again Pannenberg reworks the classic doctrines, dealing with problems he perceives in the tradition. Impressive as his account is (and it most certainly is), I argue that his very method of theology precludes him from incorporating important biblical themes. The conclusion offers some reflections on what Pannenberg has achieved and what other Christians can learn from engaging with him.

My own theological convictions are reformed and evangelical. I am a Presbyterian minister and happily subscribe to the Westminster Confession of Faith in the terms required by the Presbyterian Church of Australia. I have written from that point of view and many of my comments about theology relate particularly to evangelical theology. Pannenberg comes from a quite different tradition. He is a German Lutheran who has drawn on critical biblical scholarship. In these discussions I am not trying to press him into my theological mould, nor am I attempting to defend my own convictions over against his. No doubt my convictions show through and my critical comments about Pannenberg hint at how I would defend my position. My goal has been to build a discussion of theology, learning from Pannenberg. Folk from my theological persuasion can live in a very confined theological world and I have found Pannenberg personally helpful in expanding my horizons and encouraging me to think more carefully about how I approach theology. I hope you will find a discussion with him helps in the same way.

My research into Pannenberg's thought led to a doctoral thesis on *Anticipation in the Thought of Wolfhart Pannenberg*.[2] The thesis contains a study of the philosophical background of Pannenberg's thought and more technical discussions of his metaphysical proposal. It also has more detailed interaction with his theology. This book develops much of the material from the thesis; if you want to follow up some of the detailed arguments the thesis is available on the electronic repository of the MCD University of Divinity.

My language about God is gender-specific. If that is not your style I hope you will not find it overly grating. I think something is lost if we entirely avoid calling God 'he'. The alternatives of constant use of 'God' or resorting to the adjective 'divine' are cumbersome, to say the least. There is a theological point at stake as well, as Pannenberg points out.[3] Like him I am persuaded by the argument that God's own revelation of himself as the One God who is Father, Son and Spirit is best reflected by retaining the common biblical pattern of using male personal pronouns for God.[4]

1.

God, History and Hope: Introducing Pannenberg

When we open Wolfhart Pannenberg's *Systematic Theology* we find a dense discussion of abstract ideas which seem removed from the details that fill our daily lives. Yet appearances deceive, for everyone is connected to a time and place and even the most abstract discussions turn out to have a historical context. As we explore Pannenberg's thought we need to see something of the culture in which he has lived and note the events, traditions and teachers that influenced him. This chapter traces Pannenberg's life and career to show why God, history and hope are important themes for him. Some authors make very clear the issues that concern them in their context. For Pannenberg it takes a little more digging to discover such issues. A study of his life suggests why some things have turned out to be very important to him.[1]

Flooded by Light

Wolfhart Pannenberg is one of the generation who came of age in Germany in the years after World War II. He was born in 1928 in Stettin (now Szczecin in Poland) and his family moved to Schneidemühl (now Piła in Poland) and then to Aachen and finally to Berlin in 1942. His was a secular family that had separated from the church when Pannenberg was a very young child. He loved music and as a young boy learned to play the piano, wrote music and enjoyed listening to the local orchestra. Toward the end of the war, when he was in his mid-teens, he came close to being killed by

Allied bombing on Berlin and only a few months later his family home was destroyed and he moved to live with relatives back to the east in Pomerania. There he had his first introduction to the Christian faith, by one of its most trenchant critics. Pannenberg's love of music led him to read *The Birth of Tragedy from the Spirit of Music* by the philosopher Friedrich Nietzsche (1844–1900).[2] This early work of Nietzsche led Pannenberg to explore more of his writings.[3]

Nietzsche has been called 'the most lethal adversary of the Christian faith in modern times'.[4] He was convinced that the 'God-hypothesis' and all religious and metaphysical interpretations of the world and humanity are untenable.[5] In his view, the world has no created order but 'is to all eternity chaos; not by the absence of necessity, but in the sense of the absence of order, structure, form, beauty, wisdom, and whatever else our aesthetic humanities are called'.[6] It is interesting to imagine a young man watching his nation collapse in the last stages of the war, and facing conscription himself, reading Nietzsche's radical philosophy. It clearly had an impact on Pannenberg and in later years he came to the view that Nietzsche must be answered before theology can proceed to talk about God.[7]

Not long after discovering the writings of Nietzsche, Pannenberg had an experience that opened him to the possibility of the existence of God.

The single most important experience occurred in early January 1945, when I was 16 years old. On a lonely two-hour walk home from my piano lesson, seeing an otherwise ordinary sunset, I was suddenly flooded by light and absorbed in a sea of light which, although it did not extinguish the humble awareness of my finite existence, overflowed the barriers that normally separate us from the surrounding world . . . I did not know at the time that January 6 was the day of Epiphany, nor did I realize that in that moment Jesus Christ had claimed my life as a witness to the transfiguration of this world in the illuminating power and judgment of his glory. But there began a period of craving to understand the meaning of life, and since philosophy did not seem to offer the ultimate answers to such a quest, I finally decided to probe the Christian tradition more seriously than I had considered worthwhile before.[8]

Pannenberg's probing remained a matter of personal reflection for the time being, as he was recruited into the German army. After training, he was posted to the front but developed scabies and so did not see action. Soon the German Army was defeated and Pannenberg was a prisoner of the British in Germany for a short while.

Later in 1945 Pannenberg returned to Berlin to continue his schooling. Around the same time he met Christians who were, surprisingly, 'jolly and joyous human beings', nothing like the portrait of Christians drawn by Nietzsche. One was his teacher for German literature. These acquaintances, along with his light experience, led him to enrol in Humboldt University to study philosophy and theology.

In these formative events for Pannenberg's faith and career several themes are already apparent. Having come to Christianity from secularism he was very aware that faith is not straightforward for many modern people. He was very sensitive to Nietzsche's criticisms of Christianity and more generally to the strain of intellectual atheism that was very influential in German thought. His description of the light experience had obvious mystical dimensions. Pannenberg is usually considered anything but a Christian mystic, yet his initial steps to faith were prompted by a vision which seemed to him to be a foreshadowing of a revelation of God's glory which would fill the whole world and include him. It is fascinating to see how such a vision plays a key role in the structure of his thought and how it guides his response to the questions of intellectual atheism.

Studying Theology

Pannenberg began to study theology with some of the great German scholars of the era. He studied with Karl Barth (1886–1968) in Basel for a semester. Barth set much of the future context of his thought (in agreement and disagreement). He retained from Barth the emphasis on the sovereignty of God in revelation and God's sublimity and majesty. However, he saw that Barth's position implied a dualism.

> It seemed to me that the truly sovereign God could not be regarded as
> absent or superfluous in ordinary human experience and philosophical

reflection, but that every single reality should prove incomprehensible (at least in its depth) without recourse to God, if he actually was the Creator of the world as Barth thought him to be. Increasingly it seemed to me inconsistent with that assumption that Barth presented God's revelation as if God had entered a foreign country instead of 'his home', as the Gospel of John tells us (1:11). Therefore, I felt that my philosophy and theology should not be permitted to separate, but that within their unity it should be possible to affirm the awe-inspiring otherness of God even more uncompromisingly than Barth had done.[9]

Gerhard von Rad (1901–71) introduced Pannenberg to an approach to Old Testament exegesis which was both critical and theological. He says of Von Rad, 'his thesis, that God is acting with Israel and with all humanity in history and that history is constituted by the acts of God, has influenced me more than any other thing that I learned as a student'.[10] Throughout Pannenberg's thought, the relationship of God to history has been a constant theme.

Philosophy Teachers

Much of Pannenberg's early training was in philosophy and philosophical theology. The way in which philosophical and theological thought have developed alongside each other and have interacted has been an important part of his thought and he has written several accounts of the historical development of philosophy and its relation to theology.[11] The teacher who introduced Pannenberg to the formal study of the history of philosophy was Karl Löwith (1897–1973) at the University of Heidelberg.[12]

Löwith had studied under two of the great philosophers of the late nineteenth and early twentieth centuries, Wilhelm Dilthey (1833–1911) and Martin Heidegger (1889–1976), and was greatly influenced by Heidegger and Nietzsche.[13] Dilthey and Heidegger were part of the great movement in philosophy that rejected any notion of a reality that lies beyond the immediate human experience. Both of them held that whatever truth we may be able to access is available to us only in the realm of history and concrete human experience. For most of Christian history most people in the West have been happy to accept that there is a transcendent

God who exists outside of our realm and is the basis for truth. This kind of view can be found in thinkers such as Plato and Aristotle (though they would not necessarily call the ultimate reality 'god'). Dilthey argued that all such metaphysical thought happens in a historical context which means that claims about the Absolute are always changing (and so not absolute). Pannenberg came to have a high regard for Dilthey; Gutenson records that in his last lectures before retirement Pannenberg attributed to Dilthey the greatest influence on his historical view of truth.[14] Heidegger disagreed with Dilthey in many ways, however he also rejected any attempt to develop 'metaphysics'. He insisted that an attempt to understand 'being' must start from a concrete, specific, local setting; not from some grand idea of a god.

Löwith, who had to live in exile from Germany for eighteen years because of his Jewish background, traced what he saw as the demise of Western civilization to a philosophical decay. This decay, he felt, came from the rejection of metaphysics found in Nietzsche and Dilthey and culminating in Heidegger. However he also included Christianity in his critique, since he thought that it led to a hope that meaning could be found in a historical process with a messianic redeemer. This hope had allowed Heidegger to hail Hitler as the Führer. Löwith proposed a return to classical Greek thought and Stoicism which finds meaning in the structure of nature rather than in history.[15] In this case, Pannenberg came to share much of his teacher's assessment of the problem, but sought the answer in demonstrating that the Triune God of Christianity unites history and nature in a way that restores meaning.

So in his early years Pannenberg was influenced by Nietzsche, Dilthey and Heidegger, three powerful German thinkers who rejected belief in God at the most basic level. Despite these influences Pannenberg was becoming a Christian theologian. The questions which these thinkers raised continued to challenge him, and answering their challenge became a major goal for Pannenberg's theological work. It is impossible to understand his project in depth without some familiarity with Nietzsche, Dilthey and Heidegger.

Pannenberg completed a doctorate, writing a dissertation on predestination in the thought of the medieval theologian Duns Scotus and his *Habilitationsschrift* on the concept of analogy in medieval theology. Thus he received a thorough grounding in the history of theology and particularly in medieval theology. Pannenberg's theological method has relied heavily on the exposition of historical theology and his early work as a scholar helped to lay a foundation for this. Pannenberg completed his doctorate in 1953 and was ordained as a Lutheran pastor the same year.

Heidelberg, Hegel and History

Pannenberg began his career as a theological teacher at Heidelberg. During this time he realized how important Hegel was for modern theology. Hegel's approach is very different from the anti-metaphysical approaches of Nietzsche, Dilthey and Heidegger. He offers an account of reality in which God (or rather the Absolute) is found in history. For him the historical process is an unfolding of the existence of *Geist* (spirit), which is both collective human insight and the infinite God. Here was another thinker who held that history is the key to reality, though this time he found a metaphysic within history. There is no doubt that Hegel had a significant influence on Pannenberg, though the exact nature and extent of the influence is debated by interpreters.

Pannenberg's early theological work was done with a group of friends in Heidelberg and they formed what was sometimes called the 'Pannenberg circle'. In the 1950s the issue of revelation was a focus of discussion in German theology which was dominated by the 'kerygmatic' approach of Barth and Rudolf Bultmann (1884–1976). The term comes from the Greek work *kerygma* which means 'a proclamation', that is the message of the gospel. Barth and Bultmann called theology to focus on a preached message, not on the results of historical investigation of the events which may lie behind the text.[16] For Bultmann revelation occurred 'in the moment of faith connecting with the word of the cross', while for Barth revelation was 'in the person and work of Jesus Christ' and was unapproachable from any human perspective. Against these views, Pannenberg and his group called for a return to a focus on history as the realm of revelation. They published a collection of essays titled *Revelation as History*, to which Pannenberg contributed the introduction and a chapter titled 'Dogmatic Theses on the Doctrine of Revelation'.[17] In this he identifies divine revelation with universal history which is only completed in the eschaton, that is in the final state of God's kingdom. That is, against Barth and Bultmann, he asserts that God is revealed in the whole of history (not simply a few special events). The revelation in the whole of history only becomes apparent at the end of history in the consummation of God's kingdom. Does that mean that Pannenberg thinks that revelation is entirely delayed? No, he claims that there is a proleptic revelation, that is a revelation which anticipates the full event. He describes revelation as first realized in 'the fate of Jesus of Nazareth, insofar as the end of all events is anticipated in his fate'.[18] These theses of a universal future revelation and its anticipation in Jesus became programmatic for his entire project.

Wuppertal and Eschatology

Pannenberg became a professor of theology and a colleague of Jürgen Moltmann (b. 1926) in Wuppertal. Pannenberg and Moltmann appeared to have a great deal in common. Both had been students of Karl Barth soon after World War II, both interacted with Bloch and emphasized the importance of hope and the future. This meant that in the early years they were often grouped together as theologians of hope. However over time they took very different approaches to theology. Both emphasized the importance of eschatology for theology. Eschatology (from the Greek word *eschaton* – the end) is used in theology to refer to the hope of full and final redemption for the individual and for the cosmos. Different theologians can have radically varying eschatologies. Both Pannenberg and Moltmann learned something of the importance of the future from the German Marxist philosopher Ernst Bloch (1885–1977).[19] As you would expect from a Marxist thinker, Bloch was an atheist. However, he took from Aristotle the idea that the material world and human history are full of possibilities and he thought that history had 'a promise of ultimate redemption'.[20] He saw that humans live with a hope which turns them toward the future.

Moltmann's first great work, *Theology of Hope*, was a response to Bloch's philosophy of hope.[21] Pannenberg was not as closely engaged with Bloch, but seems to have found a 'provocative confluence' in Bloch's thought which assisted him to articulate his position.[22]

Chicago and Process Theology

In 1961 Pannenberg took the chair in systematic theology at the University of Mainz and in 1963 he visited the University of Chicago as a guest professor. There he encountered process philosophy and the thought of A.N. Whitehead (1861–1947). Pannenberg recalls that in theological circles in Chicago, 'you couldn't survive intellectually at that time without having read everything of Whitehead'.[23] Whitehead was a British mathematician who finally became a professor of philosophy at Harvard University in Massachusetts. In his thought about reality he rejected the idea that existence depends on underlying 'substances'.

On the traditional view, any thing (a human, animal, object) has a nature (for example it is a person). Over time the thing is acted on or it acts (the person grows and learns and changes cities and has children). Those changes alter the attributes and relationships of the thing but its underlying nature (the 'human nature') remains because that is what it is. Whitehead thought that reality consists not in the underlying nature but in events. Reality is a process, not a process which happens to things but a process in which 'things', including minds, are always changing. Rethinking reality in this way meant rethinking God as well, which Whitehead was quite ready to do. On his view, the traditional picture of God was too much like an ancient monarch, God remained too much like an Egyptian or Mesopotamian king, transcendent, independent, unchanging and 'internally complete'.[24] In Whitehead's version God is the totality of the process and is thought of as having a twofold nature. There is a 'primordial nature', which is the sum total of all the possible events in the universal process and the 'consequential nature' in which God consists of all events which take place at every time. The primordial nature supplies to reality the possibilities which unfold under God's influence, though not under his control. On this view, God is not the omnipotent ruler but 'the lure for feeling, the eternal urge of desire', 'the poet of the world' and the fellow-sufferer with the universe. As we explore Pannenberg's thought there are some intriguing similarities between his view and Whitehead's. Yet Pannenberg rejects the idea that he is a process theologian and claims that his approach is quite different. At this stage it is important to notice that Pannenberg saw process theology as an important idea which needed to be discussed.

Pannenberg's time in the USA also led to him becoming well known there. Like several other German theologians of the twentieth century, Pannenberg was at least as well known in North America as he was in Germany, and US theologians were important interpreters of his thought.

Jesus – God and Man

Pannenberg's famous christological work, *Jesus – God and Man*, was written during the 1960s and develops the same programme as *Revelation as History*.[25] Although the philosophical questions were very important to him, so were the questions of history and the historical study of Jesus. Part of his genius is that he has been able to draw the philosophical concerns and New Testament history questions together. This combination has not satisfied everyone, and both New Testament scholars and philosophical theologians often look askance at what seems to them to be a strange amalgam. We will return to Pannenberg's integration of the two sets of questions in a later chapter. For now we can concentrate on the main points he makes in *Jesus – God and Man*.

The New Testament scholarship which Pannenberg encountered as a young theologian was focused on the historical study of Jesus.[26] In the generation before him Bultmann had declared that almost nothing could be known of the historical Jesus and that theology should think of itself as independent of the historical Jesus. Pannenberg's contemporaries Günther Bornkamm (1905–90) and Ernst Käsemann (1906–98) led what came to be known as the 'New Quest' for the historical Jesus. From 1949 Bornkamm taught at Heidelberg where Pannenberg both studied and taught, and Bornkamm's book *Jesus of Nazareth (Jesus von Nazareth)* was the most influential work on the historical Jesus at the time.[27]

Several claims made by Bornkamm became central for Pannenberg's approach to Jesus. Bornkamm did not think that Jesus had claimed to be the messiah or called himself the Son of Man (he argued that for Jesus 'the Son of Man' was the future judge of the world). 'There is in fact not one single certain proof of Jesus' claiming for himself one of the Messianic titles which tradition has ascribed to him ... nowhere does this seem to be of any importance either in his preaching of the coming of the kingdom of God.'[28] Rather than his claims about himself, Bornkamm thought that it was Jesus' actions and his message which brought the kingdom into the present. 'It is the special character of his message and work, that Jesus is to be found *in* his word and *in* his actions, and that he does not make his own rank a special theme of his message prior to everything else ... His word is action and event, and his ministry a sign of the reign of God which is already dawning.'[29]

For Bornkamm what the New Testament gospels record is not the mere historical Jesus but the historical Jesus understood in the light of the resurrection. The Jesus of the gospels is not a fantasy, Bornkamm views him as the risen Lord, however his identity is only revealed (even to himself) in his resurrection which casts its light on his message and actions. 'The Messianic character of his being is contained in his words and deeds and in the unmediatedness of his historic appearance ... the secret of his being could only reveal itself to his disciples in his resurrection.'[30]

Pannenberg pursues a 'Christology from below'; that is one that starts from the historical Jesus, not from the assumption that Jesus is divine. He takes up Bornkamm's idea 'that Jesus' claim [that the kingdom is present with him] results from the presence of the expected eschatological future in [his] activity'.[31] If Jesus makes such a claim, how can it be considered true? Pannenberg finds the answer in the resurrection. He argues that Jesus expected 'the imminent universal resurrection from the dead', and this was the 'expected eschatological future'. When Jesus rose from the dead it was apparent that the kingdom had been already present in his miracles and teaching. The logic of this claim may be seen clearly in the reverse: if Jesus had not risen, then the expectation aroused by his ministry would have been shown to be misdirected, since he would have been a messianic pretender and blasphemer. However, he did rise again and that event confirmed the truthfulness of earlier hopes.

Thus the expectation of the resurrection for the saints at the end of time gave Jesus' own resurrection 'immediate, inherent significance' and implied his unity with God, and hence his divinity.[32]

Apart from the resurrection Pannenberg would have no Christology.[33] He states that the 'resurrection event has retroactive power' and confirms Jesus' pre-Easter claim to be the Son of God. Pannenberg claims that 'what has become evident in the resurrection . . . has been on the stage from the very beginning' and 'it had been on stage from the very beginning because Jesus has been raised from the dead'.[34] Notice in this statement the interplay of time frames. The resurrection reveals what has always been true and it is true because of the resurrection. The fundamental importance of the future for determining all reality is a sustained theme in Pannenberg's thought, and I will argue that it is a key aspect for understanding and assessing his thought.

Munich and Method

In 1967 Pannenberg became Professor of Theology at the University of Munich. After the publication of *Jesus – God and Man*, Pannenberg's published work focused more on theological method. One of his concerns was to argue that theology is a science. The idea that theology needed to establish itself as a 'science' has a particular background in Germany. In the nineteenth century Wilhelm von Humboldt had organized the University of Berlin as a model of Enlightenment education. The faculty of theology had to concede primacy to philosophy, and theology was widely criticized for its failure to be a 'science' (*Wissenschaft*). Various proposals were made about how theology should be reformed.

The term *Wissenschaft* is often translated as 'science' but it is not equivalent to what English speakers might mean by 'natural sciences'. Rather it refers to 'scholarly enquiry'. It was used from the early nineteenth century for disciplines which operated with the ideal that 'no predetermined conception of truth should interfere with the pursuit of science and learning' and both teachers and students should be free from any confessional limits (or concern about the practical value of their study). *Wissenschaftsideologie* was the ideal of 'pure' research in which scholarly inquiry was answerable only to reason.[35] Theology which held the biblical texts as norms and was constrained by commitments to creeds or confessions did not fit the ideal.

Pannenberg takes up this discussion and insists that as a science theology must interrogate the truth of its own claims. In this he is sharply critical of Barth. He believes that Barth does not allow theology to examine its own truth claims, but rather demands a positivistic approach to Christian truth. He explains that 'Barth's apparently so lofty objectivity about God and God's word turns out to rest on no more than the irrational subjectivity of a venture of faith with no justification outside itself'.[36] Pannenberg argues that theology is a science (or at least it can be) since theological statements should strive to be realistic and demonstrably so. To be 'realistic' in this context means that there is a reality outside of the words themselves which the words describe and against which the words can be tested for their truthfulness.

Taking theology as the science of God, Pannenberg treats the truth of God as the central hypothesis of theology. He claims that the idea of God must be 'measured and verified *on its own implications*', and since God is the reality which determines all other realities then the implications of the idea of God must be tested against all reality.[37] Pannenberg calls for theology to test its hypotheses for coherence with biblical tradition (or whichever religious tradition they seek to explain) as well as human experience and thought.[38] Pannenberg gives each of these areas a very wide brief. For instance human experience and thought include individual experience, the disciplines of psychology and sociology and the natural sciences as well as philosophical reflection. The test of coherence is that the claims of theology must be able to be shown to make sense in the light of all these areas and to make sense of all these areas. It becomes clear from this why Pannenberg interacts with a vast range of disciplines.

Pannenberg accepts a view that science always works with hypotheses which are open to testing and either refutation or confirmation. However this confirmation is never final, the process of questioning and testing must always continue. According to Pannenberg the hypotheses of theology only find full confirmation in the eschaton, for this is the final revelation of God. Pannenberg holds that the statements of theology, to the extent to which they are true, are true in anticipation of what will come about in the end. In fact he thinks this is the case of all statements, but more obvious in Christian theology since the final revelation of the truth is in the kingdom. This leads to Pannenberg's account of theological language as doxological, that is it is framed as praise of God (doxological comes from the Greek word *doxa* which means 'glory' and it refers to giving God glory). So in theological statements 'the speakers rise above their own finitude to the thought of the infinite God'.

God, Hope and History

Pannenberg remained as a professor in Munich until he retired in 1994. In those years he wrote prolifically and the next chapter surveys some of those books and the themes which develop in them. What Pannenberg writes in his mature works continues and consolidates the themes already apparent in his developing years. Indeed, his work develops so consistently that it is impossible to mark out clear periods in his thought. This chapter has focused on the influences on him and summarized his response to some of them. The next chapter will focus more on the details of his responses (though we will encounter some further influences along the way).

Pannenberg's big question for theology is, 'Is God true?', that is, 'Is the Triune God, the God of Jesus, the reality which determines all other reality?' If this is true, then it will only be true when it is completely apparent that God does determine all things, and that will only occur in God's future kingdom when God is 'all in all' (as the apostle Paul writes in 1 Cor. 15:28). That is, Pannenberg's view of truth is 'eschatological', reality comes from the future.

In the meantime, theology is left with the task of seeking to test and confirm its own claims. How can it do that? It will involve patiently examining the breadth of human experience and considering if it is coherent with the claims. Because of this Pannenberg increasingly felt that he had to show the interaction of theology with a range of other academic disciplines.[39] In particular he has focused on history as the realm in which there are anticipations of the fullness of reality which God will bring. Pannenberg's theology seeks to show the truth of God who is at work in history and who will bring all things into harmony from the future. That is not an abstract theological programme, it is one that he has come to because he wants to answer the questions which confront him as someone in a secular society who surprisingly encountered God and has been convinced that life and history will not make sense apart from God.

2.

Thinking about Everything: Themes in Pannenberg's Thought

Wolfhart Pannenberg is convinced that the true God is the One who determines all reality, so when he comes to think about God he has to think about everything else at the same time. If the idea of God does not bring light to everything else, then it is not a sufficient idea of God; and if Christian theology cannot provide a way of thinking about God that succeeds in this, it has nothing to offer. On the other hand, once you start thinking about the God who created and redeems all things and brings them to perfect unity, you cannot help but think about everything else. In this chapter we will see the wide sweep of Pannenberg's theological interests.

While in principle theology should think about everything, there are some particular areas of life which Pannenberg focuses on and he understands these by engaging with the disciplines which study them. So as well as noting his areas of interest we also need to get some sense of the phenomena he is interested in and the discussions he has about them. In this chapter I will highlight four areas of special interest for Pannenberg: philosophy, anthropology, natural sciences and religions. These themes combine in his work *Systematic Theology* and I will give an outline of that work and some of the features which stand out in its approach to theology.

Philosophy

Philosophy has always been an important part of Pannenberg's thought – Nietzsche gave him an introduction to Christianity! His reflections on the history of philosophy and its interaction with theology culminated in the book *Metaphysics and the Idea of God*. The term 'metaphysics' is difficult to define.[1] Understood in its broadest sense as 'the philosophical investigation of the nature, constitution, and structure of reality', metaphysics involves any view about what exists. On that definition there can be a wide range of metaphysics proposed by various philosophers.[2] Pannenberg uses the term for something more specific: 'the metaphysics of the Absolute' which seeks 'God' in a conceptual 'ascent above everyday experience'. Metaphysics, for Pannenberg, involves the claim that there is an Absolute transcendent reality.[3] This discussion is the central question for both his philosophy and his theology (and their interaction) and that is the focus of *MIG*.

Pannenberg confronts the 'end of metaphysics' – the rise of intellectual atheism and the accompanying demise of metaphysics. His response to the emptiness of the idea of God in the modern world is that 'if the word ["God"] is like a blank face to us, it reminds us by its very strangeness of the lack of meaning in modern life, in which the theme of life's unity and totality is missing and the wholeness of human existence has become an unanswered question'.[4] Pannenberg seeks to re-establish a metaphysical account that can stand with Christian belief.

Some commentators have assessed Pannenberg's thought as more 'philosophical' than 'theological'.[5] Pannenberg would not accept that differentiation since the Christian self-description must be correlated with wider philosophical questions.[6] At the same time he is critical of theology which relies on philosophical systems to provide it with its conceptions.[7] He sees a model of a healthy relationship between theology and philosophy in the confidence of the theologians of the early church. They were convinced that Christian faith had a universal truth and on that basis they competed with the philosophical schools to provide a 'true philosophy', that is to give a definitive account of the 'ultimate basis of reality', as well as of the nature of humanity and the world.[8]

Pannenberg claims that theology makes a special move when it deals with philosophical ideas. The word he uses is that philosophy 'sublates' the themes and concerns of philosophy. To 'sublate' (the German term is *aufheben* of which *Aufhebung* is the cognate noun) is to take up an idea and include it in a new concept so that the original idea is partially negated and yet at the same time it is retained and included in a synthesis. Perhaps the easiest way to imagine sublation is to think of a piece of music in which a particular phrase is repeated, varied and developed. So, for Pannenberg, theology sublates philosophical concepts when it takes them up and shows that they are only fully understood in relation to God, and in doing so transforms them.

In 1996 Pannenberg published *Theologie und Philosophie* which surveys the interaction of Christian theology with philosophy from Plato, Aristotle and the Stoics to the twentieth century. The discussion of recent thought is, not surprisingly, focused on German philosophy, especially on the development of philosophical anthropology. Philosophical anthropology developed in Germany following the demise of metaphysics.[9] Older philosophy took for granted a human nature which was given expression in life. This newer approach saw the self and identity coming into existence through interaction with its environment, both physical and social. This prompted a philosophical discussion of human existence in interaction with biology, psychology and sociology. A key thought was the idea of 'openness to the world' (*Weltoffenheit*) which means that all beings, especially humans, become what they are through a process of interaction with their world. How radical the idea of openness is for these thinkers is shown by their description of humans as *exocentric* (having a centre outside). That is, we are not merely 'open' to the world, we have our centre in our surrounding context, not in ourselves.

Anthropology

Pannenberg engaged with such philosophical anthropology in *Anthropology in Theological Perspective*.[10] He is critical of an approach to theology that is only grounded in human 'subjectivity and self-understanding', yet he affirms the need to deal with anthropological questions.[11] He asserts that 'anthropology has become the terrain on which theologians must base their claim of universal validity for what they say'.[12]

Ludwig Feuerbach (1804–72), the first public German intellectual atheist, argued that religion is an expression of human consciousness, so that the idea of God is not given to human thought, but produced by it. That is, God is a projection of human nature.[13] This means that religion is anti-human and alienating: 'to enrich God, man must become poor; that God may be all, man must be nothing'.[14] Pannenberg notes that modern atheism has continued to argue that God is unnecessary for 'enlightened exercise of human existence' and, in fact, is alienating.[15] Feuerbach's arguments show the failure of any attempt to establish the existence of God based on anthropology. Pannenberg holds that theology must respond to these.

Responding to Feuerbach and philosophical anthropology Pannenberg calls theology to attend to the philosophical debates about freedom and subjectivity in relation to the religious dimension of human experience.[16] His aim is to show that the existence of God is a dimension without which human life, in its historical reality, is incomprehensible. He builds from the idea of human exocentricity to argue that humans are, at base, open to God and have their true identity in him. This identity only comes in the perfected fellowship of the eschaton, so again Pannenberg stresses the future as the source of reality in his thought.[17]

Natural Sciences

Beyond anthropology Pannenberg also interacted with a wide range of sciences.[18] From the late 1960s Pannenberg had been convinced that theology must re-engage with the natural sciences. He recognized that the sciences had proved problematic for Christian theology, and often the two have moved apart.[19] He also criticized Barth for making theology immune from any scientific criticisms. Pannenberg's view is that if the God of the Bible is the Creator[20] of the universe, then it is not possible to understand fully, or even appropriately, the processes of nature without any reference to God. On the contrary, if nature can be adequately understood without reference to the God of the Bible, then that God cannot be the Creator of the universe, and consequently he cannot be truly God.

In contemporary theology a dialogue with science is a common feature. At the stage when Pannenberg began this dialogue it was a relatively new venture, and he is one of the theologians who has continued it in a very sustained way.[21] He met with a group of scientists to discuss their fields and the possible overlaps and together they produced a volume of essays.[22] Some of Pannenberg's thought about science is found in a series of key articles collected in *Towards a Theology of Nature: Essays on Science and Faith*. A later volume, *The Historicity of Nature: Essays on Science and Theology*, contains several further essays in which Pannenberg develops this interaction.[23]

Pannenberg engages extensively with science in his doctrine of creation. He draws on cosmology, particle physics and evolutionary biology to present a vision of 'the expansion of the universe as the Creator's means to the bringing forth of independent forms of creaturely reality'.[24] One of Pannenberg's key questions to scientists concerns the principle of inertia, which he perceives 'played a major role in depriving God of his function in the conservation of nature and in finally rendering him an unnecessary hypothesis'. Related to this is the question of the real contingency of nature and the reversibility of natural processes, which have implications for whether reality can be understood historically, or if scientific abstraction gives the truer picture. If processes are truly reversible, then the apparent directionality of history is an illusion. Finally, 'perhaps the most difficult question' is whether Christian eschatology can be reconciled with cosmological predictions of the future.[25]

The Religions

An area of growing interest for Pannenberg is the place of 'religions' in world history (and theology).[26] As with Pannenberg's discussion of science, part of his motivation is the simple recognition that Christian theology cannot ignore such an important feature of modern life. He opens one article on religions: 'In the present situation of the world the dialog between the religions becomes an important contribution toward the conditions for a peaceful coexistence of nations and cultures'.[27]

Interaction with religions is also a point of contact between Pannenberg's philosophical and anthropological interests. His philosophical claim that 'the idea of God' implies the unity of all reality has a complementary anthropological reality: 'If the one God is to be Creator of the human race, then as self-conscious beings we must have some awareness, however inadequate, of this origin of ours.'[28] He holds that religion is the realm in which this 'unthematized' knowledge of God is found, and God's reality is first indicated by the fact that religion is a 'constitutive part of human nature'. Pannenberg then claims that the knowledge of God is found in 'the history of religions', which he sees as a history of conflict and criticism between religions. This is also 'a history of the manifestation of the divine mystery that is concealed in [the historical religions]'.[29] That is, revelation comes in the process of conflict between religions, rather than first of all within a religion.[30] He then focuses on the historical process in which God's self-revelation in Christ emerges from the religious conflict and he moves quickly to biblical revelation and revelation in Christ as the truth which emerges from religion. He states that 'theology examines the historical religions to determine how far the all-determining reality of God makes itself known in them as the unifying unity of all reality distinct from itself. Christian theology devotes itself to a similar examination of Christianity.'[31]

Pannenberg claims that Christian interaction with other religions must allow for plurality, because of the 'provisional character of human beings in relation to the one divine truth'. This plurality of religions is not presented as 'pluralism in principle', for there is also a christological exclusivism.

As long as Christians take their faith in the eschatological revelation of God in Jesus Christ seriously, they will also stick to the exclusivism in Jesus' challenge of confessing him and to the sentence of Peter that salvation is accessible to human beings in no one else but Jesus Christ.[32]

Pannenberg also insists on an inclusivism based on the reality of God as the Creator of all and the identity of the Creator with the Redeemer. According to Pannenberg, pluralism, exclusivism and inclusivism must be held together in the Christian assessment of other religions. He argues that it is only possible to do so on the basis of a recognition of the provisional nature of present knowledge of God in the light of the final eschatological revelation.

Scripture

It should be evident from the last chapter that Pannenberg seeks to present his theology as a reflection on and account of the teaching of Scripture. There is no doubt that Pannenberg takes this dimension of theology very seriously. Grenz notes that he 'includes lengthy and illuminating discussions of biblical materials throughout the dogmatics'.[33] The influence of Pannenberg's early teachers such as Von Rad is obvious and he has continued to draw on biblical scholarship as a guide to appropriating the biblical message in his theology. Pannenberg's basic method of proceeding in systematic exposition is to examine the relevant biblical material on a particular topic as it has been understood in historical-critical interpretation and then to outline the church's ongoing discussion of this area. Within these discussions, Pannenberg introduces interdisciplinary discussions that he considers relevant. Pannenberg names Gerhard von Rad, Günter Bornkamm and Hans von Campenhausen as important influences on his approach to understanding the Bible. He quotes Von Campenhausen, who taught him that 'you have to be critical with regard to the [biblical] tradition, but no less critical regarding the critics of the tradition'.[34] The indexes of *Systematic Theology* also indicate the extent to which he interacts with critical scholars such as Rudolf Bultmann, Oscar Cullmann, Joachim Jeremias, Walter Kasper, Martin Kähler, H. Merklein, Rudolf Pesch, Rolf Rendtorff, Odil Hannes Steck and Ulrich Wilckens.

Grenz's survey of Pannenberg's theology identifies three central concerns which characterize approaches to systematic theology and which are apparent in Pannenberg's thought: the Bible, the Christian heritage and the contemporary world. He argues that Pannenberg 'seeks to present a delineation of the Christian faith that reflects the main themes of the Bible as he understands them'. He views Pannenberg as having a more conservative approach to theology, in the sense that he seeks to conserve traditional theology (with some reconfiguration) rather than trying to radically rethink it. He also argues that Pannenberg shares many of the concerns of 'confessionalist theologians' though Pannenberg is no 'mere confessionalist', and that his theology is often shaped by 'ecumenical concerns'.[35] Grenz supports the conclusion that Scripture and classical theological tradition are the key sources in Pannenberg's thought.

How Did Pannenberg's Thought Develop?

It is only natural that a thinker develops new themes and insights during a long productive career. Pannenberg has been remarkably stable in his approach to theology and he records that 'when I search my memories and other evidence, I find it difficult to discern any fundamental change in my theological perspective since 1959, when I published an article on "Redemptive Event and History"'.[36] Occasionally critics claim that Pannenberg only develops trinitarian thought late in his career or that his view of God and eschatology has shifted. Although there are changes in emphasis and developments in presentation and argument it is difficult to find any radical new directions within his work.

Systematic Theology shows that Pannenberg's thought has developed along consistent lines from his earlier thought.[37] Christoph Schwöbel notes that through his career Pannenberg has been willing 'to subject his arguments to constant re-examination' and he finds 'significant shifts in emphasis' in Pannenberg's thought.[38] Charles Gutenson gives an overview of Pannenberg's publications that he can describe as 'recounting a course of research that led to . . . *Systematic Theology*'.[39]

The changes which we can detect in *Systematic Theology* reflect this pattern of careful revision and re-expression along consistent lines. For example, the doctrine of the Trinity becomes central and essential in a way that was not obvious in earlier works. In this shift Pannenberg makes explicit what was implicit (and almost hidden) in his earlier work.[40] He also revises his 'Dogmatic Theses' in the light of changes in his description of the relationship of word and Spirit in revelation.[41] In *Jesus – God and Man* Pannenberg states that Christology must be further developed from a different perspective. *Systematic Theology* then offers this development, in the course of which he revises his earlier rejection of the Reformation doctrine of the threefold office of Christ.[42] He also seems to have shifted from stressing God's 'futurity' to thinking in terms of 'eternity', which is understood as God being his own future, and of eternity entering time from the eschaton.[43] This shift is primarily one of emphasis rather than thoroughgoing revision.[44] Eliers finds a shift from *ST* 1 in which divine and human actions are strongly distinguished to a view in *ST* 3 that believers participate in God's actions through their union with Christ.[45]

Thinking about Everything

Pannenberg sets himself an impossible task as a theologian – he has to show that the true God is the reality which determines all other reality. It is an impossible task because that reality is established from the future, in the fullness of the kingdom of God. Pannenberg is convinced that Christians are right to see Jesus Christ as the presence of the kingdom in history and Christian theology as the testimony of the church to that conviction. Pannenberg seeks to continue that witness by working within the great Christian tradition and engaging with a wide range of disciplines. The Bible is foundational for his approach to theology, although it is certainly not the only source to which he appeals. Rather he presents the conclusions of biblical scholarship and a discussion of the development of Christian theology and weaves into that fascinating discussions of philosophy, anthropology, natural sciences and religions. As he does so he seeks to build a coherent vision of the true God that can serve as both a hypothesis to be tested and a doxological witness.

3.

Thinking about God: Pannenberg and Systematic Theology

Pannenberg is committed to thinking about everything because he is committed to thinking about God. He has a sweeping range of interests because he wants to show that God is required in order to make sense of every other part of reality and this, in turn, is required to show that Christian claims about God are valid. Hence all his thinking finds its integrating point in the discipline of systematic theology because he brings all discussions about various topics back to the point where he can show the connection between that topic and the existence of the Triune God. The move to relate consistently thinking to God as the central theme is typical of systematic theology as a discipline, certainly as Pannenberg practises it. This approach is most fully expressed in his magnum opus, the three-volume *Systematic Theology*.

Pannenberg is sometimes described as being an apologetic theologian – which means he is committed to defending the Christian faith against criticisms and objections. That is true in a sense; certainly the need to counter the atheist critique of Christian faith is central to his work. However, it can be rather confusing to think of him as an apologist, since apologetics usually takes the claims of Christian faith for granted and sets out to defend them. Pannenberg, in contrast, allows the question of the validity of the Christian faith to be an internal question for theology. Theology takes its own claims as hypotheses to be tested. This means that the whole of his *Systematic Theology* is an exploration of the truth of the assertion that the Triune God present in Jesus Christ is the Creator and Redeemer of the universe.

This chapter focuses on Pannenberg as a systematic theologian and considers some of the 'systematic' characteristics of his thought. From that it is natural to turn to some of the assessments various commentators have made of his overall approach to theology. That will help to draw out further some of the major themes of his thought. On the basis of this broad survey of Pannenberg's work I will point out some of the ways we can learn from him about how to go about doing theology. The chapter finishes with some reflection on the discipline of systematic theology.

Systematic Theology

Pannenberg begins *Systematic Theology* by setting theology the task of testing and confirming the truth of Christian claims about God. To do so, the 'idea of God' must be examined for its implications and this first comes from a general discussion of the existence of religion and what that says about God. Pannenberg suggests that it is in the historical interchange and conflict between religions that claims about God can be tested, and he considers Christian claims about revelation in that setting.

From this point Pannenberg begins to work his way through the usual range of theological topics. Volume 1 finishes with chapters on the doctrine of revelation (4), and doctrine of God (5–6). Volume 2 begins with creation (7) and humanity (8). Chapter 9, which considers the connection of Christology and anthropology, is unusual in systematic theologies and reflects the importance Pannenberg places on Christian theology making sense of human existence and experience. The following chapters return to a more usual set of topics: the deity of Jesus (10) and the reconciliation of the world which focuses on the work of Christ in reconciliation (11). Volume 3 then considers the Spirit, the kingdom and the church (12) as an orientation to the work of the Spirit who now brings an anticipation of the kingdom in the life of the church. In Chapter 13 Pannenberg develops his thought about the development of the individual in a social context in a discussion of the messianic community and individuals. The final two chapters deal with election and providence (14) and the consummation (15).

In *Systematic Theology* Pannenberg's discussion is in very close interaction with the history of theology. Most sections consist of a survey of the historical discussion of a topic, through which Pannenberg makes his own comments and observations. He is testing Christian claims by seeking the clearest expression of those claims in the light of all the factors involved. His historical method certainly does not mean that he simply accepts the most recent views as correct. Generally he accepts the challenges of contemporary scholarship but offers a reconfiguration of classical orthodox theology.

In the opening pages of *Systematic Theology* Pannenberg aligns himself with the approach of Vincent of Lérins (d. c.445) who famously argued that church doctrine was to be found in that which was believed 'always, everywhere and by all' (*semper, ubique, et ab omnibus*).[1] Pannenberg's discussions of the history of theology reflect his commitment to the so-called *Vincentian Canon*, though Pannenberg is not willing to accept Vincent's approach as a rule (that is a 'canon'). Rather it is the aspiration of theology. Pannenberg notes that 'the criterion of consensus' is 'not . . . easy to apply' and he is not willing to grant to ecclesiastical consensus, whether Eastern, Roman or Protestant, the authority to determine the truth of dogma. He views the church's consensus on dogma as instrumental, giving expression to understanding which arises from Scripture and must be tested by Scripture: 'content and truth of dogma do not rest . . . on the consensus of the church' but 'knowledge of the subject matter of scripture produces consensus'.[2]

Assessments of Pannenberg

At this point it is worth noticing some of the overall assessments other scholars have made of Pannenberg's thought. Here I am not looking at the points of detail which have engaged commentators with delight, puzzlement or disagreement but at some general assessments of Pannenberg's whole project and his method of executing it. This will help to point out some issues we should think about as we consider his theology.

Grenz observes that some consider Pannenberg is 'too optimistic and too bold in constructing a systematic theology' since he admits that theological claims are provisional and yet presents his work as 'in some sense transcultural and transtemporal'. Similarly, Pannenberg has been criticized for being rationalist, allowing 'rational inquiry as the central, if not the only, arbiter of truth'.[3] Grenz agrees that Pannenberg views the central task of theology as giving a rational account to the world of the Christian faith. While Grenz does not offer an explicit conclusion on the accusation that Pannenberg is 'rationalistic' his positive exposition of Pannenberg's thought suggests that he finds the use of reason appropriate. Grenz highlights the orientation of Pannenberg's thought to the future of the kingdom of God. The elaboration of a 'reason for the Christian hope' is, for Grenz, the 'overarching contribution' of Pannenberg's work.[4]

Shults also takes up the question of how 'rationalist' Pannenberg is, noting that most English-speaking critics have been concerned at Pannenberg's apparent 'foundationalism' and 'rationalism'.[5] In much theological discussion 'rationalism' is used as a negative assessment, suggesting that the thinker is overly dependent on reason, or particular forms of reason. It is a vague criticism which is hard to respond to unless the critic gives specific examples of the claimed 'rationalism'. 'Foundationalism' is a somewhat clearer term. It refers to an approach to knowledge which assumes that the whole edifice of knowledge rests on the foundations of some incontrovertible truths available to human 'reason'. Foundationalism claims that starting from basic   experiences (such as self-awareness and the existence of the world), rational thought can carefully put various bricks of confirmed knowledge in place and finally form a strong wall of truth which is true for any person from any time and place.[6] To call Pannenberg a foundationalist means that he follows this path in theology, so that, starting from the historical evidence for Jesus' resurrection, he argues step by step to show that the claims of Christianity are true. The converse of foundationalism is nonfoundationalism which views human knowledge as 'a web of mutually supporting beliefs, which are mediated through a particular community', that is it is relativistic.[7]

Shults thinks it is a misunderstanding of Pannenberg to describe him as a foundationalist (though clearly he is not a nonfoundationalist). He argues that Pannenberg's approach is postfoundationalist: it accepts that interpretations are dependent on prior commitments and particular communities, but also that knowledge seeks a truth which is not limited to particular contexts. Shults argues that Pannenberg's approach is typical of postfoundationalism since it is interested in fundamental or foundational issues and in offering a coherent account which enhances the understanding of a particular community. Shults argues that Pannenberg's 'rationality' can be seen in the reciprocal relation between 'fundamental' concerns (anthropology, philosophy) and 'systematic' concerns, a relationship that displays 'asymmetric bipolar relational unity' in Pannenberg's thought.[8] Shults illustrates this relationship as a 'mobius strip' which appears to have two sides but turns out to have a single continuous surface. In terms of Pannenberg's thought, this means that the systematic movement 'sublates' the fundamental, and so has a measure of 'control', yet the full unity of seeing all things *sub ratione Dei* (in their relation of God) is only available when the two perspectives are grasped in unity, though retaining their own unique character.[9]

Christoph Schwöbel describes Pannenberg's theology as 'rational orthodoxy'. It is 'rational' in that 'he never ceases to argue for his position and seeks to make his reasoning transparent for his readers' and orthodox in that it displays 'wide-ranging agreement with the teaching of doctrinal orthodoxy in regard to the material content'.[10] While Pannenberg's concern to argue his case carefully cannot be disputed, commentators have taken differing views on the extent to which Pannenberg is orthodox. Clayton notes a 'mixed reaction to Pannenberg' on this issue and he observes that Pannenberg is 'criticised both for not doing theology in the traditional mode . . . and for being *too* traditional'.[11]

Schwöbel comments on the 'combination and mutual interpretation of historical and systematic reflection in arguing for the truth of dogmatic statements', which he describes as a historico-dogmatic method. He also observes that Pannenberg's arguments always relate to historical revelation in Jesus Christ. He further describes Pannenberg's method as that in which 'a historico-hermeneutical investigation, trying to assess the contemporary validity and relevance of doctrine, is constantly combined with the methods and criteria of a systematic-analytical inquiry, attempting to uncover the conditions for the truth of doctrine'.[12] Schwöbel's hyphenated adjectives reflect the complexity of Pannenberg's methodology.

Mark Worthing considers the difficulty of classifying Pannenberg's theological method. He notes Clayton's suggestion of 'pervasive criticisability' as the central tenet of Pannenberg's thought yet finds that, while this is a major concern, it 'alone does not do justice to the full range and complexity of Pannenberg's method'. He rejects Schwarz's grouping of Tillich and Pannenberg as 'dialogical', since this fails to deal with the 'significant differences' in methodology between the two. Moreover, Pannenberg's approach strives for a far closer integration of various disciplines into a fully theological one than is suggested by the term 'dialogue'. Worthing also observes that describing Pannenberg as doing 'theology from below' is too simplistic, for he includes metaphysical and even speculative aspects in his doctrine of God. Worthing offers 'pan-critical-historico-hermeneutical' as a description of Pannenberg's method.[13]

The concluding chapter of Timothy Bradshaw's *Pannenberg: A Guide for the Perplexed* focuses on the place of eschatology and anticipation of the end in Pannenberg's thought, suggesting that Bradshaw holds that these lie at the heart of Pannenberg's thought. The chapter includes general comments about Pannenberg's project. He describes Pannenberg's thought as 'a subtle Christian trinitarian theological ontology working off an Hegelian base and seeking to revise it through a profound engagement with the figure of Jesus in his thought context, particularly apocalyptic, in continual dialogue with the secular world'. He praises it as 'a patient and meticulously argued case of total consistency' which uses eschatology 'in the most interesting way' and develops 'all major doctrines of the Christian faith in an indisputably intriguing and often convincing way'.[14] Peters' comment on the content of Pannenberg's project also reflects the all-embracing scope of his thought and the importance of history and eschatology in relation to God: 'Pannenberg projects on the screens of our imaginations a theological phantasmagoria that unites creation with eschatology, that places the history of the cosmos past and future within the trinitarian life of an eternal God.'[15]

This review of critical appraisals of Pannenberg's work suggests questions that are important in understanding and assessing his thought. There is considerable discussion about whether Pannenberg's thought is 'rationalistic', if his claims are too sweeping and universal, or if he is overly confident about what theology may achieve. By contrast, some commentators put more emphasis on Pannenberg's view that all theological claims are provisional and so view him as less enamoured of modernity.

Hermeneutics: Pannenberg's Method in Theology

Several assessments of Pannenberg describe his method of theological reflection as hermeneutical. In noting this feature, they reflect the fact that Pannenberg seeks to understand and interpret biblical texts, theological concepts, historical events and human experiences, and to show the connections between these. Pannenberg's discursive and synthetic writing style relates to this conviction. There are many extended discussions as he explores various aspects of a particular topic. As he examines each theme in *Systematic Theology*, he considers it in the light of historical theology, scriptural testimony and other relevant material (which may be religious history, anthropology, science or history). He develops his own position through this discussion. Typically in *Systematic Theology*, a section will finish by pointing forward to the next section, and the whole work, for the full exposition of the theme at hand. For instance, the opening discussion of the truth of Christian doctrine concludes that the question will be a theme in all theology. Likewise, the discussion of the Trinity concludes that 'only the process of expounding the divine economy of salvation will yield the degree of clarification that theological reflection awaits'.[16] Pannenberg's hermeneutical approach is the reason for the density of his presentation. His work, particularly in *Systematic Theology*, is closely argued, often dealing with several issues at the same time, and expressed with great precision.

An understanding of Pannenberg's work requires an awareness of why he adopts this method, since he does so on the basis of assumptions which are fundamental to his project. An assessment of his work requires careful exposition of his thought, taking into account the thinkers and issues with which he interacts.

God: the Centre of Pannenberg's Theology

Most commentators recognize that the reality and nature of God are key themes in Pannenberg's thought. Shults proposes that the *Grundprinzip* (the basic or fundamental principle) of Pannenberg's project is to view all things *sub ratione Dei*. This reflects the centrality of God in Pannenberg's thought.[17] Shults' interpretation of Pannenberg, taken out of context, could suggest that Pannenberg proposes a self-evident, or at least easily established, idea of God, to which he relates all other reality. This is not Pannenberg's approach, nor is it Shults' understanding of Pannenberg. Shults' claim that Pannenberg's method is postfoundationalist highlights the reciprocity in Pannenberg's approach. This means that for Pannenberg, there is a reciprocal relation between God and all other reality. On the one hand all reality is what it is, in relation to God; on the other hand God's divinity is established in his lordship of all that is. The reciprocity between God and his creation is a constant theme in Pannenberg's thought since the task of theology is the demonstration of God's lordship which can only be done by showing that God is the lord of all. The way in which this dynamic is conceived and how it is related to the eschatological metaphysic is another important question for an assessment of Pannenberg.

Philosophy: the Partner in Pannenberg's Theology

Hans Frei is an example of a commentator who holds that Pannenberg allows philosophical questions to dominate over theological concerns. Frei's typology categorizes theologians on the basis of his analysis of the relation of philosophy to theology in their thought.[17] His categories run from Type 1, in which theology is a philosophical discipline and any distinctively Christian note is subordinate to a philosophical description, through to Type 5, in which 'there is not even a subordinated place for philosophy within theology'.[18] He categorizes Pannenberg as a Type 2 theology, in which philosophical and theological understandings are 'merged' and a systematic foundational philosophical scheme justifies the result.[19] Frei's Type 2 allows a specific Christian self-description (which Type 1 does not) while insisting on a systematic relation between theological and philosophical understandings. It allows that a specific Christian understanding is valid as a 'regional aspect' of a wider philosophical understanding and insists that the meaningfulness of Jesus must be demonstrated in wider terms.[20]

How well does Pannenberg fit into Frei's Type 2? Pannenberg does demand that Christian self-description must be correlated with wider philosophical questions. However, he offers critical discussions of a wide range of philosophers and disavows the connection of his thought with any particular philosophical position: 'I must warn against any tendency to link this presentation to any particular philosophical theology, even my own.'[21] He holds that, while philosophical reflection provides 'criteria for presenting the understanding of God within a religious tradition', it does not supplant the tradition, which reflects directly on religious experience, nor can philosophy 'claim the character of a definitive foundation'.[22] Theology must demonstrate its truth in critical conversation with philosophy, yet it succeeds in doing this when it sublates the themes and concerns of philosophy in its own discussion and shows that they are only fully understood *sub ratione Dei*.[23] In Pannenberg's work, theological language, in a rather traditional form, is the fullest available description of reality. Thus, according to Pannenberg's own account, his method lies somewhere between Frei's Types 2 and 3. Of course it is possible that the critics are still correct. It could be that by insisting on such a close engagement with philosophy Pannenberg allows philosophy to set the terms of discussion and to subvert Christian claims (rather than theology sublating philosophy). That is a question we will return to in later chapters.

Appreciating Pannenberg

The rest of this book will focus on detailed issues in Pannenberg's thought as a way of understanding and assessing his theology. The wider survey already allows us to appreciate some of the strengths of his approach and to reflect on what Christians who wish to think seriously about their faith can learn from him. His theology raises a whole host of questions and this chapter only hints at some of them. Those questions are testimony to the scope, integration and precision of his thought. Pannenberg's theology is a brilliant synthesis and I think it is appropriate to refer to his genius. Consider a few features of his theology which are particularly impressive and worth emulating.

First, Pannenberg has worked from a commitment to take as seriously as possible the questions of his context. From his initial questioning of Nietzsche to his discussion of the natural sciences, Pannenberg has insisted that theology cannot hide from the hard questions asked by secularism and he has led the way in engaging those questions (in principle he is also interested in questions raised by other religions, though his actual discussions of religions are shaped by the questions of the secular West more than by Islam or Hinduism). There are two reasons that he puts forward for this engagement. Primarily, if the true God is the reality which determines all other reality, then reality will only make sense in light of understanding God. Second, the existence of God is under question in many ways in contemporary (Western) thought and if the church is going to bear witness to the true God, then theology must apply itself to examining and re-examining its case for God.

In contrast, a great deal of evangelical theology seems able to proceed relatively untroubled by the hard questions of the context, often consumed by its own internal squabbles over relatively minor issues while ignoring the major challenges which surround it. Pannenberg may not always have the right answers, but it is undeniable that he is aware of very important questions. Evangelical theology would do well to give more attention to the questions raised by other religions and secular thought.

Second, Pannenberg's theology is an impressive synthesis of a wide range of material. He integrates discussion of biblical texts with insightful assessments of the theological tradition and moves from that to discuss physics and metaphysics. Because he is concerned to present Christian theology as coherent, he constantly ties his various discussions into each other so they become a tightly woven conceptual tapestry. If God determines all reality, then when we view reality in his light we should be able to understand it. The way in which Pannenberg shows that various aspects of reality relate to each other and make sense together is what makes reading him difficult and exciting. The difficulty is that as you read you have to keep a whole host of discussions in mind; the result is an often-breathtaking Christian synthesis.

Theology often misses this element of integration. A common criticism of the modern theological academy is that it is populated by specialists who know a great deal about one area but are not ready to relate their speciality to any wider discussion. A biblical scholar may have studied the opening verses of John's Gospel in detail and a historian may know a great deal about the debates in the early church about Jesus' deity but they do not interact with each other even though their specialities overlap significantly. If there is one discipline which has the role of bringing all the diverse elements of Christian thought together it is systematic theology. Pannenberg helps to show how exciting and persuasive systematic theology can be when it offers a thoughtful integration. He helps to set for us a very high standard of careful integration in theology.

Third, Pannenberg is aware that theology is a limited human exercise. He considers theological claims to be hypotheses which have to be constantly tested and which may need to be expressed in new ways or even abandoned. He makes this point by calling theological claims 'doxological' because speech about God is rooted in adoration of him and is uttered in hope of its final confirmation. In a similar way, medieval scholastic theology spoke of language about God as analogical, which is to say that it expresses a truth about God but falls short of the reality of God in ways which we cannot know. Pannenberg argues that 'the concepts by which we praise God's essence become equivocal in the act of the sacrifice of praise'. Equivocal language is insecure, uncertain and open to more than one interpretation. That is, Pannenberg is pointing out that as we discuss God we admit that what we think falls far short of the reality. This is a feature of any serious thought about the God of the Bible and one that I often notice in the theology classroom. As we walk along well-travelled paths in orthodox theology, such as the doctrine of the Trinity, we constantly reach the limits of our ability to understand or express the truth about God. These limits make us realize that much of what we have already said in following classic formulations of the doctrine is not as clear as we first imagined. The whole discussion of God, to which theology must constantly return to be true to its calling, traces the edge of a chasm of mystery.

Pannenberg stresses the same humility in the face of God's mystery as did the medieval approach, but by viewing this in an eschatological perspective he offers a note of confidence which is missing in traditional discussions of analogical language. For Pannenberg, doxological statements of theology are made 'in the hope of a fulfilment which by far overcomes the distance fixed in the analogy'.[24] They anticipate their confirmation and clarification in the eschaton. Pannenberg's stance gives theology an appropriate mixture of confident assertion and cautious humility which looks to God's final revelation for both the vindication and judgement of our words.

Fourth, Pannenberg takes the Bible and Christian tradition very seriously. He is not willing to allow theology to float free in a kind of unguarded speculation. It may seem unfair to accuse other theologians of indulging in speculation, but in much contemporary theology it is difficult to find any commitments which introduce a serious limitation on its thought. The Enlightenment rejection of authority and a postmodern propensity for playfulness and imagination can combine to allow theologians to develop incredibly fanciful schemas. Pannenberg strives to test his theology by the classical sources of Christian thought.

Finally, Pannenberg knows that theology must be about God. This may seem obvious from the derivation of the word, yet it is not always the case. During the Reformation Melanchthon announced that 'To know Christ is to know his benefits, not, as they teach, to reflect upon his natures'.[25] Later theologians adopted Melanchthon's phrase to imply that seeking to know anything about the nature or mode of the incarnation was an empty and pointless quest. What mattered, they thought, was knowing the human experience of faith. In a similar way some contemporary theology has more to say about society and culture than it does about God. Pannenberg, however, is convinced that theology must be the science of God. It is the human attempt to think about and speak of God and in doing so to show the truth of God's reality. This engages theology in considering all of reality, including human experience, society, history and cosmology. It considers all of this in relation to God. In doing so, theology is proleptic; it does not have the final word.

Pannenberg sets out an exciting and challenging view of theology and there is a great deal to learn from him. The rest of this book will follow Pannenberg in his thinking about several areas of theology. I hope that the discussion of Pannenberg's thought has already shown that he is worth understanding simply because he is an interesting theologian. His ideas are developed carefully and across a very wide horizon. Anyone who is interested in theological thought will find his project engaging. Each of the following chapters will lay out part of the fascinating project. There is no reason that we must follow Pannenberg entirely, and at several places in this book I will explain some of my criticisms of his thought, yet his approach will challenge us to reflect on our own theology and how we develop it.

What Is Systematic Theology and Why Does It Matter?

Pannenberg's theology invites us to consider how we do theology. At this point it is worth thinking a little more about the discipline of systematic theology, taking Pannenberg as a guide. Titling his major work *Systematic Theology*, Pannenberg places it in a long line of similar volumes. The term was first used by post-Reformation theologians and the discipline developed into one which seeks to describe and understand Christian teaching 'in its full scope and in its integrity'.[26] As with most disciplines of its kind the exact nature of systematic theology is a matter of debate. There is no single neat definition with which all systematicians agree. This is because a view of systematic theology will always depend on the content of theology. If a theologian has the view that we encounter God in numinal experiences which cannot be reduced to words the resulting theology will be quite different from that of a theologian who sees the Bible or church tradition as the key to knowledge of God. Given this wide variety, there is not a great deal to be gained in long debates about the precise definition of systematic theology. That being said, Pannenberg's presentation of systematic theology can stimulate us to think about what systematic theology is and, more importantly, why it is worth doing.

Pannenberg does not quite offer a definition of systematic theology, though he comes close when he says that it 'should be an effort in constructive thought in order to exemplify how the God of the Bible can be understood as the creator and Lord of all reality'.[27] It does this by giving an account which is based on the Bible but is often a reformulation of the biblical witness. By presenting this understanding systematically he tries to show how the claims of Christianity cohere with one another and seeks to integrate a synthesis of Christian claims with the insights of secular disciplines.[28] All of this is to aid the great goal which Pannenberg sets for systematic theology – to establish the truth of Christian claims. He explains that Christian confession requires us to say that we believe certain things to be true about God and Jesus. If these things are not true then we cannot follow Jesus nor entrust ourselves to God.[29]

I take a somewhat different view of systematic theology. It does not seem to me that the question of the truth of Christian claims has to be *the* central question for theology. Truth matters very much and when Christians live in a culture which questions their claims then theology will have a very lively interest in the truth. Yet if theology is our account of the biblical revelation of God, then it is important to recognize that the issue of the truthfulness of its claims is not the most significant question in the Bible's own record. The Bible accepts God's identity, the claims of Jesus, the announcement of life in his name and the gift of the Spirit, and exults in all of this with a joyful confidence. Theology should reflect this by quite often getting on with the task of understanding God's revelation and helping believers to grasp it and live it, without constantly turning back to test its truth. Let me repeat that this is not to sideline the question of truth, simply to suggest that it is not the only question or the central question.

In my view systematic theology is the discipline which seeks to serve the church by giving a coherent account of the Christian knowledge of God and of knowledge of all things in their relation to God. It seeks to develop an account of the living Triune God who is known in redemption by the incarnate Son, Jesus Christ and through the Holy Spirit. This account is governed by Scripture in careful conversation with the 'great tradition' of orthodox theology and responds to the context of the church which it seeks to serve. Each element of this definition needs some further explanation.

The central task of theology is to help us understand the Triune God revealed in Christ. This focus itself flows from key theological claims: that the true God is Father, Son and Spirit and the *summum bonum* (the highest good) and so is worth knowing above all else, and that God invites his human creatures to know him by redemptively revealing himself in his incarnate Son, Jesus Christ, and by the Spirit. Genuine systematic theology develops from the gospel announcement. Theology cannot successfully proceed by simply trying to collect knowledge of God from a range of sources and integrate it in a way determined by the theologian. Theology exists because God has acted and called us to know him. Here we can follow Pannenberg closely since, as Shults points out, he is post-foundationalist. If Pannenberg were truly a 'rationalist' who looks to reason to lead us to God he would have little to offer to genuine Christian theology. Shults shows that through all the complexities of Pannenberg's discussion he is not 'arguing up' to God from a foundation but seeking to relate knowledge of God in Christ with the questions of philosophy and other disciplines in order to understand God better and demonstrate the validity of claims about him. While I think that the focus on the question of truth is somewhat distorting for Pannenberg, I affirm the centrality he gives to the Triune God known in Christ.

If the primary role of systematic theology is to serve the church, this presumes that what it does is helpful! I am convinced it is. Christians believe a whole host of things: from 'God is triune' and 'angels exist' to 'humanity is redeemed by Jesus' death and resurrection'. It is important for Christians to have some idea of why they believe those things and how the various beliefs fit together into an overall picture of the world in which we live for God. Systematic theology helps with this. When we ask what Christians think about God or science or humans or music – we ask systematic questions. To answer those questions it is not enough to say that a part of the Bible says something relevant or even to summarize several relevant passages. We need an overall picture and have a sense of proportion in that picture.

Kevin Vanhoozer describes the task of theology as 'dramaturgy', which is the art of understanding scripts to help actors perform them well.[30] He makes the analogy that the theologian works to help Christians understand the drama they are involved in so they are able to participate as truly as possible. Useful dramaturgical guidance does not come from piecemeal comments or mere lists of features of the script; it requires clear insight into the developing plot, the key themes, the crucial scenes and the presentation of the various characters. Similarly, theology aims to help the church understand what God has done and is doing and how it should respond to God. The Bible is the 'script' as it were, but is not the drama itself – the drama is God's great work in all of history and in the lives of each of his people. If systematic theology can help in that task, then it truly can serve the church. If this is the way we think about the work of systematic theology, then it is not as fully focused on the demonstration of truth as Pannenberg makes it.

The Bible is basic to doing theology, since Christians believe that God reveals himself through the Bible. That is not a straightforward matter since various Christians view the Bible in quite different ways and some of the major disagreements within theology are about how we should think of the Bible and how it informs our beliefs. All Christian theology holds that God's redemptive revelation is in Christ by the Spirit and that this redemptive revelation is shared with us in the Bible. A theologian who has no place for knowing God through Christ, the Spirit and the Bible has forfeited any serious claim to be a Christian theologian. Approaches to theology can differ a great deal in how they think the revelation in Christ by the Spirit connects with the Bible and how they think God relates to the Bible. One of the important theological tasks is to reflect on how the Bible should inform our thinking. In the next chapter, as we consider Pannenberg's view of God's revelation, we will be able to think about how he sees the Bible.

We do not read the Bible alone. God has called us to be his people together and has promised his Spirit to his church. So we understand God better by learning along with the whole church, specially from the tested answers of previous generations. It is this accumulated wisdom that I am thinking of as 'the great tradition'. This tradition does not speak with a unified voice; there are certainly varying emphases as well as some clear contradictions. Yet Augustine, Luther and Wesley, and a whole host of others, held to common creeds and we can discern many common threads running through this whole tradition. Theology should do its thinking as part of this great tradition. Even though Pannenberg positions himself somewhat differently in relation to the tradition than I do, a great deal of his theological discussion happens in careful interaction with the tradition. His conclusions are usually a careful reconfiguration of the classic traditions, never an outright rejection of the tradition.

Evangelical theology has been wary of appeals to tradition, especially if that tradition included thinkers from the medieval and early church. Fortunately this situation has changed in recent years. Contemporary scholarship reminds us that classic Reformation theology developed from earlier thought and never imagined that it was starting all over again. Even a thinker as avowedly Protestant as John Owen, a Puritan independent who was an outspoken opponent of Catholicism, was quite self-conscious in his dependence on thinkers from the medieval tradition.[31] The same point can be made for other Reformed evangelical theological 'heroes' such as John Calvin, Jonathan Edwards or Herman Bavinck. A renewed interest among evangelicals in knowing the great tradition and thinking from within it is a healthy sign.

Along with Pannenberg, I agree that exploring coherence is an important part of systematic theology. My interest in coherence is primarily because a coherent account is part of helping us understand God and his ways, only secondarily does it serve to validate the claims of the faith. It is just as important, then, to be aware of elements in Christian belief which, at least from our point of view, seem irreconcilable and incoherent. We need to know where there are tensions in our knowledge of God, tensions which have to be maintained not relieved.[32]

Systematic theology typically sets out to show what Christians believe and how the various aspects of that belief fit together. There are some obvious points at which there are real questions about how Christian beliefs fit together. For instance, can Jesus be truly and fully divine and human or can God be intimately present to all things and yet transcendent and sovereign? There are other points at which the questions about how beliefs fit together may be less obvious, but sometimes the answers are more interesting. For instance, how do redemption by Christ, the work of the Spirit, the existence of the church and Christian hope all fit together? Are they simply four things Christians have beliefs about which do not relate much to each other? There are fascinating and important connections between the four theological themes. In brief, the Spirit indwells Christians so that we now share in what Christ has achieved in redemption. We share redemption together as God's people but not yet fully. In the New Creation we will share fully all that Christ has done for us. So the work of Christ and the Spirit, church and hope are interwoven in a single story of God's redemption of his people. As we explore the interconnections, each of these aspects of redemption opens up in new ways. That exploration is one of the important tasks of systematic theology.

Some critics of systematic theology are very suspicious of the way in which it appears to change radically its material as it presents it. If the Bible is taken as the primary source of theology, then the discussions of theology can seem far removed from the biblical text. An old accusation which continues still is that theology represents an illicit Hellenization of the Bible. This criticism is that theology takes its lead from Greek philosophy and uses terms and ideas which come from there rather than from the Bible. If the key source for theology is thought to be religious experience then the same kind of question arises – is the experience lost in the analysis and discussion? Similarly, systematic theology is criticized for being, in general, too affected by philosophy or simply too abstract. For instance, Goldingay comments that 'if systematic theology did not exist, it might seem unwise to invent it – at least, unwise to begin the devising of grand schemes that are bound to skew our reading of Scripture'. He argues that 'quite different assumptions about God feature prominently in biblical narrative' than in traditional systematics.[33]

Such criticisms offer systematic theology a very important warning. It is naive to think that restating Christian faith in different terms and laying out responses to new questions will have no effect on the content of the faith. The process of developing systematic theology will change what is being presented in subtle ways, or at times not so subtle ways. While this is something of which to be aware, it is not something that we should try to avoid. As John Webster points out, in order to develop a useful systematic account of the Christian faith, a certain transformation is required. 'It is difficult to imagine a systematic account of Christian teaching which simply recorded positive data, for it would lack the abstraction and schematization necessary for a conceptual representation of the material.' Webster reminds us of something about which Pannenberg is very clear, stating that 'to make a representation of Christian teaching is to construe it, to commend a version of it which may not be made up but is certainly made'.[34] Pannenberg deals with the same issue by saying that theological statements are hypotheses and have their truth in doxology. That is they are human attempts to say something about God and they do not fully correspond to what they describe, but strive to praise the true and living God and have their truth in that praise.

A common way of describing theology as something believers make and as an abstraction is to compare it to a map. A map, no matter how accurate, is not the same as the area it represents. If it were identical to the ground it mapped, it would not be any use, since the value of a map is that it allows us to gain perspectives which we never could form from simply being in the landscape. The test of a map is how well it represents for users the relevant information. Systematic theology offers maps of the Christian faith. It is not the same as Christian faith or the Bible or religious experience and it is important not to confuse theology with the immediate realities. Vanhoozer's comparison of theology with the work of the dramaturge makes a similar point.

Finally, one of the attractive things about Pannenberg's theology is that he is fully engaged in his context. Certainly, theology should not be slavishly driven by its context, but be interested first and foremost in God and his redemption. Yet as we try to think about all things in the light of God, then we do think about human experience. Further, if theology is to serve the church then it will need to deal with the context in which the church exists. The questions which believers face, as well as those asked from outside the church, should be answered as well as possible. As we seek answers there is an inevitable process in which our answers are included in our exposition of the faith and become part of the systematic theology which we develop. Thus theology develops as a response to a particular context.

Pannenberg's interaction with science is an excellent example of his engagement with his context. He lives in an era in which science is a major cultural influence. Most traditional theology has had very little to say about science, perhaps largely because science has not always been the dominant cultural and intellectual force which it became from the early twentieth century. Pannenberg is right to recognize that theology has to engage with science. This engagement can and should be critical. Pannenberg calls for 'critical reflection upon the methodical framework' of other disciplines.[35] As with other aspects of context, theology should not be determined by science but it should be engaged with it.

Conclusion: Doing Systematic Theology with Pannenberg

Systematic theology is worth doing, in fact it is essential if the church is to chart its ways in a complex world. Wolfhart Pannenberg offers one of the pre-eminent examples of contemporary systematic theology. His project shows how relevant and exciting systematic theology can be and how important it is for the church that theology be done well. Theology which is genuinely centred on God and based on revelation in Christ, which is governed by the Bible and seeks to show how God is related to everything else, and does that it in a way that deals with the questions of its own context, is a project worth pursuing. Done well it can be a real help to the church during its pilgrimage. Pannenberg shows us what theology can aspire to be. The rest of this book is an exploration of some specific areas of Pannenberg's thought. This will let us consider in more detail how he does theology and will let us start to do some theology with him, learning from him both in agreement and disagreement.

4.

Jesus, History and God: Pannenberg and Revelation

The idea of revelation presents a problem for modern theology and the question of what to make of the Bible presents this question in its most pressing form. Paul Avis thinks that revelation is 'the only problem' for theology.[1] While Avis overstates the case (there are other problems in theology), he reminds us how intensely contemporary theology feels the questions about revelation. For Pannenberg questions associated with revelation have been major ones and his first well-known publication was the essay 'Dogmatic Theses on the Doctrine of Revelation' in the volume *Revelation as History*.[2] The best way to unpack Pannenberg's theology is to begin with the theme of revelation and see the problems and challenges he faced in that area and how he responded to them. This chapter will look at some of the developments in thought about revelation which set the scene for Pannenberg's work and then consider his own approach.

Biblical Criticism

The straightforward element to the challenge Pannenberg faces is that several generations of critical study of the Bible changed the way most Christians view their Scriptures. Pannenberg is convinced that the Scripture principle of the Reformation is no longer tenable, since critical study seems to show that parts of the Bible are historically unreliable and that not even the New Testament provides a 'contradictionless doctrinal unity'.[3] Pannenberg's early training introduced him to some of the leading critical scholars and he is well aware of the impact this approach has had on the doctrine of Scripture. As we will see he does not abandon a Scripture principle, but he does think that the authority and reliability of the Bible needs to be established through theological discussion rather than merely be accepted as an axiom. For many evangelicals who read Pannenberg, his acceptance of this heritage of the critical study of Scripture is surprising. It is important to remember that this was the standard view which he met in his education; it is also important to understand that these scholars were not aiming to destroy or reject the Bible but to understand it.[4] This chapter will finish with some more reflections on Pannenberg's stance toward the Bible.

Philosophical Challenges

Rationalism: Kant

The more complex elements of Pannenberg's discussion of revelation are the philosophical challenges from three significant philosophical movements in the nineteenth century. The first is the rationalism of Immanuel Kant. Kant was disturbed by the challenge of David Hume's scepticism and sought to show that human knowledge could be set on a secure basis through careful critical examination of reason itself. He argued that the concepts and categories by which we understand the world (such as 'cause and effect') are not supplied by sense experience but are given by our mind. We understand the world through these categories and rational reflection on them can clarify them and show they are needed for us to grasp the world.[5] Kant thought of the categories as something like the windows through which we view the world. From our position inside a closed room we could not see out at all except for windows. We need them. Yet what we see is determined by the windows. Their frames set the limits of our vision and the ripples and colours in the glass are inevitably part of how we view the scenes outside the room.

The implication of Kant's view is that humans never know things-in-themselves (*noumena*) but only as they appear to us (*phenomena*). The windows are always part of our view and, since we cannot see apart from looking through them, we can never untangle what in our perception is window and what is part of the things-in-themselves. For Kant, our concepts allow us to work very successfully with sensory data and provide a basis for the natural sciences. However, these concepts do not grant us metaphysical knowledge. Kant argued that when our innate concepts are applied to the idea of God we end up with irrational, nonsensical conclusions. This reinforced his claim that we cannot know anything about metaphysics or God.[6] He offered different grounds for postulating God's existence. He claimed that moral truths are inherent in the universe and known by reason and that God's existence was itself a postulate of practical reason. That is, moral experience (which is a given) requires that God's existence must be postulated.

Kant's approach ruled out the possibility of revelation as it had traditionally been understood. Revelation was traditionally understood as God bringing people to knowledge of himself, but Kant did not allow that the human mind could have genuine and direct knowledge of God. Instead Kant asserted an 'inner revelation' based on reason which establishes practical dictates for the moral life. This revelation is the measure which judges all other claims to revelation. If a claim about God supported reasonable morality, then it could be accepted because it was a condition of morality. So, it was important to hold that God was the judge of all, since this supported the universal law which Kant held was the basis of moral living. On the other hand the doctrine of the Trinity had no moral relevance and had to be discarded. In Kant's view God's existence is a postulate of practical reason, not a matter of revelation. He recognized the importance of Scripture for ecclesiastical religion, but did not accept that such religion was of any great value; it certainly had no basis on which to claim that its dogma was true.[7]

Romanticism: Schleiermacher

Romanticism was an obvious reaction to Kantian rationalism.[8] If rational thought is not able to receive knowledge of God or the infinite, human feelings and experiences of beauty and transcendence offered a different route to God. This romantic inclination developed into a programme interested in poetry, arts and religious experience.[9] Friedrich Schleiermacher (1768–1834) offered a romantic basis for theology, giving feeling and intuition fundamental places as the essence of religion.[10] For Schleiermacher, the feeling of absolute dependence was the basic religious experience and the source of theological reflection, so that 'Christian doctrines are accounts of the Christian religious affections put forward in speech'.[11] Romanticism also tended to put an emphasis on the miraculous events 'which cannot be explained in the stricter context of natural occurrence' and so point to 'a higher power which is at work in the world'.[12]

Idealism: Hegel

Idealism responded to Kantian dualism by placing the whole emphasis on the mind, so that all reality is seen as the product of an Absolute Mind. G.W.F. Hegel (1770–1831) was the great systematizer of idealism. According to him, reality is a dynamic process in which the Absolute Mind or Spirit (*Geist*) is expressed. Hegel presented Christianity as the revelation of the Absolute because in it there is 'an immediate relation of God to the mind'. For idealists in the Hegelian stream, revelation occurs in the entire process of history as God is revealed through and to himself by human consciousness which is the product and sum of history. Thus idealism views revelation as God's self-revelation on the basis of whole historical process, focused in human consciousness.[13]

Pannenberg's Response to the Nineteenth-Century Challenges

Pannenberg's theological context was shaped by rationalism, idealism and romanticism since these three movements were the source of most views of revelation in nineteenth- and early twentieth-century German thought. Each of the movements challenged the traditional view of revelation which was that God inspired the words of the Bible and these words can be taken as direct revelation from God and of God. Rationalism questioned the possibility of any revelation, Romanticism sought revelation in religious experience, and idealism found it in the cultural-historical process. Pannenberg's account of revelation is a response to each of these positions, and takes something from each.

The importance of these three movements is indicated by the attention Pannenberg gives to the thought of Richard Rothe (1799–1867).[14] Rothe's theology combined Hegelian speculative idealism with a strong supernaturalism which was similar to romanticism.[15] Although Rothe is less dependent on Kant, romanticism and idealism were both ways of overcoming Kant's criticism of the idea of divine revelation. Pannenberg finds some appeal in the idealistic approaches to revelation. His idea of God as the true Infinite, who transcends and includes all other reality resonates with the idealist view.[16] Yet he fears that the idealist approach seems to imply 'a pantheistic equation of the cosmic process with God'.[17] More precisely, when revelation is the totality of history then it is difficult to conceive of a specific event – even the life, death and resurrection of Jesus – as revelation, let alone the final revelation. Pannenberg shares Kierkegaard's protest that Hegel's approach cannot hold that Christ is the absolute revelation.[18]

Rothe's view can be thought of as a 'romantic' one because it views revelation as an inner experience, though brought about by Christ's miracles which 'can be explained only by the idea of God' and which allow the human mind to 'arrive, with evidence, at the idea, the true idea, of God'.[19] Pannenberg takes this as a step toward a view in which revelation is public and located in the work of Christ. However, he acknowledges that Rothe fails to reach this idea himself and criticizes him for retaining a view in which the public events of Christ's miracles are not revelation in themselves but must be supplemented with an experience of inspiration for those who receive revelation.[20]

Barth and Bultmann

Rationalism, romanticism and idealism are the general background to Pannenberg's thought about revelation. There is also a more immediate background in German theology in the period during which Pannenberg matured as a theologian. The two great

German-speaking theologians of the mid-twentieth century, Barth and Bultmann, both held revelation as a key concept, though each conceived of revelation and the task of theology quite differently from the other.

For Barth, revelation is the event in which God makes himself known and is an act of the free sovereign God who uses his creation but whose freedom is not constrained by the forms of revelation. Central to Barth's theology is the claim that God has revealed himself in Jesus and, because in Jesus, then in Scripture and the proclamation of the church.[21] Revelation in these forms does not depend on the capacity of the historical events or the written or spoken word; God in his sovereign freedom transcends the limited capacities of events and words in the miracle of revelation.[22] This approach released Barth from some of the pressing questions of nineteenth-century theology and the critical study of Scripture. Revelation is not an event which theology can 'produce' in order that it be interrogated and tested; rather Barth says we can only let the event 'speak for itself'.[23] In the event of revelation a person is confronted by God and called to know God and this involves a personal encounter which has conceptual and cognitive aspects as well as a personal, moral, self-involving dimension.[24] Because of the cognitive aspect there is a content which can be unfolded and proclaimed, but the event of revelation can never be pinned down in order to be assessed by the historian (or the psychologist or theologian). Thus Barth could deal with the historical events referred to in the Bible as revelation and view the Bible itself as revelation, and yet isolate revelation from the acidic scepticism of critical scholarship.

> A singular concern may be identified in Barth's writing on the theme of revelation: namely, to give an account of the reality of this event in which the proper (and vital) distinction between God and the world is maintained at every point. God is known in the midst of historical existence . . . But in the midst of this miracle God remains the one who is wholly other than us, and we, for our part, remain human.[25]

Bultmann allowed critical scholarship a far more direct impact on theology with the result that traditional theology could not be sustained.[26] For him the theological content of revelation is existential, that is it opens up the experience of human exist-ence and, secondarily, allows reflection on that experience. This occurs through encounter with the Christian message found in the New Testament, but the medium of revelation is almost inci-dental. Bultmann declared that 'by tradition Jesus is named as the bearer of the message . . . if it proves otherwise, that does not change in any way what is said in the record'.[27] For Bultmann the particularities of history were not at all involved in revela-tion. Bultmann, inspired by the existential thought of Heidegger, was interested in how the message of the New Testament casts light on human existence, or rather how it enables an enlightened human living. For Bultmann, faith is 'self-understanding' or 'a new understanding of existence'.[28] He does not mean that faith is a self-understanding achieved by an isolated individual on the basis of self-analysis. As Myers has pointed out, Bultmann's view is that identity and self-understanding are possessed by historical individuals who exist in encounter with others. 'For faith can exist only in the context of a living encounter – and that means, for Bultmann, encounter with the Word of God. Faith is the event in which I hear God's Word through scripture "as a word which is addressed to me, as *kerygma*, as a proclamation".'[29]

Bultmann is quite explicit that there is a close parallel between the New Testament message and the thought of Heidegger. He explains that Heidegger's analysis of human existence is 'no more than a secularized, philosophical version of the New Testament view of human life'.

> For him the chief characteristic of man's Being in history is anxiety. Man exists in a permanent tension between the past and the future. At every moment he is confronted with an alternative. Either he must immerse himself in the concrete world of nature, and thus inevitably lose his individuality, or he must abandon all security and commit himself unreservedly to the future, and thus alone achieve his authentic Being. Is not that exactly the New Testament understanding of human life?[30]

There is, of course, far more that could be said about the approach of Barth and Bultmann to theology and revelation. These brief surveys will, however, serve for the purpose of understanding

Pannenberg's approach to revelation. In a theological context dominated by these two great thinkers Pannenberg had to address the question of revelation as a central question in his theology, especially since he thought that both Barth and Bultmann gave truncated accounts of revelation. He argues that both tended to leave a distance between revelation and the full range of human experience, particularly in its historical dimension.[31]

Pannenberg describes Bultmann's view as 'the purest and . . . classical expression of *kerygma* theology' which reacted against rationalist historical method but comments, with dry understatement, that as a result Bultmann tended 'to lose sight of the historical basis of the biblical witnesses'.[32] Pannenberg's complaint against Barth is not only the distance he puts between revelation and history but also his refusal to relate philosophy to theology.

> It seemed to me that the truly sovereign God could not be regarded as absent or superfluous in ordinary human experience and philosophical reflection, but that every single reality should prove incomprehensible (at least in its depth) without recourse to God, if he actually was the Creator of the world as Barth thought him to be. Increasingly it seemed to me inconsistent with that assumption that Barth presented God's revelation as if God had entered a foreign country instead of 'his home' as the Gospel of John tells us (1:11). Therefore, I felt that my philosophy and theology should not be permitted to separate, but that within their unity it should be possible to affirm the awe-inspiring otherness of God even more uncompromisingly than Barth had done, since he returned to reasoning by analogy.[33]

While Pannenberg has clear criticisms of both Barth and Bultmann he also draws important themes from each. Echoing Barth, Pannenberg insists that the majesty of God demands that 'God can only be known if he gives himself to be known'.[34] For Pannenberg, as for Barth, theology has a 'constitutive correlation with revelation' and is founded on revelation which has a christological focus.[35] Similar themes can be seen in Bultmann.[36] However the way in which Pannenberg will develop these themes is quite different from Barth and Bultmann, and is often in direct contrast to both of them.

It might seem that Barth has already united the emphasis on revelation as self-revelation with a focus on the one unique event of Christ. Yet Barth applies his definition of revelation so strictly that nothing apart from Christ can be considered revelation; anything else is a witness to revelation. Pannenberg argues that this is not consistent with the biblical concept of revelation.[37]

Pannenberg also objects to the dialectic in Barth's thought in which the revelation of God in Christ is also a veiling (a view Barth shares with Bultmann).[38] Pannenberg argues that if revelation is also a veiling then it is not divine self-revelation. In *Revelation as History* he argues that in this dialectic both Barth and Bultmann risk reducing revelation to an existential encounter which cannot be given any public examination or assessment.[39] In *Systematic Theology* Pannenberg comments that this critique was 'one-sided', yet he still resists a conception of revelation in which the Word of God can be considered apart from a historical demonstration of the truth of God.[40]

Pannenberg's Doctrine of Revelation

Keeping in mind the wider discussion of revelation to which Pannenberg was responding, we can now turn to his own contribution. His position can be summarized with five assertions.

1. Revelation is self-revelation

While Pannenberg criticizes Hegel, Rothe, and Barth, he does not deny their conception of revelation as self-revelation. He agrees that Christian theology has always held that 'in every revelation God's prime disclosure is of himself'.[41] 'Revelation in the strict sense' requires that the means and act of revelation must 'not be seen distinct from [God's] own essence'.[42] Revelation must be from God and through God as it is revelation of God. The identity of God with his revelation is the basic axiom of Pannenberg's view of revelation. On the one hand this axiom comes from the Bible – an encounter with God is an overwhelming experience. An example, which Pannenberg does not discuss, is found in the experience of Israel and Moses at Mt Sinai. Israel must be consecrated (Exod. 19:10–11,15) before the Lord appears and then limits are set round the mountain on the threat of death (Exod. 19:12–13,21–5). The

Lord's appearance is not described directly, rather the Lord's presence shakes the mountain and envelops it in smoke and fire (Exod. 19:18). Even then the people say to Moses: 'You speak to us, and we will listen; but do not let God speak to us, or we will die' (Exod. 20:19). Moses, with the elders of Israel sees God and survives (Exod. 24:9–10), yet in Exodus 33 God says that Moses cannot see his face but only his back because 'no one shall see me and live' (Exod. 33:20–23).[43] Whatever Pannenberg would make of the historicity of the Mt Sinai account, he would agree that this theme in Exodus shows that God's self-revelation is incontestable. The idea that revelation is self-revelation also flows from Pannenberg's 'philosophical' view that God is the true Infinite which embraces all reality even as it is transcendent.

Pannenberg holds that God's self-revelation will be clear in itself without any resort to a supplementary explanation (contra Rothe) and cannot be a veiling of God (contra Barth). What view of revelation can meet these criteria? Pannenberg's answer is that this revelation can only be found in the eschatological revelation of God.

2. Revelation is eschatological

According to the second thesis in *Revelation as History*, 'revelation is not comprehended in the beginning, but at the end of revealing history'.[44] In *Systematic Theology* Pannenberg defends his early theses against criticisms and offers some clarifications and modifications, yet the emphasis on eschatological revelation as the full form of revelation has not changed. He explains that his aim in the 'Dogmatic Theses' was to return to the view of revelation found in idealism, that all history is divine revelation.[45]

Pannenberg's argument that revelation is eschatological comes largely from the prophetic and apocalyptic strand of Old Testament literature, in which revelation is 'the self-demonstration of the deity of the God of Israel to all peoples'. He appeals to passages such as Isaiah 40:5 which express an expectation of universal eschatological revelation: 'the glory of the LORD shall be revealed, and all people shall see it together' (see also Hab. 2:14; Isa. 11:9; 1 Cor. 15:28; Eph. 1:10,21–3; Rev. 21:22–5; 22:5). The full revelation of God in his glory will not be open to dispute and will need no further interpretation.[46]

Not only will the revelation be indisputable, it will be a full self-revelation of God. Since God's own glory will fill the whole of creation, this means that God will make his own being and reality apparent. Pannenberg develops this biblical motif in a more abstract discussion. He argues that the eschaton is the entry of the eternity of God into history and since eternity is something that God is in himself, then this is the act of God in his essence.[47] Further, Pannenberg's understanding of eternity is the 'simult-aneous presence of life as a whole', and so is truly the presence of history as a whole.[48] In the eschaton Pannenberg can point to a revelation which is the public and self-interpreting summation of all history in the direct appearing of God.

Recall Pannenberg's description of the task of theology: the truth of God is the key hypothesis of theology which can only be demonstrated when God is shown to be the true God of all creation. Such a demonstration must relate to the human experience of the world and to the intimations of the unity of all reality expressed in the religions and in the historical conflict of religions. The idea of revelation as eschatological divine demonstration answers the demands for such a demonstration, especially since in the Old Testament the appeal to eschatological revelation is often made in the context in which Israel asserts that their God is the one true God. So, in his account of the revelation of God in history, Pannenberg can appeal to a notion of revelation which performs, in biblical history, the function he requires of it. What remains to be demonstrated is how this eschatological revelation is related to the Bible, which has been the focus of traditional Protestant doctrines of revelation, and how it relates to the particular historical events of Jesus' life, death and resurrection.

3. Present revelation is indirect and provisional

Pannenberg is aware that there is much material in the Bible which does not fit well into the definition of revelation as self-revelation. He holds that there is present revelation which is indirect and provisional.[49] It is provisional because it anticipates the eschatological revelation;[50] it is indirect because it is not immediate revelation of deity, but is a revelation from God about something else (that is, humanity and the world). This indirect nature of revelation is expressed in the first Dogmatic Thesis: 'the self-revelation of God in the biblical witnesses is not of a direct type in the sense of a theophany, but is indirect and brought about by means of the historical acts of God'.[51] Pannenberg argues that even the forms of revelation which involve the apparent immediacy of God are 'only a provisional self-disclosure of God'.[52]

Pannenberg uses the distinction between provisional, indirect revelation and eschatological revelation to explain several 'problems' which theology faces. One problem is that while a revelation of the one true God would be a single all-embracing event, Christians claim that there is a variety of forms of revelation (the different biblical texts, the teaching of the church, personal religious experience) which differ from each other in form and content.[53] However if these various forms are provisional, indirect anticipations of the final revelation, then their variety is not so much of a problem.

The partial status of current revelation also explains why present revelation and the reality of God remain contestable. If Christianity were to claim to have a present form of revelation which indisputably closes off any questioning of the existence of God, it would have to be considered to be falsified, for it is plainly the case that the existence of God is questioned. So, Christian claims are in fact strengthened when they allow for the contestability of God's existence and promise a future answer to the contest; both features show that the claims have a 'capacity for truth'.[54] Pannenberg holds that part of the test of theological ideas is whether they help to explain how various ideas cohere. On that test the idea of a final eschatological revelation now anticipated by partial, indirect revelation is very successful.

4. Revelation is historical

For Pannenberg revelation must occur in history. He finds the basis for this in the historical awareness which developed in Israel. In contrast to the mythical view, Israel came to see God as acting in history and held that God would act decisively at the end of history. As Israel learned to look to the future for their hope 'normative significance could finally be ascribed to the future rule of God'.[55] As with the axiom of revelation as self-revelation this emphasis also has a philosophical source – Hegel's insistence that revelation is the sum total of history.

The public nature of history provides the opportunity for the rational investigation into claims for revelation. Since present revelation is provisional, the results of the investigation are provisional. However, there is the opportunity for a genuine investigation which may falsify claims for revelation. So Pannenberg considers discussion about the historical evidence for Christian claims, and specially for Jesus and his resurrection, an essential part of theology.

Pannenberg's conception of history does not divorce human history from cosmic history. For Pannenberg human history happens within cosmic and biological processes, and all find their fulfilment in the eschaton. He argues that the eschaton will bring the fulfilment for which all of creation is open from its origin. Humanity has a special role in this, but human freedom arises from a biological process, and humanity brings all creation to its goal.[56] Chapter 1 noted the correspondence Pannenberg finds between the natural sciences and the human sciences. For him, both are part of the one total reality and can be understood in analogous ways since both find their end in the eschaton.

Pannenberg's appeal to history would be empty apart from history finding a unity in the eschaton, for at present history has no demonstrable unity as a revelation of God. All claims about revelation in history are made in anticipation of its fulfilment. Once again, eschatology and anticipation of the eschaton are prominent in Pannenberg's thought.

Pannenberg's account of revelation as eschatological and historical with a present indirect and provisional form relies heavily on his view of apocalyptic literature. He sees the emergence of apocalyptic writing as a full expression of views of revelation which were implicit in much of the Old Testament. In this section of the Old Testament, revelation is not claims about God so much as a promised final appearance of God himself to redeem his people and establish his kingdom. Apocalyptic literature gives its readers a glimpse into a future revelation in which God will act historically to demonstrate his own identity and sovereignty. It typically asserts the future kingdom of God against the claims of rival gods and empires. Pannenberg argues that the apocalyptic strand of the Old Testament provides the typical New Testament view of revelation as 'a present disclosure and then a future universal disclosure' of God himself.[57]

5. Revelation is christological

For all Pannenberg's emphasis on universal and eschatological revelation, he also insists that revelation is christological, a conviction he shares with Barth and Bultmann and Rothe.[58] At the same time he points out that history continues beyond Jesus' death and resurrection and so the events of Christ's life, death and resurrection cannot meet the absolute criteria for revelation. He integrates the universal and christological by asserting that in Christ there is a unique anticipatory revelation of God.[59]

Apocalyptic revelation characteristically gives a glimpse of a future reality. Pannenberg argues that with Jesus there is something far more than such a disclosure, for in him the kingdom is present as 'a power that shapes the future' so that it 'is already an event . . . without ceasing to be future'.[60] Those who encountered Jesus met more than a prophet; they met the one who embodied the kingdom and its claims in his life and teaching. Yet this anticipatory revelation was still indirect. Pannenberg points to Jesus' hesitancy in identifying himself as the Christ.[61] This hesitation is observable in the gospel accounts as they stand, though Pannenberg is not working directly from the gospels. He appeals to the reconstruction of Jesus' history from Bornkamm and others who hold that the more direct claims of Jesus in the gospels are not historical. This critical account of the historical Jesus suggests strongly that during Jesus' ministry it was not at all clear who he was or how he related to God. When we consider Pannenberg's Christology we will see how important this historical reconstruction is for his Christology.

For Pannenberg, it is the resurrection which removes the ambiguity from Jesus' claims and clarifies his identity.[62] He does not think that the resurrection simply lifts the veil to show what was always the case. For Pannenberg, Jesus' identity is established by the resurrection: 'the Easter event determines what the meaning was of the pre-Easter history of Jesus and who he was in his relation to God'.[63] In this statement the word 'determines' is very important. The resurrection is the event which creates the meaning for events which occurred before it. To put it the other way round, Pannenberg argues that the pre-Easter ministry and identity of Jesus anticipated what Jesus became in the resurrection.

Pannenberg notes that the New Testament texts which are often used when theologians seek to show that revelation comes in Christ (John 1:1–4; Rom. 3:21; 16:25–6; Heb. 1:1–2; 1 Tim. 3:16) do not quite deliver what is hoped for! They present Christ as the decisive revelation of salvation but not the final self-revelation of God.[64] Yet there is a crucial connection between salvation and revelation which allows these texts to be the basis for a claim about Christ and revelation. Pannenberg develops the idea that salvation involves the manifestation of God's glory (e.g. 1 Cor. 2:7–9). As salvation dawns in Christ so too does the revelation of the deity of God and this salvation will ultimately involve the full revelation of God's glory. If salvation comes with Christ, then revelation comes with him as well. With this argument, Pannenberg asserts that the texts which he says present the 'New Testament revelation schema' allow 'an express statement about God's eschatological self-revelation in Jesus Christ'.[65] Although historically such revelation is indirect, it has its full meaning in that which it anticipates.

Pannenberg approaches a christological view of revelation very differently from Barth. He accepts that in the life of Christ there are hints and glimpses of the presence of God's kingdom, yet it is only because of the resurrection that Christ's life becomes the revelation of the kingdom. The resurrection is revelatory because it anticipates the eschatological glory of God and it, in turn, allows the glory of God to be seen in Jesus' whole life. The structure of Christology becomes the structure of revelation for Pannenberg.

Anticipation

Pannenberg's central claim about revelation is that Jesus is the anticipatory revelation of God's final all-encompassing self-revelation. This idea of 'anticipation' is one we will meet many times in Pannenberg and Chapter 5 will explore it in detail. At this point it is important to have some idea of what Pannenberg means by 'anticipation'. Initially it may seem quite odd. How can a later event (Easter) change or create the meaning of an earlier event?

One way to understand what Pannenberg is doing is to remember that he is dealing with the meaning of events. In history we commonly recognize that the meaning of an event depends on later ones. What happened when Archduke Ferdinand was assassinated in June 1914? What did that event mean? At the time it was the demise of the heir of a fading military power, yet it turned out that the assassination was the spark that set Europe alight. By Armistice Day in 1918 the assassination had a terrible significance that had only developed with the near self-destruction of Europe in bloody war. You may respond to this example by arguing that it deals with the meaning of the event and not the event itself. Pannenberg would answer that events and their meanings are intertwined. He appeals to the hermeneutical tradition of Schleiermacher which sees understanding and meaning as basic to what things are.

The pattern of anticipation is repeated when Pannenberg argues that the resurrection has significance as it anticipates the eschaton. Jesus' resurrection is a revelation of God's eschatological kingdom: 'if Jesus . . . is ascended to God and if thereby the end of the world has begun, then God is ultimately revealed in Jesus'.[66] Pannenberg's claim that revelation has a christological focus depends on the anticipatory relation between Jesus' ministry, the resurrection and the eschaton.

Revelation and Word

So far the summary of Pannenberg's view has been concerned with revelation in historical events. Yet in German theology there were important strains which emphasized the word of God as revelation. Pannenberg deals with three ways of viewing 'God's word' as revelation: the term can refer to the eternal *Logos* who reveals God, to the preaching of the apostles and to the words of Scripture. Pannenberg is wary of the total identification of revelation with word. On the one hand he does not accept that the mere form of preaching as a challenge or call is sufficient to render a message as God's revelation (a view he associates with Barth and Bultmann). On the other hand he rejects Rothe's view that events are not revelatory but need to be interpreted by an accompanying word.[67] He is also critical of Jüngel's immediate association of the 'word of God' with Christ. It is not that he finally denies this link, but rather that he views it as one which needs to be developed and demonstrated not merely assumed and asserted.[68]

Pannenberg develops the links between Christ, revelation and word by starting with revelation as history.[69] He argues that where revelation is proleptic and debatable (as it is now), words are essential.[70] So there must be testimony to Jesus' life, death and resurrection, and interpretation of them. Yet the apostolic testimony does not supplement an event which is 'dumb'; it 'simply spreads abroad the radiance that shines from Christ's own glory'.[71] The message comes from the events and it is revelation because the events it reports are true revelation.[72] So Pannenberg has a place for apostolic testimony as the explanation of Jesus and his resurrection. He recognizes that this preaching has a subjective element and a call for response, but holds that it is revelation not because of its form, but because of its content.[73] Thus, Pannenberg ascribes to the apostolic gospel the task of giving the knowledge which is the basis of faith.

We might wonder if Pannenberg is not simply capitulating to the pressure of tradition when he includes the notion of a word in his account of revelation. Would it not be more consistent for him to say that revelation is the eschatological summation of history and so anticipatory revelation is also a historical event and the words that report the event are clearly secondary and dependent? Pannenberg offers a reason for giving words a place in revelation alongside event. He begins with Ebeling's claim that words have an ability to 'make what is hidden present . . . especially what is past and future'.[74] Ebeling's claim, in the first instance, is about all words, though he and Pannenberg both make the claim on a theological basis and apply it particularly to words of divine revelation.[75] That is, language has a unique ability to give 'an anticipation of the totality of truth'. In *ATP* Pannenberg offers a long anthropological argument to show that language arises in human culture, and culture is always based in a view of the whole of reality. He argues that language conveys some premonition of and participation in that view.[76] If language in general does this, the Christian message is a special case, for by proclaiming the identity of God it makes the theme of the totality of the world explicit. Language has the capacity to give an anticipation of the unity of all reality and in the gospel this capacity is most fully realized.

So Pannenberg concludes as follows: 'We can thus see why mediation by word and speech was an essential element in the anticipation of the future of God in the coming of Jesus, and why the revelatory meaning of his person and work needed the Word as the medium of its articulation.'[77]

From this line of thought Pannenberg appeals to the *Logos* concept. The second person of the Trinity was termed the *Logos* because he was the creative Word of God who made all things and sustains all things and will unite all things. So Pannenberg draws the *Logos* tradition and the *kerygma* tradition together to conclude: 'the world order that is manifest in Jesus Christ is thus a historical order, the order of the divine plan for redemption of the world which is revealed in him'.[78] For Pannenberg, the event of revelation is itself the content of the 'comprehensive idea of Word of God'. This alone 'can be called the Word of God in the full sense'. He concludes that 'Jesus Christ, then, is the Word of God as the quintessence of the divine plan for creation and history and of its end time but already proleptic revelation. We may thus speak of the self-revelation of God by this Word . . . so long as the Word is the same as the deity of God.'[79]

Revelation and Scripture

At the start of this chapter we saw that Pannenberg shares the conclusion that the Reformation Scripture principle cannot be presumed. He argues that a doctrine of Scripture must be a goal, not a foundation.[80] Pre-Enlightenment systematic theology would usually include a discussion of Scripture in the prolegomena or introductory material. Scripture was put forward as the reliable foundation for theology, and real theology proceeded from that. Such discussions might offer reasons for the acceptance of Scripture, but were preliminary to the real business of theology. Pannenberg, however, thinks that a doctrine of Scripture can only be substantiated in the process of the exposition of the whole of the Christian faith. Like other elements of theology, claims about the Bible are hypotheses which have to be developed and tested through the discussion.

Pannenberg proposes an approach to Scripture that aims 'to discover . . . [the] unity of Scripture in the Christ-event attested by its different witnesses'.[81] He hopes to achieve this in a historical study in which the Christ-event, as it 'bears its own meaning in itself', is examined and becomes the standard by which New Testament witnesses are judged. He expects that this study will show that the New Testament witnesses are held together by 'the unfolding unity of the inherent meaning of the Christ-event'.[82] His claim is that the Bible's narratives have a realism which is best honoured by a critical historical examination, rather than treating them 'simply as literature in which the facticity of what is recorded is a subsidiary matter'.[83]

Pannenberg looks to the gospel as that which unites the New Testament witness. It is this, he says, which 'unfolds' and 'brings home' the significance of the Spirit-filled eschatological revelation in Christ and 'lays hold of hearers' so that 'Jesus Christ himself . . . speaks and acts through the word of the gospel'.[84] The gospel is the source of the church and 'represents the authority of Jesus Christ'. This is the basis of the authority of the Bible: 'insofar as they bear witness to this content [the gospel] . . . the words . . . of Scripture have authority in the church'.[85] The gospel is present in the statements of Scripture, but the two are not identical and they can be differentiated sufficiently that 'scriptural statements' may be measured 'by the content of the gospel'.[86]

Pannenberg makes material revelation expressed in the gospel the ground on which to establish any formal claim to revelation (that the Bible is the form of God's revelation). The message of the dawning kingdom in the resurrection of Christ is also the criterion by which to judge claims to revelation. His view means that 'the authority of the Bible . . . does not guarantee . . . the truth of individual statements in biblical books' and the inspiration of Scripture is a conviction arrived at on the basis of its witness to Christ. He claims that this leaves room for 'individual judgement regarding the content and truth of the scriptural witness' and the 'free recognition of the truth' in which the reconciliation of God with the world reaches its goal.[87] A further implication is that the question of the canon is a subordinate one, in which each writing is tested for its witness to Christ.[88]

Pannenberg's Theology: a Theology of Revelation

Pannenberg's whole project is based on eschatological revelation since it is oriented around the action of God to reveal himself to his creatures as the true Infinite.[89] This theology of revelation provides the architectonics of his thought. Grenz describes the chapter on revelation in *Systematic Theology* 1 as 'pivotal to the whole', claiming that 'the doctrinal delineation that follows is but the unfolding of what lies undeveloped in revelation'.[90] As we examine some key doctrines in Pannenberg's thought we will see how he builds from his view of revelation to give a systematic account of Christian theology.

When we locate Pannenberg's approach to revelation in his wider project, it is clear why the question plays such an important role in his thought and how his particular view of revelation helps his project. Pannenberg accepts the critiques of Dilthey and Heidegger that absolute claims are untenable and metaphysics has come to an end. He also recognizes that after the Enlightenment mere claims to authority are inadmissible. This raises the question of how Christian theology can make anything like its traditional claims to the universal and absolute truth of a particular revelation. His answer builds on the idea of anticipatory revelation. This claim is both a positive assertion and an important qualification. The assertion is that revelation is anticipatory. Present revelation genuinely, if only partially, grasps God's future and is truly characterized as 'revelation'.[91] On this basis the Christian can speak and think about God and metaphysical discussion is reopened. The qualification, made at the same time, is that revelation, and reflection on it, are multiform and remain open to contention and revision. The Christian, and especially the theologian, ventures hypotheses and seeks to verify them as far as possible. This task of theology corresponds closely with Pannenberg's account of revelation.

Scaer criticizes Pannenberg for making absolute claims about Christ based on 'the probabilities of historical investigation' and thinks that 'there seems to be an inherent self-contradiction in his entire system of thought'.[92] This misses the basic point of Pannenberg's appeal to an anticipatory revelation. He is very aware that Christian theology makes claims about the whole of reality but cannot fully substantiate them. This is part of his reason for saying that present revelation is anticipatory. This claim may not convince a critic but it cannot be dismissed as self-contradictory. Pannenberg would reply that Scaer's preference for an 'absolute' basis for claims about God is doomed to fail since at present claims about God clearly are contestable and so cannot (yet) have an absolute basis.

Learning from Pannenberg's Doctrine of Revelation

I want to highlight three striking features of Pannenberg's present doctrine of revelation. First, his axiom that revelation is God's eschatological self-revelation correctly orients his doctrine of revelation. Paul writes that 'now we see in a mirror, dimly, but then we will see face to face' and he looks forward to the time when he will 'know fully' (1 Cor. 13:12). The Christian hope is to 'see God', sometimes called the blessed (or beatific) vision. Molnar criticizes Pannenberg for failing to appeal 'directly to God acting *ad extra* in his Word and Spirit' and for holding instead 'that meaning should be seen "in the light of the temporality of reality and *experience* of reality, as an anticipation of the totality of truth which will be complete only in the future" '[93]. Surely it is part of the strength of Pannenberg's theology that he recognizes that there is a necessarily provisional nature to present revelation. Molnar seems not to grasp the importance of Pannenberg's recognition of the plurality and provisional status of present knowledge which means that theology cannot build merely on a simple and direct appeal to God's action in Word and Spirit. Nor does he seem to appreciate the controlling role of Pannenberg's appeal to the Bible's eschatological orientation.

Many discussions on the doctrine of revelation hardly mention eschatological revelation, but surely Pannenberg is right to insist that it is revelation in its full and proper form. All other forms of revelation are on the way to the final revelation and find their completion in it. This recognition can help to relieve the pressure in some formulations of the doctrine of revelation. For instance evangelical theology sometimes talks about the 'absolute' truth of the Bible. I do not want to diminish the truth and reliability of the Bible; however it is worth noting that 'absolute' is probably not the right word to use about the Bible. In its more technical use 'absolute' means that something is independent, not viewed in relation to other things or in comparison to them. The Bible is not 'absolute' revelation in that sense. It is dependent on God's actions to reveal himself, it does not give us God's own knowledge of himself and it promises a fuller final revelation than it now offers. One task of theology is to give us a sense of proportion and to see how various things that Christians believe fit together. Setting present revelation on its eschatological horizon helps to do that.

A second strength of Pannenberg's approach is that he addresses the doctrine of revelation in the midst of his full discussion of God and deals with the doctrine of Scripture within that. A great deal of evangelical doctrine of Scripture suffers because neither of those steps is taken. Many theology texts and courses begin with doctrine of Scripture. This pattern developed in the post-Reformation period when Protestant theology had to establish its ground in Scripture alone rather than in Scripture and tradition together. In the Enlightenment era questions about the basis of knowledge were primary and so doctrine of revelation naturally remained the first (and foundational) issue. This reinforces the idea that we can think about how God reveals himself without giving serious consideration to God himself or to the purposes of his revelation. It also seems to assume the foundationalist approach which assumes we can establish a firm basis for knowing and then work on the project of building knowledge. It is important to recognize that any doctrine of revelation and Scripture already assumes a doctrine of God and of redemption. I also think that a postfoundationalism which deals with the justification of claims in the midst of the exposition of those claims is a far better method.

It is not that a theology book or course can never begin with a discussion of revelation (any discussion has to start somewhere). Rather it means that we should be aware of what is being assumed when we do this and especially how doctrines of God and redemption have to be included in any account of revelation.[94] There is no reason that the doctrine of revelation should always be treated as the first step in theological exposition and it would be good to see more evangelical theology starting with the gospel and allowing that to shape our doctrine of revelation.

The third strength of Pannenberg's approach is that he does just that – the gospel leads to his doctrine of Scripture. Pannenberg develops his doctrine of Scripture within this Christology. God's anticipatory self-revelation is in Christ and the apostles' message comes from him and his resurrection. This message is then the basis for the New Testament and so for Christian Scripture. This approach does not have an obvious place for the Old Testament as Scripture, and that is one of the signs that Pannenberg's thought needs a more robust doctrine of Scripture (more of that below). However he is right to move from Christ to the gospel and then to Scripture.

Some Questions for Pannenberg on Revelation

There are two significant questions I want to raise about Pannenberg's view of revelation. The first stems from the fact that his view is drawn from his Christology which is, in turn, based on a reconstruction of the historical Jesus. It has to be admitted that his approach will only be as strong as this reconstruction. In Chapter 7 I will suggest that there are good reasons to question the critical reconstruction on which he relies. If that is questioned, then Pannenberg's doctrine of revelation will have to be given some reformulation.

The second question relates to Pannenberg's doctrine of Scripture. His overall doctrine of revelation is rich and complex, so it is somewhat surprising that his account of Scripture is rather attenuated. He affirms the inspiration and authority of Scripture, but offers little more and his brief comments do not provide a clear theological foundation for biblical interpretation.[95] One aspect which seems to be lacking from his doctrine of Scripture is discussion of how the events of history relate to the biblical texts as two loci of revelation. He discusses the connection between the events of Jesus' life and the apostolic witness, but not the broader question of the connections between events and text.

A treatment of this relationship is important for Pannenberg because he puts significant emphasis on both loci. On the one hand in Pannenberg's description, the primary locus of revelation lies 'behind' the biblical text in the events to which the text witnesses. Consistent with this view, his theological method rests on historical investigation of the events. Yet on the other hand he seeks to examine the texts themselves; he writes that 'the accounts themselves must also figure in any presentation of the history of Israel and primitive Christianity'.[96] In accord with this his work makes extensive reference to the biblical writings. Yet I will argue later in this book that there are important features of the biblical texts themselves to which Pannenberg pays little attention.[97] I suspect that one reason for his lack of engagement with the details of biblical texts is that his theological account of Scripture is thin and lacks a positive account of the literary features of the biblical text, or any of its features beyond its witness to the events of revelation. Pannenberg does not provide a theology of Scripture which is sufficient to accommodate the 'literary turn' in biblical studies and so his practice fails to include fully this approach.[98]

In evangelical theology the connection between the events of revelation and the text is usually dealt with by affirming a doctrine of inspiration. This doctrine describes how the text of Scripture is divinely intended revelation. Pannenberg's theology lacks a sufficient doctrine of the inspiration of Scripture, or something equivalent. Based on the affirmation that the proclamation of the gospel is Spirit-filled, Pannenberg argues that it is justified to conclude 'that the writings of the New Testament also participate in some way in that divine inspiration'. Yet this is the case 'only insofar as those writings witness to the Pauline gospel of God's saving activity in Jesus' death on the cross and in his resurrection'.[99] This does not take us any further than the statements about the gospel and does not provide for an orientation to the texts as texts, rather than as witnesses. I am not arguing that Pannenberg's position requires him to adopt a classic evangelical version of the doctrine (if we can identify what that is). My argument is that looked at on its own terms his theology requires an analogous doctrine to give an account of Scripture which will be sufficient for Pannenberg's actual practice of scriptural interpretation.[100]

Pannenberg's approach to the doctrine of revelation already offers the resources for a fuller doctrine of Scripture.[101] A starting point for this development would be Jesus' view of the Hebrew Scriptures. Jesus' life and his relation to God are formed in the context of listening to and meditating on Scriptures. Jesus shared the common view of first-century Judaism that the Scriptures were divinely inspired and the instrument through which the covenant of God worked. He himself appealed to and lived by the Scriptures (e.g. Matt. 5:38; Mark 2:25; 7:6–7,10; Luke 4:16–30).[102] The importance of the Scriptures in Jesus' life and ministry is an obvious feature of the gospel records. Ben Meyer argues, in a way which would likely satisfy Pannenberg, that Jesus' awareness of his mission includes 'the conviction that in this last, climactic mission to Israel, and therefore in the bearer of this last, climactic mission, the Scriptures . . . had, of divine or prophetic necessity, to come to fulfilment'.[103] As well as the role the Scriptures played in his own life, Jesus gave his disciples a practice of reading the Hebrew Scriptures which paid close attention to its wording and accepted its teaching as authoritative. In doing so he gave Christianity a Scripture principle and directed Christian theology to allow the texts of the Hebrew Scriptures to shape an understanding of God. From this historical basis a fuller doctrine of Scripture could be developed which would support a practice of reading Scripture with greater attention to the texts and their literary features.

What I have suggested above is not a doctrine of inspiration *per se* but is a more robust doctrine of Scripture. Pannenberg is wary of a claim of authority for Scripture which is separate from the truthfulness of its content. There is, however, no need to assert the authority of Scripture independent of its content and the truthfulness of that content. Scripture conveys the provisional revelation in the history of Israel and in Christ, and as they share in the anticipation of truth, so they share anticipatorily in the freeing authority of God's final revelation. This claim does not bar historical-critical investigation of Scripture, nor does it attempt to foreclose investigation of 'the difference between the biblical texts and the events to which they point', which Pannenberg identifies as 'the central problem of historical study'.[104] It would, on the other hand, direct theology more immediately toward Scripture as the foundational source of theology.

So we can conclude our review of Pannenberg's doctrine of revelation noting that he offers a complex and satisfying view which presents revelation as personal, historical, eschatological, christological, evangelical and scriptural. The key to his position is the claim that Christ is the anticipatory revelation of God's final revelation. Along with several strengths, we have noted that this approach depends on a historical reconstruction which has been questioned and that needs to be developed to offer a fuller doctrine of Scripture.

5.

How the Future Makes the Past:
Pannenberg and Metaphysics

Pannenberg's project requires him to explain how it is possible to affirm the truth of a transcendent God, who is the reality which determines all other reality, when philosophical reflection has come to view reality as fragmented and shifting. Pannenberg accepts much of these philosophical claims, but appeals to God's eschatological revelation as the point at which reality finds its unity. His argument is that we can make a valid appeal to God's future because there are, in the present, anticipations of the final revelation. The pattern of final unity of reality in God and a present anticipation is not only a revelational pattern. For Pannenberg it must also be a metaphysical one. It is not merely that we know partially now but will know fully in the eschaton. Knowledge must reflect the structure of reality, or it is not truly knowledge. Pannenberg insists that this is especially so if we are thinking about God. Since God is the one who unites all reality, his existence is only established when such unity occurs, so not only knowledge of God but God's very existence must come from the eschaton. That then demands a new way of understanding reality – a new metaphysic. So Pannenberg sets out to rethink reality!

This chapter considers Pannenberg's metaphysical proposal. I begin by identifying the criteria that Pannenberg's metaphysical proposal has to meet and then tracing his presentation of the proposal and his view of the relationship of time and eternity. I am going to lay out the criteria and Pannenberg's argument for his proposal in some detail (although it will still be a summary). It is only when you see the challenges Pannenberg is trying to overcome and all the various factors he is seeking to integrate that the power of his proposal becomes evident. His metaphysical proposal is very surprising and I will look at some reactions to it before thinking about how we can assess it.

The Criteria for Pannenberg's Metaphysical Proposal

Theology has been built on a metaphysical account which Feuerbach, Nietzsche, Dilthey and Heidegger have dismantled. If theology is going to continue, it will have to rebuild metaphysics in a way that overcomes the problems these critiques have revealed. Pannenberg holds that there is no place for simply reasserting a traditional foundation for theology, that has already been shown to fail. From his interaction with the critique of metaphysics and broader themes in his work, it becomes clear that there are several criteria that a new metaphysical proposal will have to meet. Pannenberg does not gather these into a list, but each can be identified in his thought and once they are spelled out it is easier to see why his proposal takes the form it does. These criteria are interdependent so that each could be viewed as an implication of the others in the list, yet each is sufficiently distinct that it deserves separate treatment.

1. Anthropological validity

One criterion Pannenberg has for metaphysics is that any proposal will have to be validated by anthropology. Although critical of views which assume that the human mind determines truth, he accepts that they make an important point: that an idea of God must illuminate human experience.[1] Importantly, Pannenberg rejects deterministic views, which he thinks are the implication of Augustinian theology, and holds that any metaphysic must give a proper account of human freedom.[2] Freedom is established by historical contingency, so a metaphysic which deals with contingency will offer a better account of human freedom. Pannenberg does not, however, hold that freedom consists of simply acting in a contingent history, for his full account of freedom involves humanity reaching the destiny of fellowship with God.[3] He therefore seeks a presentation of God in which he is 'the origin of freedom' in being the goal of human life.[4]

2. Asserting universality

Pannenberg holds that a convincing metaphysical proposal must be universal; it must show how God is related to all reality: 'the final tenability of any idea of God which is put forward depends . . . upon the understanding of the world, that is, upon how far the God who is asserted is comprehensible as the reality which determines everything'.[5] In one sense, to insist that a metaphysic be universal is a truism. The point Pannenberg is making is that, though the possibility of such an account has been denied, if theology is going to speak of a God who determines all reality then it must have an account of the existence of the whole.

3. Allowing for historicity

We have seen that Pannenberg is concerned about history. He emphasizes that revelation occurs in history and that meaning develops historically and he stresses that human existence is historical. Pannenberg makes this point emphatically in the concluding chapter of *Anthropology in Theological Perspective*: 'Human life, whether it is the life span of the individual or the larger story of peoples and states, takes concrete form in history . . . of all the disciplines that have the human being as their subject, the science of history and historiography come closest to grasping human reality as it is experienced.'[6]

He finds a weakness on just this point in the atheistic tradition, which stresses the historicity of human life, yet cannot determine if humans are 'constituted prior to history' and create history, or if the historical process creates them. He claims that only a theological perspective can answer this question by providing an understanding of God who is the goal of history and who co-operates with his human creatures.[7]

4. Articulating meaning

The dual stress on universality and historicity draws from Dilthey, who held that meaning comes from the relationship which a part has to its corresponding whole. In line with Dilthey, Pannenberg argues that genuine understanding transcends any general explanation provided by a wider law or principle. A particular is understood as more than an instance of a general law.[8] Genuine understanding transcends an 'explicit frame of reference' and reaches that point at which a particular is perceived to fit into the whole, and in this case 'the semantic horizon of this basic understanding fades into the indefinite distance'.[9] The particular is no longer referred to a general law but is understood in the light of 'all reality', even though this cannot be fully articulated.

In assuming that reality may be understood in this way, Pannenberg is standing apart from Kant and with Hegel. Kant recognizes the need for human reason to discover a unity in the experience of diversity, but holds that this could not be reached from empirical experience. In contrast, Pannenberg seeks to show that the universe is meaningful and that this meaning is not grounded on human perception but in the world as it is in itself.[10] Hegel's response is that understanding draws on the concepts provided by the cosmos itself.[11] Pannenberg agrees, though he holds that the claim can only be made in anticipation.

5. Allowing for incompleteness

Related to the historicity of human experience is its incompleteness. Pannenberg agrees with Dilthey and Heidegger that traditional metaphysics does not recognize this incompleteness.[12] He argues that a revised metaphysic must include this feature: 'since reality is still in process, still open, our experience of reality is always at any given moment necessarily incomplete'.[13]

Pannenberg's Metaphysical Proposal

Pannenberg offers the fullest exposition of his reworked metaphysic in the first five chapters of *Metaphysics and the Idea of God*, which were originally a lecture series.[14] Each chapter deals with a major question suggested by the criteria listed above. In the conclusion of each step of the argument Pannenberg appeals to Christian theology. He does so, not because his philosophical reflections have proved the theological claims, but because the claims meet the demands laid out by philosophical criticism.

The Absolute

The end of metaphysics is the claim that there is no 'Absolute' or, to use Pannenberg's parallel term, no 'Infinite'; the finite, empirical world is the only reality.[15] Pannenberg argues that a systematic exclusion of transcendent perspectives makes it impossible to view reality as a unified whole. At the conclusion of the discussion of the Absolute, Pannenberg states that 'it is for the sake of . . . the task of achieving a comprehensive interpretation of the finite world that metaphysics attempts to rise above the multiplicity of the finite toward the idea of the One, a One that grounds the unity of the world and provides the unifying context for the multitude of things within the world.'[16]

For Kant the unity of reality is supplied by the knowing subject; Pannenberg asserts a more objective unity. His argument, adapted from Hegel, is that the concept of all finite objects in general must imply the Infinite. Conversely, if we cannot meaningfully think of 'all reality' then we cannot make sense of individual objects. Pannenberg's argument is that the thought of a finite object implies other finite objects because the finite is, by definition, limited in space and time, and in perception it is differentiated from other objects. Thus if one can conceptualize a finite object, then there must be other objects by which this object is limited and from which it is differentiated. In turn, the concept of all finite objects must, in itself, be a finite group. So what is it that stands over against this group and makes it possible for us to grasp the idea of the whole of finite reality? Pannenberg's answer is that we must have the concept of the Infinite. In making his point, Pannenberg appeals to Hegel's claim that 'whenever we think of a border, we have always thought at the same time of a something that lies beyond the border, however vaguely'.[17] Pannenberg does not contend that this argument provides a clear conception of the Infinite, but rather states that the idea is intuited and is unthematized.[18]

The Infinite in Pannenberg's scheme is not a mathematical infinite (an unceasing numeration), but the 'concept of an actual

Infinite', as found in Christian thought, that is a personal, infinite God. Is it coherent to think of a being who is personal and infinite?[19] To show that it is, Pannenberg returns to the Hegelian argument that the Infinite is the basis of the perception of the finite. As such, the Infinite must be that which relies on nothing else. So Pannenberg identifies the Infinite with the Absolute as 'all-sufficient'.[20] He adopts a further conclusion from Hegel arguing that if the Infinite is genuinely unlimited then it must also include the finite within it. It must be both 'transcendent' and 'immanent', producing and embracing all finite reality.

With Hegel, Pannenberg admits that the arguments do not bridge the gap between 'the idea of the infinite' and 'the idea of an existing being'.[21] He does not try to argue further but rather turns directly to Christian theology: only the Christian doctrine of the Trinity meets the requirement of speaking of a reality which is all-sufficient and both 'transcendent' and 'immanent'.[22] His appeal to the doctrine of the Trinity is an example of philosophical reflection performing the critical function Pannenberg ascribes to it: showing what a proper conception of God must include but also revealing its own need for 'religion' to provide the material with which it will work.

What has Pannenberg achieved at the conclusion of this stage of his metaphysical argument? He claims to have shown that if the world is to be understood, it requires the idea of a true Infinite which is the basis and origin of all reality and is, in turn, not dependent on anything else but is both transcendent and immanent. He has argued that the Christian doctrine of the Trinity meets these criteria. So he has begun to provide a new way of conceiving of the Infinite as the Triune God. However, he has not yet addressed those criteria that particularly relate to human experience.

Self-consciousness

When Pannenberg turns to anthropological themes he faces the question of the existence of 'the soul', the existence of which has been widely denied in Western thought since Hume. The other obvious alternative, provided by Kant, is that the human soul, as self-consciousness, is what unifies perception of reality.[23]

But Pannenberg maintains that Kant replaces God with human consciousness. He must show how the idea of the soul is sustainable, without making it constitutive for reality.[24]

In order to show that human self-consciousness is not self-positing, Pannenberg first seeks to establish that 'the consciousness of objects is, in principle, independent from self-consciousness'. His argument is empirical, drawing on a wide range of thinkers. He takes up the ideas of thinkers such as Hume, Locke, James, Mead, Freud, Erikson and Bergson, all of whom are sceptical about the notion of a metaphysical soul. He uses their arguments to build the case that perception of the world (as a unified world) is not grounded in the consciousness of the self, but rather 'the ego's unity is mediated through the experience of the world'.[25] Having established that self-consciousness cannot be treated as the basis for knowledge of the world, he explains the aspect of Kant's approach which he considers valid: that the capacity to integrate and refine knowledge depends upon self-knowledge.[26] So he denies Kant's claim that the unity of reality is based in human self-consciousness but grants the claim that modern empirical-scientific knowledge with its discursive method relies on self-consciousness.

Having critiqued and then partially affirmed the Kantian axiom, Pannenberg extends the argument beyond the realm considered by Kant. First, he argues that self-consciousness is not a prior given but develops through experience of the world, and thus identity, which is mediated by self-consciousness, also develops through time, both in an individual life and in a wider cultural history. Even the socio-cultural horizon is too limiting however, for a full explanation of human consciousness must 'ascend above the context of society'. So finally, Pannenberg concludes that self-consciousness requires metaphysics. Grounding the rise of self-consciousness in awareness of the Absolute explains 'the roots of a society's cultural identity, the constitution of individual subjectivity, *and* the individual's ability occasionally to turn against society out of motives that need not be solely egotistical'.[27] At this point Pannenberg's consideration of anthropological questions converges with theistic metaphysics: 'The metaphysics of Absolute I am proposing would not merely attempt, on the grounds of subjectivity, to reconstrue the constitution of the subject through some source in the Absolute that precedes it. Instead, it would carry out the "rising above" toward the idea of the Absolute from a starting point which encompasses worldly experience, self-consciousness and their reciprocal mediation.'[28]

Pannenberg concludes that the idea of human subjectivity is not inimical to Christianity; indeed he argues that it has Christian roots. It is only when the self is conceptualized in total independence from God that the emphasis on subjectivity comes into opposition to Christian thought. He draws on his lengthy discussion of the issue to assert that, in fact, such a conceptualization 'cannot be successful'.[29]

Pannenberg concludes that humans do have something like the traditional 'soul', but that this is a self-awareness which develops over time in interaction with others and in dependence on the Absolute. A metaphysic must account for this and for how 'we know or feel ourselves to be identical with ourselves', so that in the present we are 'everything that we were [in the past] and will be in the future'. This time-bridging unity is, Pannenberg suggests, 'appropriately described only as participation in eternity'.[30] Thus he begins to examine directly the temporality or historicity of human experience of the world.

Being and time

Pannenberg takes up the question of the relationship of being and time by reviewing the ancient roots of the discussion. He summarizes the way in which Plato, and even Aristotle, held to the view that there is 'a distinction between real being (and unchanging identity) and the realm of becoming and passing away'. For Plato the distinction was between two realms, while for Aristotle it was between attributes and underlying essential forms. Pannenberg explains that process philosophy offers an alternative to the classical view, but he concludes that this fails since it cannot offer an adequate explanation of the unity of the many elementary events.[31] He traces a parallel pattern in Heidegger's thoroughly temporal view that the totality of life, which is never completed within the history of a life, serves as the basis for the meaning of all individual experiences, and that this meaning therefore changes over the course of a life history.[32]

Pannenberg responds to Heidegger's position in a way that supports a theistic metaphysic. He finds resources for this in the

Neoplatonic thought of Plotinus (*c.*204/5–70) and its Christian adoption. It is common to think of time and eternity as opposites: time is change and movement, and eternity is timeless and changeless. Plotinus however had a more positive view of the relationship and thought that eternity was the unity of all time in the transcendent One and was the basis for time. We experience time and not eternity, yet we remain aware that our time has a unity and we strive for a future unity of the whole.[33] Pannenberg summarizes Plotinus' view as: 'the whole is present only in the sense that it hovers over the parts as the future whole' and points out that 'Plotinus . . . first maintained the primacy of the future in the understanding of time', and this was a primacy grounded 'in the fact that the totality of existence is possible only from the standpoint of its future'. Plotinus' thought touches on several of Pannenberg's criteria for a metaphysical proposal. Most importantly, Pannenberg can point to Plotinus' emphasis on the future as the point in which a present unity of experience is grounded. However it seems that Plotinus' future is infinitely removed.[34]

Augustine was very influenced by Neoplatonism but made a distinctively Christian contribution to the understanding of time by affirming the doctrine of creation. Since God is the good Creator, our participation in time is a gift, not the result of a fall. Augustine does, however, lose Plotinus' recognition of the priority of the future. Augustine does offer an analysis of how the soul experiences time. In a famous reflection in *Confessions* Augustine considers how the soul remembers the past, pays attention to the present and expects the future, and in this way draws together the divisions of time.[35] According to Pannenberg the time-bridging function of the soul has significance for metaphysics because it reflects the fact that the soul has a kind of participation in eternity.[36] Pannenberg combines three ideas – Plotinus' view of the unity of time lying in the future, Augustine's positive account of time and eternity, and his view that the soul unites the moments of time because it participates in eternity – to provide a basis for a theological response to Heidegger.

Pannenberg contrasts the Neoplatonic-Augustinian conception of the soul participating in time which is united in a future eternity with Kant's view that the self provides the basis for unity and Heidegger's claim that the unity of the self is constituted in the anticipation of death.[37] Pannenberg disputes Heidegger's claim that there is a true totality in death. Death, in itself, fragments life so, says Pannenberg, any unity of life must be found in a 'possible totality of an existence always extended beyond whatever death makes of it'. His argument is that if life is going to have a totality, this will only be seen by 'another light'. This, says Pannenberg, points to religious hopes for life after death as an expression of the need for a different source of totality.[38]

From these reflections Pannenberg concludes that only the future offers the possibility of the wholeness of life and so it has 'the leading role in our consciousness of time'.[39] With this Pannenberg comes to a crucial conclusion: 'The essence of a life as a whole is temporal; it depends upon whatever future it is whose coming will bring about the wholeness of this whole' so the self 'exists in the mode of anticipation'.[40] This is a remarkable and counter-intuitive claim. It means that a thing is what it truly is (it has its essence) because of its future.

Pannenberg understands that this conception of essence applies to all existence. 'Everything that exists is what it is only as the anticipation of its future, in which . . . the wholeness of each being might be established: as long as something is, its end remains before it; still it is what it is always in anticipation of its end and from its end.'[41] Pannenberg says that he has 'something in mind along the lines of Dilthey's hermeneutic of historical experience . . . a descriptively demonstrable fact with ontological implications'. This new interpretation of essence can be termed Pannenberg's 'temporalized essentialism'.[42]

Just as Pannenberg's argument for the Absolute could only be completed by Christian theology so his reflections on self-consciousness, time and eternity appeal to Christian eschatology. Apart from a genuine hope for life with God, Heidegger would be right that wholeness can only be found in non-existence. Such hope can only exist because Jesus claims to bring the kingdom and his claim is confirmed in the resurrection.

Concept and anticipation

Pannenberg then clarifies his metaphysical proposal and seeks to validate it in the context of philosophical discussion. Dilthey's argument against metaphysics was that while it claims to discuss an unchanging reality its own concepts are constantly changing. According to Dilthey, all systems of metaphysics are historically conditioned and none gives a true description of 'reality'; he was 'convinced that the ensuing conflict of [proposed metaphysical] systems would eventually lead to scepticism'.[43] Pannenberg argues that one strength of his view is that it does not rely on unchanging concepts. Rather he offers a 'conjectural reconstruction' of the history of metaphysical discussion.[44] His view is that reality is developing in anticipation of a final unity, and so changes in how that unity is perceived can be incorporated into an account which holds that reality is developing. Human understanding is incomplete and can only offer hypotheses which it anticipates may be confirmed. Pannenberg views this anticipatory structure as not only noetic, but also ontological: anticipation is not 'external to the content' but is 'a form appropriate to its own content'.

To justify this claim, he turns explicitly to theology, and two cases in which anticipation has ontological implications: Jesus' message as an anticipation of the kingdom of God and his resurrection as an anticipation of the general resurrection. In both these cases anticipation is more than an announcement that looks to the future, but 'the future . . . is viewed as already and actually having broken into history'.[45] In both cases there is a 'presence' (not simply a prediction), but there is also a future event that 'will reveal the truth about the present'. The explicitly theological orientation of the kingdom and the resurrection may seem to distinguish sharply these concepts from others but Pannenberg draws on his previous discussion of being and time to assert that 'all created life is . . . a form of participation in the divine eternity, however weak or limited this participation may be'.[46]

Pannenberg claims that the New Testament can provide a missing element for the philosophical discussion.

It is just this . . . basically apocalyptic characteristic of the ministry of Jesus that, by means of its anticipatory structure, can become the key to solving a fundamental question facing philosophical reflection in the problematic post-Hegelian situation . . . It is possible to find in the history of Jesus an answer to the question of how 'the whole' of reality and its meaning can be conceived without compromising the provisionality and historical relativity of all thought, as well as the openness to the future on the part of the thinker who knows himself to be only on the way and not yet at the goal.[47]

He holds that the destiny of the cosmos is revealed in the resurrection of Jesus, and this shapes his metaphysics.

Some students of Pannenberg dispute his claim that his metaphysic is based on biblical eschatology. Lösel describes Pannenberg's model of religions (in which he has shown anticipation is a key element) as 'a "joint venture" of theological Hegelianism and religious Darwinism' and Molnar views it as a direct adaptation from Heidegger.[48] However, Pannenberg sharply distinguishes his view from those of Hegel and Heidegger and does so in order to reflect Christian eschatology. The same observation can be made about his points of differentiation from Plotinus, Dilthey and even Augustine. Pannenberg's proposal has important elements grounded in the claims of Scripture about Jesus' resurrection and the eschaton.

Pannenberg applies the insights drawn from biblical eschatology to the problem of developing a metaphysic which allows for historical contingency and also universal rationality. According to Pannenberg, all concepts have a 'two-sidedness': an aspect of identity and one of difference. In one aspect, a concept claims to give access to a particular object and this can only be so if it has an identity with the object. In the other aspect, the concept remains distinct from its object and requires 'verification' through the thing it denotes. This need for verification shows the difference between the concept and its referent, while the possibility of verification shows the possible identity of the two. According to Pannenberg, the gap between concepts and their objects is only fully closed eschatologically. He argues from this that 'the anticipatory form of knowledge corresponds to an element of the "not yet" within the very reality toward which knowing is directed', for 'the identity of things themselves are not yet completely present in the process of time'. That is, in the light of Christian eschatology, Dilthey's insight into the historical structure of the meaning of human life must be extended to 'the question of the essence of natural events and things'. Pannenberg states that 'the decision concerning the being that stands at the end of the process [of a thing becoming what it is] has retroactive power'.[49] When Pannenberg refers to a 'decision' he uses the word in a metaphorical sense as we might about a war being 'decided'. He does not, in the first instance, mean that God 'decides' the outcome, though as he explains his metaphysical proposal it becomes apparent that the locus of decision is the eternity of God.

Pannenberg's metaphysical proposal accepts 'time and becoming as the medium that constitutes the "whatness" of things'. The obvious sense of this is that substance or essence emerges through time. Pannenberg's proposal also claims that the essence of an object already exists as future. From this discussion a new temporal definition of the concept of substance emerges: 'things would then be what they are, substances, retroactively from the outcome of their becoming on the one hand, and on the other in the sense of anticipating the completion of their process of becoming, their history'.[50] Pannenberg admits that this counterintuitive proposal is hardly necessary when thinking of typical and self-repeating forms such as plants or geometric shapes. The power of temporalized essentialism is that it describes human lives and societies which have their identity more obviously decided in historical development. Pannenberg's proposal reconfigures classical metaphysics to deal with the historical nature of reality without adopting the atomism of process thought.[51]

Pannenberg extends the connection between this philosophical reflection and Christian eschatology. Heidegger focused entirely on the life of an individual. According to Pannenberg, this fails to deal with the fact that all reality is intertwined and the context of any event, form or individual is the whole of reality. Jewish apocalypticism expresses a better view: 'that the end of world history will bring fully to light all of its events and the life of each individual'. Further, this 'end of history' is not 'nothingness' but 'eternity'. So the 'essence of each individual thing' will be decided from eternity, and this is already present in the 'manner in which it has anticipated eternity'.[52]

Time and eternity

Pannenberg's view of anticipation is related to his view of the relationship of time and eternity. He concludes the presentation of his metaphysical proposal with a claim that can be made only on the basis of Christian revelation. 'But the end of history is not nothingness. The end of time (as we saw in Plotinus) is eternity. It is from the standpoint of this end that the essence of each individual thing, the manner in which it has anticipated eternity, will be decided.'[53]

Pannenberg has given two extensive treatments of the relation of time and eternity, in *Systematic Theology* and in a later article.[54] In these presentations the theological foundation of Pannenberg's metaphysic is made very clear. He presents his view in contrast to the classic view of divine timelessness taken by Augustine and in contrast to more recent views of divine temporality.[55] His position is also a contrast with views typical of process theology, which do not allow for ontological distinction between the immanent and essential Trinity meaning that the divine essence is what God becomes through history.[56]

Pannenberg appeals to the Bible's presentation that 'all time is before the eyes of God as a whole', while God is the source of life and creation but is always unchangeably himself. Moreover, the Bible presents God as one who acts in time. He argues that Christian thought erred when it accepted the view that time and eternity are antithetical. Instead he thinks that Christian theology can claim from Plotinus the idea that eternity is the simultaneity (not the denial) of all reality and that it becomes divided in time and so as the source of time and the goal of time-bound creatures. In this view eternity is not the antithesis of time but is 'constitutive of the time that is distinct from it'.[57]

Despite his high regard for Plotinus' conception of time and eternity, Pannenberg is not entirely satisfied with it and notes two significant limitations. The first is that the Neoplatonist has no eschatology but holds that the participation with God for which the soul strives is reached only in 'the self-abnegation in the experience of mystical union'.[58] The second, related, limitation is that Plotinus has no way of relating God to the future. In contrast, Pannenberg argues that God's eternity has a structure that reflects the priority of the future. He argues that Exodus 3:14, which is often used to show that God's eternity is atemporal, in fact hints at the priority of the future for the God who *will be* who he will be. More importantly, Pannenberg appeals to the New Testament presentation of the kingdom, which is present in Jesus' ministry but lies in the future. The kingdom establishes God's identity (or essence): 'with the manifestation and recognition of [God's] kingship his divine nature itself is at stake'.[59] In other words, the eternal identity of God is established in the life, ministry, death and resurrection of Jesus.

Pannenberg claims that, based on an appeal to God's eternity coming into history from the future, we can affirm that God's identity is established in history and yet that it is not identical with that history. He argues that when 'the divine identity of the Father is conceived in terms of the power of his future' and this future is understood as the source of new events in history then events of history may be held to establish God's identity without compromising God's transcendence.[60] This conception is in accord with Pannenberg's claim for the power of the future, for eternity establishes the nature of things and unifies history from the eschaton.

Pannenberg's view of the relationship between time and eternity is therefore grounded in his view of the relationship between God and time. We have already seen that for Pannenberg the true Infinite, or the Absolute, is a philosophical expression which finds its reality in the Triune God. In the same way, he does not propose an abstract 'eternity' which is different from God. He argues that the concept of God as both transcendent over changing time and having a real relationship with time, mediated via the future, is only coherent if God is an 'intrinsically differentiated unity', as the doctrine of the Trinity affirms. This trinitarian approach must include an emphasis on the economic Trinity, for God is not only eternally differentiated, but each person of the Trinity is related differently to time, and together they draw temporal creation into unity with God's own eternity. Pannenberg holds that God 'does not have ahead of him any future that is different from his present'; he is his own future, and that is 'perfect freedom'.[61] Pannenberg holds that temporal distinctions are not lost in the eternal present of the Triune God, but are brought into a perfect unity. Pannenberg's view that in eternity time is united in simultaneity but retains the differentiation of moments means that his ontology affirms genuine temporality and also affirms the unity of reality.

This theological exposition of God's relationship with time is reciprocally related to the more philosophical discussion of 'concept' and 'anticipation'. Temporalized essentialism is incoherent apart from the claim that events in history depend upon and are gathered up into the eternal present of God in the eschaton, so that what seem to be fractured and separated parts are found to share in a unified whole. Pannenberg's theological claims are given credence by their capacity to suggest resolutions to apparently intractable philosophical puzzles about being and time. At the same time, the metaphysical proposal can be tested for its coherence with biblical revelation and Christian eschatology. Meanwhile, both elements of Pannenberg's thought await final verification in the eschaton itself.

Anticipation and Pannenberg's Metaphysical Proposal

At this point in the discussion it is possible to venture a description of Pannenberg's metaphysical proposal by way of a definition of 'anticipation'.[62] When Pannenberg uses the concept of anticipation he expresses a notion that is both epistemological and ontological.[63] The epistemological notion is straightforward: a thing is revealed as it is and known and understood in its essence at the end of its existence and fully at the end of the historical process. It is only when all events have played out that we can finally say what each thing is. The ontological notion is counterintuitive: what is revealed as the essence is *determined* from the end of the process, so that a thing has its essence during the temporal process in anticipation of the final reality. The correlate to this claim is that because the essence has been present, anticipatorily, throughout the process it can be known provisionally before the end.

The fact that what exists at the end of history is constitutive for present reality is what Pannenberg in an early article calls 'the power of the future'. There he states that 'the future creates the past and the present'.[64] In *Metaphysics and the Idea of God* he makes a similar assertion: 'the future is to be construed as the source of the wholeness of finite being, and its being as the anticipation of its future'.[65]

In Aristotelian metaphysics, essences determine ends. A thing exists for a certain purpose or goal because it has an essence and this essence brings the thing into existence. Taking the example of a sphere, Aristiotle concludes that 'there is no other cause of the potential sphere's being an actual sphere; this was the essence of each'.[66] Pannenberg reverses Aristotle's claims and argues that ends determine essences because what comes about at the end constitutes identity, which has been present, in anticipation, all along. Pannenberg argues that this might have led Aristotle to perceive the principle of 'retroactive causality'.[67]

The motif of anticipation allows Pannenberg to deal with the fact that truth claims and interpretations shift through time. This shifting threatens to overwhelm an epistemology based on a static metaphysic, for if truth is that which is stable and unchanging then the historically conditioned nature of truth *claims* makes them seem very distant from truth itself. Pannenberg argues that an anticipatory view allows for the historicity of knowledge without conceding the case to a thoroughgoing cognitive relativism.[68] This is particularly important in theology, for discussion of the Absolute in any meaningful way is impossible if the case of cognitive relativism is granted, since true knowledge of the Absolute cannot be ultimately relative.[69]

What to Make of Pannenberg's Metaphysics?

Incredulity is a common response to Pannenberg's temporalized essentialism! Roger Olson identifies the 'futurity principle' as the 'most difficult problem in Pannenberg's doctrine of the Trinity' and the idea which has 'perplexed and delighted interpreters for over two decades'.[70] William Hill calls it a 'somewhat idiosyncratic idea' as does John Polkinghorne who rejects it on both scientific and theological grounds.[71] David McKenzie finds what he calls Pannenberg's 'future principle' to be unclear.[72] David Pailin asks, 'Is the notion of the future's influence on the processes of the reality plausible?'[73] George Pattison not only wonders whether Pannenberg's metaphysical proposal is justified or justifiable, but even if it is meaningful.[74] The detailed examination of Pannenberg's metaphysic in this chapter should show that it cannot be dismissed as meaningless, unless all metaphysics is arbitrarily ruled inadmissible. Pannenberg relates his proposal to a wide range of thinkers and seeks to solve many classical and modern problems. His approach may or may not finally be convincing but it should be recognized as a proposal that deserves a careful hearing. It may strike us as very unusual but it deserves more than incredulous dismissal.

Mostert summarizes five, more precise, criticisms of Pannenberg's use of anticipation:

1. It is an ontological claim which lacks support;
2. His whole theology is overly concerned with ontological questions;
3. It is determinist;
4. The consummation of history is unthinkable;
5. His use of the motif is not consistent.[75]

In early works Pannenberg did not explain his metaphysical proposal in detail. At that stage the criticism that the proposal lacked support had some validity. Clayton comments in his preface to *Metaphysics and the Idea of God* that 'one might argue that this was a book that Pannenberg had to write', since both English-speaking critics and philosophers at the University of Munich were demanding that he explain and defend his elusive comments. Clayton suggests that even *Metaphysics and the Idea of God* does not deal with the question as fully as might have been hoped.[76] However, after its publication Pannenberg cannot be accused of making unsupported claims about his temporalized essentialism and anticipation. His case may not be convincing to all critics, but it has been presented carefully and in considerable detail.

The claim that Pannenberg's thought is overly concerned with ontological questions usually rests on a misunderstanding of his project. Although Pannenberg devotes considerable attention to metaphysics, he does so for the sake of theological exposition. He has argued persuasively that theology must engage with ontological questions, and he seeks an 'asymmetric bipolar relational unity' between fundamental and systematic theological concerns. It is only at the end of a careful exanimation of Pannenberg's project that it is possible to conclude whether he has, or has not, placed too great an emphasis on ontological concerns.

The objection that, despite his claims, Pannenberg's view does not preserve human freedom is one that has been made by Clayton,

Ford, Polk and Pailin.[77] Ford and Polk take a process view and would presumably raise this objection to any account which treats God as 'all-determining'. Thus Polk repeats Gilkey's criticism that Pannenberg's view is 'a kind of Calvinism set into temporal reverse gear'.[78] Mostert defends Pannenberg against charges of determinism.[79] Pannenberg states in his doctrine of election that 'there is no guarantee of an ultimate universal reconciliation, but in a history that is still open the possibility of forgiveness is promised'. This view is less deterministic than traditional Augustinian accounts.[80] So those in the Augustinian tradition (like myself) will not judge Pannenberg's account to be overly deterministic; those who are critical of Augustine may well do so.

The objection that the consummation of history is unthinkable rejects a claim for which Pannenberg presents considerable evidence. To sustain this objection, the critic must reject a creedal statement of the Christian faith. From Pannenberg's point of view, the claim that history has a consummation is open for debate and, like all theological claims, can only be held provisionally. However the argument of *Metaphysics and the Idea of God* makes a good case for regarding the idea as thinkable.

The objection that Pannenberg's use of anticipation is inconsistent is the most serious of the five areas of criticism. Both Clayton and Olson point out that Pannenberg assumes the unity of thought and being (or the epistemological and ontological) but that he also sets the two against each other.[81] Olson accepts that the analysis of other views offered in *Metaphysics and the Idea of God* has shown their shortcomings and that Pannenberg's approach, if valid, 'is a creative advance in thinking about the God-world relationships'. But he suspects that Pannenberg's linking of the noetic and ontological concepts is 'more asserted than actually defended' and that it is not a coherent metaphysical solution.[82] Clayton also comments that Pannenberg shares the idealist assumption of the unity of thought and being. Pannenberg does reflect the tradition of German idealism. However, on the whole, he more fully reflects the Christian view that in the light of the revelation of God's reality humanity can think about reality and 'true being'. Pannenberg's move to ground this eschatologically reflects the Christian view that only in God's light do we see reality fully (Ps. 36:9; cf. 1 Cor. 13:12; 1 John 3:2).

Mostert recognizes the power of Clayton's criticisms and views them as leaving questions for Pannenberg to answer, rather than being decisive objections to his view.[83] He provides the defence that he perceives Pannenberg's approach requires, by showing that Pannenberg's thought must be understood in terms of his trinitarian doctrine of God. He concludes that in Pannenberg's thought 'the theology of the eschatological kingdom of God and the theology of the Trinity coincide' and that this is the best defence of Pannenberg's metaphysical proposal.[84]

Assessing Pannenberg's Proposal

It is certainly difficult to assess Pannenberg's metaphysical proposal. It is a surprising idea – but I hope I have shown that this is not, by itself, a reason to reject it. His arguments in support of the idea are extremely complex. They do not provide a single line of argument which can be accepted or rejected. His case is developed by showing tensions and problems in both classical metaphysics and the denial of metaphysics, then suggesting on the basis of these discussions that it is possible and even necessary to hold to the existence of the Absolute. He then appeals to Christian theology as the adequate source of this idea. Even if a critic finds parts of the argument unpersuasive, Pannenberg can easily point to other lines of argument. What is more, it is an implication of his position that his own account is a provisional claim, which can only be confirmed or negated directly in eternity.

The key to thinking about Pannenberg's proposal is to note that he has carefully intertwined it with his presentation of Christian theology. He appeals to theology as the source of his most significant ideas, such as the existence of the Absolute and the priority of the future. For Pannenberg, the Absolute or Infinite, of which philosophy offers some inkling, turns out to be the Triune God. Pannenberg has no valid generalized concept of the Absolute apart from the Christian God. He justifies his theistic metaphysic by showing that an understanding of reality requires the horizon of the Infinite, which is to be understood as the Triune God of Christian faith. Similarly, while he suggests that the priority of the future is required by various philosophies, he does not claim that the concept can be supplied apart from Christian eschatology anticipated in the resurrection of Jesus. As well as drawing on theology for the key element of his metaphysical proposal, Pannenberg uses his idea to present Christian theology. The tight interconnection of philosophy and theology suggests that Pannenberg's metaphysical proposal is properly tested theologically. If we see that Christian claims do support his metaphysic and that it helps to present and explain Christian theology then his metaphysic seems to be well supported. In the following chapters the assessment of Pannenberg's proposal proceeds through an examination of three key sections of his thought: Christology, the doctrine of reconciliation and the doctrine of God.

6.

Jesus, God and History: Pannenberg and Christology

Christology is central in Pannenberg's project. We have already seen that his theology is grounded in and developed from Christology and finds its focus in the Triune God. This chapter looks in detail at Pannenberg's Christology. Pannenberg is commonly associated with 'Christology from below' so I will start the discussion exploring what that approach entails. The next step is to see how Pannenberg develops his Christology from an account of the historical Jesus in which anticipation and Jesus' resurrection have a major role. Pannenberg reconfigures Chalcedonian Christology and so the chapter finishes by examining the relative strengths of traditional Chalcedonian theology and Pannenberg's reconfiguration.

Jesus and History: Christology from Below

'Christology from above' is the classic approach to Christology which assumes the divinity of Jesus and takes the incarnation as the framework of its view of Jesus.[1] This approach, which is classic Chalcedonian Christology, is the view that the Son, who from eternity is equal to the Father in essence or substance, has willingly taken on humanity (flesh) and exists as one person with two natures (divine and human) which remain distinct but not separated. There is a 'hypostatic union', the one person (hypostasis) has taken on human nature so he is a truly human person while still a divine person (and one person not two).

In contrast, 'Christology from below' begins by examining the historical and human Jesus and, if it comes to abstract formulations of persons and natures at all, it comes to these far later in the process of reflection. It is often assumed that Christology from below always begins with the historical study of Jesus; however Pannenberg uses it to describe a range of methodologies.[2] He considers approaches to Christology which start from Jesus' human personality or the faith-consciousness of Jesus reflected in the community of faith as forms of Christology from below because they are concerned about general anthropological issues.[3]

Pannenberg gives three reasons why Christology cannot be developed 'from above'. The first and third points are epistemological, dealing with how we could know about Jesus' divinity, while the second deals with the theological implications of Christology from above.

1. In a context in which Jesus' divinity is contested it cannot be assumed. Christology has to present reasons for the confession of Jesus' divinity.[4] Pannenberg states programmatically 'we must discover the contours of the divine sonship of Jesus in his human reality'.[5]
2. 'Christology from above' does not properly come to terms with the historicity of the human Jesus. Pannenberg claims that there is a loss of substance in Christology when the unique historical setting of the life of Jesus recedes before an 'independent incarnational theology'.[6]
3. A 'Christology from above' assumes God's point of view that is inaccessible for us.[7]

Reasons (2) and (3) relate to Pannenberg's anthropological concern. He holds that theology, and especially Christology, must illumine human life. One way in which he does this is to relate Jesus' life and ministry to the experience of all humans.[8] His concern to relate Christology to anthropology is the source of his major unease about the Chalcedonian tradition. He holds that if the human nature of Christ has a personal existence only in union with the divine person then the free humanity of Jesus will never be properly affirmed and Christology will not be fully related to anthropology. He asserts that 'in the history of early Christology the equation of the incarnation of the Logos with the birth of Jesus blocked the way to any evaluating of the human uniqueness of Jesus of Nazareth as a medium of the revelation of the divine Logos'.[9] He recognizes that this tradition sought to maintain Jesus as fully human and fully divine, but claims that it either stressed an independent humanity (the heresy of Nestorianism) or a fully dependent humanity (the heresy of Monophysitism, which approached Docetism).[10]

So Pannenberg's Christology from below has a focus on specific details which can be determined through the historical study of Jesus' life and also a commitment to interact with wider anthropological questions. We will start with his emphasis on the historical Jesus and then return to more general concerns.

As in other areas of theology, in Christology Pannenberg asserts that reflection on human, historical events properly leads to a 'rising above' which allows an appreciation of how historical reality participates in the eternal. For Christology this means that the history of Jesus is the starting point for knowledge of the Son. There is a reciprocal relation between the historical Jesus and the eternal Son, though such a relationship cannot be simply assumed but must be demonstrated. Even in *Jesus – God and Man*, Pannenberg indicates that he will 'later show the relative justification' for the 'from above' approach.[11] In *Systematic Theology* Pannenberg is more emphatic about the need to relate Christology to the Triune God and moves materially closer to 'the classical Christology of the incarnation'.[12]

Jesus' Unity with God

The claim at the base of Pannenberg's Christology is that the gospels present Jesus' unity with God. This unity is expressed in a variety of ways – for instance Jesus is the Christ, the 'Son of God', the Spirit-filled prophet, the messenger of the kingdom of God, and the Word. Pannenberg concludes that the variety of descriptions cannot be neatly resolved into a single theological picture because the gospel texts do not present a uniform Christology. While not uniform, they share a common witness to Jesus' unity with God.[13] Pannenberg understands these traditions as Christian reflections on the life and ministry of Jesus in the light of his resurrection.

Pannenberg focuses his discussion on Jesus' relationship to the kingdom. In his ministry Jesus offered an experience of eschatological salvation since 'the coming rule of God was present already to the salvation of those who received his message', and 'he was also the mediator of the inbreaking of the rule and the forgiving love of God'.[14] This is a claim for unity with God, since the kingdom is, on Pannenberg's definition, the immediate revelation of the kingship of God. Remember this is how Pannenberg understands revelation – history will end when God's glory invades the whole of reality to bring redemption to his creation and in that God will be shown to be ruler of all. So if Jesus offers the kingdom, then he offers some taste of the saving presence of God.

Following a common view in New Testament scholarship, Pannenberg thinks that Jesus did not directly identify himself as the Messiah.[15] Yet Jesus' claim to bring the kingdom had messianic implications and was an offence to many of his hearers. The offence lay not only in the claim to bring the kingdom, but also in the fact that the claim was not obviously true, for the all-encompassing glory of God was not evident. Jesus' message itself meant there was a difficult 'ambivalence' about him and his identity. Could he truly bring the kingdom, given his unimpressive appearance?

This ambivalence ultimately led to Jesus' crucifixion when the Jewish authorities executed him as a messianic pretender, while even his disciples deserted him. Jesus' fate on the cross seemed to clarify the ambiguity, showing that his claims about the kingdom were an 'illusion'. Only the resurrection reversed this denial of his claims, establishing Jesus' claim and creating the possibility that his death had 'saving significance'.[16] Here the pattern of anticipation becomes very important. It is the resurrection which gives meaning to Jesus' life and death and so, on the basis of an appeal to the retroactive power of the future, it can be truly said that Jesus always was in union with God.

Jesus' Self-Distinction from God

Along with Jesus' unity with God, Pannenberg notes a correlate theme of his distinction from God expressed in submission to the Father. The ambivalence of Jesus' identity came from the fact that although he declared the coming of the kingdom he did not exercise God's rule but rather lived in submission to God. He was not, apparently, the divine king ruling his kingdom, but a human subject of that kingdom and thus distinct from God rather than united with him.

Traditional Christology explains the submissive distinction of the Son from the Father in two ways. One is to relate it immediately to the incarnation and so to the human nature of Jesus. The incarnation is the humiliation of the Son, his lowering to take on human existence, which includes dependence upon and obedience to God, so Jesus submits to God as a human. The other is to see the submission as an aspect of the 'economic Trinity', that is to do with the work of the Son in redemption, but not related to his eternal relationship with the Father.[17] However, much contemporary theology has sought to understand the submission of the Son as related to the inner relationship of the Trinity (the immanent Trinity).[18] At this point contemporary theologians share similar motivations to those of Pannenberg, wanting our understanding of Christ to relate closely to the historical Jesus and the work of God in Christ. (We will come across this theme again when we think about Pannenberg's doctrine of the Trinity).

Pannenberg offers a Christology which meets this contemporary concern, with his own distinctive approach to the historical life of Jesus. He argues that 'the differentiation of God as Father from his own person is . . . constitutive for Jesus' message and attitude'.[19] Jesus proclaimed God the Father and his kingdom, not himself, and he did not claim that his presence was the presence of the Father's future kingdom (though it turned out, in the light of the resurrection, that his ministry was a provisional presence of the kingdom). Jesus witnessed to the Father, sought to glorify the Father and honoured the claims of the first commandment to have no other god: 'The aim of the whole message of Jesus is that the name of God should be hallowed by honouring his lordship.'[20] Pannenberg sets this differentiation alongside Jesus' 'close link' to the Father, so the use of the term 'differentiation' should not be taken to imply that Jesus is distant from the Father. According to Pannenberg, it is the resurrection that establishes the correlated truths of Jesus' 'differentiation' from and intimacy with the Father.[21]

The movement of self-distinction of Jesus from his Father is constitutive for the identity of the Son and the Father. Pannenberg uses the risky term 'subordination' (risky because it is the term used to condemn Arianism). He states that 'this uniqueness of Jesus rested on the unconditional subordination of his person to the lordship of God . . . only in this subordination to the rule of the one God is he the Son'.[22] He explains that by distinguishing the Father from himself as the one God, the Son moved out of the unity of the deity and became human, but in doing so he actively expressed his divine essence as the Son. The self-emptying of the Pre-Existent One is thus not a surrender or negation of his deity as the Son, it is its activation.[23]

The obvious danger of such an account of Jesus is that it might turn out to be 'subordinationist', which is the view that the Son is less than, rather than equal with, the Father. Such subordinationism has been rejected since the early debates about the Trinity. How can Pannenberg avoid this view? He does so by developing the theme that while the Son submits to the Father, the Father also makes himself dependent on the Son. He refers to the Father 'handing over his lordship to the Son' and thus 'his kingship [is] dependent on whether the Son glorifies him and fulfils his Lordship'. This means that the reality of God's lordship 'has its place in the intratrinitarian life of God, in the reciprocity of the relation between the Son . . . and the Father'.[24] The handing over of lordship by the Father occurs, like submission and self-differentiation, in the human history of Jesus.

For Pannenberg, Christology and the doctrine of God deal with the same biblical themes from slightly different perspectives. It is not possible to establish God's identity and show that the Son is God, and then think about the incarnation. That would be Christology from above. The identity of the Son and the Father are established in the human, historical life of Jesus. So thinking about Christology and the doctrine of God are interdependent.

The Incarnation and the Pre-Existence of the *Logos*

The movements of unity with the Father and self-distinction from the Father in the historical life of Jesus are the dynamics of Pannenberg's Christology and he relates them to each other through his temporalized essentialism. This is evident in his discussion of the incarnation and the pre-existence of the *Logos*. He views these concepts as, in themselves, 'mythic' (that is they appeal to a prehistoric, or supra-historic reality, which is not accessible to historical human knowledge). However he justifies their theological use because they describe the meaning of the resurrection for the historical life of Jesus. He explains that the paradoxes of the incarnation are only tolerated 'when one perceives the necessity of their emergence from the circumstance of the proleptic appearance of the eschaton in Jesus' history'.[25]

Pannenberg affirms the pre-existence and incarnation of the *Logos* based on Jesus' life and the resurrection. He asserts: 'we cannot separate the eternal dynamic of self-distinction (the *logos asarkos*) from its actualisation in Jesus Christ (the *logos ensarkos*)'.[26] The *logos asarkos* is the Word (or the Son) in his existence before the incarnation, that is without flesh (*sarkos*), while the *logos ensarkos* is the en-fleshed Word or the incarnate Word. Pannenberg again links the eternal reality of God *(logos asarkos)* with the historical Jesus *(logos ensarkos)* and makes the historical the 'actualisation' of the eternal.

How can the human Jesus Christ be identified with the eternal Word so that Jesus' obedience is the actualization of an eternal existence? For Pannenberg this identification depends entirely on the resurrection. Jesus' submissive self-distinction from the Father generates ambiguity which is only removed by the resurrection. Jesus is the Son of God because he has been raised from the dead. But Pannenberg's temporalized essentialism shows that what is true eschatologically is that which has always been. So, Jesus' sonship, which is actualized in history as sonship with the eternal God, must stretch back to all his life and into eternity.

Pannenberg associates his approach with that of Isaak Dorner (1809–84), an influential German theologian who faced the problem that historical criticism had made clear the full human life of Jesus including normal human development. In common with much nineteenth-century theology, Dorner thought that classic Christology could not give a sufficient account of Jesus' humanity. This is precisely the same concern as Pannenberg expresses. Dormer's solution was to propose that through Jesus' life he had a growing unity with the *Logos*: 'the Incarnation is not to be thought of as complete at once but as progressive, indeed, growing'.[27] Dorner sought to affirm much of traditional Christology and was an opponent of radical views which left no sense of Jesus' divinity. However his view falls outside the boundaries of traditional orthodoxy. The way he describes Jesus' growing unity with the *Logos* sounds like a Nestorian Christology in which Jesus and the *Logos* can be differentiated and even approaches a form of adoptionism.[28]

Pannenberg recognizes that Dorner had to abandon classic Christology, not merely reshape it. He takes from Dorner 'the interest in the becoming of the divine/human unity in Jesus' earthly life' and sets a developmental Christology in an anticipatory structure. This, he believes, 'overcomes the dilemma between a unity with God *either* already consummated in the beginning *or* only realized through a subsequent event in Jesus' life'.[29] He asserts: 'the Easter event definitively decided the personal identity of Jesus as the Son of God, but in the light of that event he was the Son of God from the very beginning . . . even from eternity'.[30]

Pannenberg then claims to reconfigure the Chalcedonian approach rather than abandon it. He overcomes the weakness of Chalcedon and gives full expression to the human, historical life of Jesus. One advantage he perceives in his approach is that it removes the need to discuss the 'renunciation' of divine attributes in the incarnation. He does so by not focusing on Jesus' birth in giving an account of his divine identity. Pannenberg argues that the New Testament passages that deal with incarnation refer to 'the totality of [Jesus'] life and work . . . not to his human birth' (John 1:14; 3:16; 1 John 4:2, 9).[31] Passages such as Hebrews 2:10 and 5:8–9 suggest to Pannenberg that Jesus' identity as Son and his unity with the Father were mediated by his whole life.[32] Since the focus is not the beginning of Jesus' life, then Pannenberg does not have to assume 'an unrestricted possession of the attributes at the beginning of the earthly history'.[33]

Pannenberg's Christology is parallel with, but different from, the classical approach.[34] Both affirm Jesus' identity as the eternal Son of God who shares in a unity of essence with the Father and the Spirit.[35] Chalcedon presents that identity as constituted by the incarnation of the eternal Son who takes on human nature, which is individuated as the human Jesus. In contrast, Pannenberg finds the identity of the Son and his unity with the Father as constituted by the human life of Jesus.

> Certainly from the standpoint of the Easter event the conception and birth of Jesus had to be seen as the entry of the eternal Son of God into union with this human life (Gal. 4:4). The union of the Logos with this human life continued throughout the whole of the earthly history of Jesus as the eternal Son of God took shape in him through the relation to the Father. We are not to take this to mean that the deity and humanity gradually grew together in the course of Jesus' history. But with the development of his human life, a relationship to the Father developed with increasing depth, and with it divine sonship.[36]

Pannenberg's comment that we should not think of Jesus' humanity and divinity as growing together reflects the fact that the divinity of the Son is constituted by the whole life of the human Jesus taken up into eternity. The relationship between Jesus and the Father grows in depth through history, but the God–human relation exists from the beginning of Jesus' life on the basis of that life anticipating its conclusion in eternity. Pannenberg differs from classical Christology by identifying Jesus' humanity, not the *Logos*, as the acting subject in the incarnation.[37]

The Resurrection

Pannenberg's Christology depends on the resurrection and he argues carefully for its facticity.[38] Equally important is the meaning of the resurrection. According to Pannenberg, Jesus shared the Jewish expectation of a universal resurrection from the dead as part of the coming unity of all things with God and looked to that for the vindication of his message about the kingdom. When he was raised on the third day he was included in the content of his own message as the messiah of the kingdom.[39]

Pannenberg contrasts his account of the resurrection with that of Bultmann and Barth, who hold that the resurrection of Christ was 'disclosure'. He argues that the Easter event 'determines' the meaning of Jesus' life and his relationship with God.[40] That is, the proper understanding of Jesus' life and his identity depend on the resurrection, not simply for their being known, but for their being what they are. 'Only by his resurrection . . . did Christ attain to the dignity of the Kyrios . . . Only thus was he appointed the Son of God in power . . . Only in the light of the resurrection is he the pre-existent Son. Only as the risen Lord is he always the living Lord of his community.'[41] What comes about in the resurrection is what has been true about Jesus from the beginning: 'what has become evident in the resurrection . . . has been on the stage from the very beginning' and 'it had been on the stage from the very beginning because Jesus has been raised from the dead'.[42]

Pannenberg's appeal to anticipation and his eschatological metaphysic allows him to move from the historical Jesus, who is not apparently divine, and to understand him as the eternal Son of God. The resurrection is the hinge point in this development because it establishes Jesus' human life as the life of the Son of God as it, in turn, anticipates the eschaton. On that basis the New Testament texts can be justified in including elements that are not strictly historical but are valid reflections of what was proleptically true and, thus, genuinely true of Jesus during his pre-resurrection ministry.

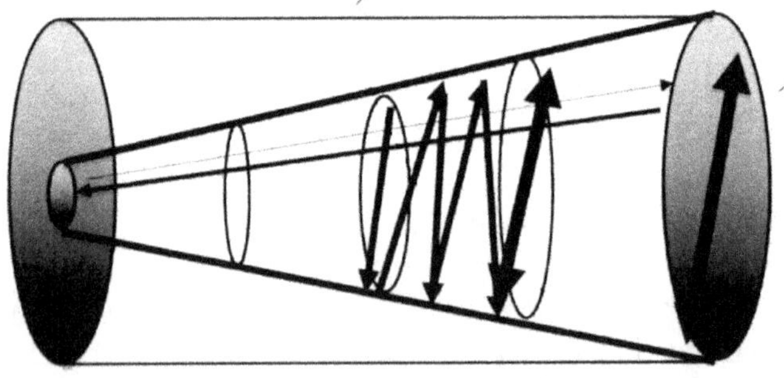

Figure 1. Christology and anticipation

Figure 1 illustrates Pannenberg's Christology in the setting of his anticipatory ontology. The series of arrows represents the historical, human life of Jesus in which he differentiates himself from the Father and in doing so actualizes his unity with the Father. (There is, at the same time, an act of the Father, which differentiates him from and unites him with the Son, and parallel acts of the Spirit, but only one relation can be shown on the diagram.) The resurrection affirms Jesus' life and claims, and in it the dynamic becomes a single movement of differentiated unity. What occurs in the resurrection anticipates what will be the case in the eschaton, in which the dynamic of the differentiating unity of Father, Son, and Spirit draws all reality into it. The arrows representing the development of history through time and the corresponding effect of the future are established on the basis of the theological claims.

Thinking about Pannenberg's Christology

There is no doubt that Pannenberg's Christology is magisterial, integrating a wide range of themes and dealing with the history of theology, biblical exegesis, the historical Jesus, and general anthropology.[43] He argues that his approach successfully reconfigures Chalcedon in a way which makes better sense of the biblical record. It is common in twentieth-century theology to observe that Chalcedonian Christology tends to detract from a proper emphasis on the humanity of Christ. Wienandy admits that 'the inherited scholastic tradition, in the light of this emphasis on the divine, portrayed Jesus as displaying little, if any, frailty and ignorance'.[44] One way to think about Pannenberg's Christology is to see how he deals with some of the material in the gospels which have been most troubling for orthodox exegetes.

Jesus' eschatological ignorance

One point in the gospels where Jesus' humanity seems most obvious is when he says that he does not know the timing of the coming of the Son of Man (Matt. 24:36; Mark 13:32). When patristic and medieval commentators dealt with Jesus' suffering and temptations they carefully distinguished between how his humanity and divinity participated in these. In this approach, however, Jesus' ignorance seems particularly baffling and difficult to conceptualize. How could Jesus have had limited human knowledge and divine omniscience? Pannenberg observes that the resulting comments often seem to downplay the reality of Jesus' human knowledge: 'a Docetic-Monophysite threat was continually present and occasionally dominant'.[45] Berkouwer also notes that these texts often seem to be explained away.[46] As recently as 1918, the Holy Office of the Roman Catholic Church issued *Circa quondam propositiones de scientia animae Christi* which concludes that it cannot be safely taught that there may be a limitation to the knowledge of the soul of Christ.[47]

There is a more consistently Chalcedonian approach to Jesus' ignorance. The early church fathers, Athanasius and Gregory of Nazianzus, explain the passages in terms of the ignorance of the human nature of Christ. They state that the *Logos* knew all things, but that the human mind of Christ did not, because the *Logos* did not reveal this.[48] B.B. Warfield defends this stream of exegesis and develops it more fully in a context in which critical-historical considerations were being pressed on Christian theology. He contends that in the New Testament presentation 'a duplex life is attributed to him [Jesus] as his constant possession'.[49] As a result, Warfield affirms both the omniscience and the ignorance of Christ.

There are two evident problems with this approach. One is that the text speaks of the 'Son' not knowing and the exegete must explain this use of a divine title in connection with an attribute of human nature. The other is that, as Warfield admits, it is very difficult to conceptualize the life of Christ in such Chalcedonian terms.[50] From Pannenberg's point of view this approach falls back on paradox and incoherence too quickly, and although it asserts the real and full humanity of Christ, he claims that this cannot be properly emphasized by Chalcedonian Christology. Even a convinced Chalcedonian must admit that resort to such explanations may be permissible but is hardly obvious in the texts.

A more common approach, found for instance in Hilary and Augustine, refers to 'official ignorance' claiming that Christ knew all things in himself but was not commissioned to reveal the day or the hour of the final judgement.[51] Scotus' suggestion was that Christ's humanity received an infinite range of truths though not simultaneously, but only in temporal succession. If he had so chosen, the incarnate Christ could have known the time of his return.[52] These suggestions deal with the text no better than the fully Chalcedonian approach and are more ad hoc, lacking a consistent theological basis. There have also been suggestions that the text itself is corrupted or that it could be interpreted differently.[53] None of these suggestions is convincing.

Pannenberg, on the other hand, deals with the texts quite straightforwardly. He includes them in a treatment of a wider theme of Jesus' lack of messianic consciousness: 'Jesus' lack of knowledge was apparently not only related to the Day of Judgement, but thereby to his own person as well.' These texts fit well with Pannenberg's anthropological concerns and are part of his anticipatory Christology. Pannenberg holds that when Jesus admits his ignorance, his identity as the Son of Man is not yet established, and so he is not aware of it. Jesus' ignorance of the future is part of his real humanity. Pannenberg adopts Rahner's claim that human freedom requires a level of nescience and states that 'as awareness of the not yet decided future, the knowledge of one's ignorance is a condition of human openness and freedom'.[54]

Jesus' obscurity

Jesus' ignorance only appears very occasionally in the gospels, the next feature I will consider is far more widespread. Especially in the Synoptic Gospels, Jesus' identity is often obscure. His disciples only gradually recognize that he is the Christ (Matt. 8:27; 16:16–17) and John the Baptist doubts it (Matt. 11:3; Luke 7:19). The crowds have, at best, a partial and wavering recognition of Jesus' identity (Matt. 9:8; 13:54–7; 16:14; 21:8–11; 22:33; Mark 11:8–10; Luke 7:16; 19:37–8). Jesus' opponents recognize his claims, or at least the implications of his words and deeds, but refuse to acknowledge him (Matt. 9:34; 12:14; 21:23; Mark 3:6; 11:28; Luke 20:1–2). A lack of faith is one explanation which the gospels give when people failed to recognize Jesus, but that is not the whole story. He seems to keep his identity hidden. He silences likely witnesses (Matt. 8:4; 9:30; 12:16; 16:20; 17:9; Mark 1:25,34; 5:43; 7:36; 8:30; 9:9; Luke 4:41; 9:21) and avoids direct claims to be the Messiah until his trial

(Matt. 26:64; 27:11; Mark 14:62; Luke 22:67 – 23:3). His parables are deliberately obscure (Mark 4:10–12; Matt. 13:10–17).

William Wrede called this strand in the Synoptic Gospels the 'Messianic Secret'.[55] His theory was Jesus did not claim to be the Messiah at all and that the 'messianic secret' was added to the gospel accounts to explain why Jesus the Messiah did not appear to be messianic. Few contemporary scholars, if any, would endorse Wrede's view, though some hold to modified versions of it.[56] Since Wrede's time New Testament scholarship has had to say something about the obscurity of Jesus' identity in the Synoptics, viewing it as either an element in Jesus' historical ministry or as an element added by Mark and adapted by the other Synoptic evangelists.

As we have seen, the obscurity of Jesus' identity in the gospels plays an important role in Pannenberg's Christology. For Pannenberg, self-distinction from the Father meant that Jesus did not directly identify himself. According to Pannenberg, Jesus' death is an act of God because it flows directly from the ambiguity of his identity. Pannenberg does not have to explain the obscurity of Jesus' identity; it is a basic element of his Christology.

Chalcedonian Christology has not found Jesus' obscurity nearly as difficult to deal with as the question of Jesus' ignorance. Tucket explains that the most common explanation of the 'secrecy texts' in pre-critical exegesis was 'that Jesus wished to reveal his identity to the disciples only gradually so that they might come to a deeper understanding of him'.[57] Another Chalcedonian approach is to explain Jesus' secrecy as part of his humiliation. For instance Herman Bavinck (1854–1921), the Dutch theologian, uses the idea of emptying (*kenosis*) not to speak of Christ giving up his deity but as a humiliation that was part of his vocation and was the Son's voluntary consecration of his life to God.[58] The two approaches to Christology offer different ways of handling the material. For Pannenberg it is a key theme in Christology, while for classical approaches it is incidental to Jesus' identity, though it can be given a place in an account of his work.

Jesus' self-awareness

It becomes apparent then that a crucial question which emerges from Pannenberg's Christology is the extent to which Jesus was aware of his messianic identity. According to Pannenberg, Jesus had a growing awareness of unity with God through his life: 'Jesus has his personal identity solely in being the Son of his heavenly Father', but 'he cannot have been aware of it from the very outset'.[59] Pannenberg gives no explicit treatment of how or when Jesus came to full awareness of his identity but the implication of his view seems to be that this must have occurred in the resurrection. If Jesus had claimed a distinctive sonship before the resurrection, there would have been a basis for the charge that Jesus made himself equal to God.

Jesus' identity as the divine Son is not equivalent to his identity as the Messiah, the Son of Man, or the Servant, nor is Jesus' identity equivalent to his self-awareness. However for Pannenberg the development of each of these themes converge. Pannenberg holds that Jesus did not identify himself as any of these in his pre-Easter ministry and each of these claims about Jesus is established by his resurrection. In this he follows what he identifies as 'the dominant view of NT exegetes'.[60] He underscores the ambivalence of Jesus' answer to Caiaphas (Matt. 26:64; 27:11; Luke 22:70; 23:3) over the more explicit assertion of Mark 14:62. Pannenberg doubts the historicity of Jesus' use of 'the Son' in Matthew 11:27, and in any of his earthly ministry, but defends its attribution to Jesus in the light of Easter.[61]

At this point, New Testament scholarship has moved from Pannenberg's view. There are, of course, scholars who hold that Jesus did not claim any status for himself. Most of these scholars are more sceptical about the historicity of gospels than Pannenberg is, and think that the claims about Jesus have no firm basis.[62] On the other hand, it is quite common for contemporary scholarship to assert that Jesus did consider himself to be the eschatological Son of Man.[63] For instance, Michael Bird challenges the idea that the resurrection established Jesus' messianic identity. He argues that Jesus' identity must be established by his self-identification before his death and resurrection, and that the meaning of his identity develops through his death and resurrection.[64] Pannenberg claims that the accusation of a messianic claim led to Jesus being recognized as Messiah. However, Bird's argument helps to show that the thesis that the origin of the charge is found in Jesus' own claims is more persuasive.[65]

The claim that the historical Jesus was aware of his pre-existence seems harder to sustain than the claim that he identified himself as the Messiah, at least on the basis of the evidence of the Synoptic Gospels.[66] Simon Gathercole has recently argued that a case can be made for Jesus' own claims to be the pre-existent Son. He focuses on the texts in which Jesus says that he has 'come' with a purpose and argues that these are authentic sayings of Jesus and mean that he was aware that he had come from God.[67] Gathercole's work is still recent and has received limited though generally positive reviews.[68] He has, at least, shown that the Synoptic Gospels allow the possibility of Jesus' self-consciousness of pre-existence.

The differences between Pannenberg's account of the historical Jesus and those discussed above reflect a shift in paradigm in the study of the historical Jesus. Pannenberg draws his insights from scholars associated with the so-called 'New Quest for the historical Jesus' while much recent scholarship is part of the 'Third Quest'.[69] It is now more common to conclude that Jesus made clear messianic claims and 'the opinion following the resurrection that Jesus was the Messiah was due to what Jesus himself taught and encouraged his disciples to believe'.[70] These conclusions are certainly not unanimous, but Evans' summary reflects the general development of historical Jesus research in the last generation. While several of the developments in the Third Quest support Pannenberg's project, its conclusions about Jesus' own claims put his portrait of Jesus' ministry on thinner ground.

It is worth noting that the transfiguration (Mark 9:2–13; Luke 9:28–36; Matt. 17:1–13) is one incident in the gospels which, if treated as a historical event, does not fit comfortably into Pannenberg's Christology for it implies that Jesus' identity as the glorious Son is already established before Easter. Pannenberg's passing mention of the event reflects Bultmann's view that it is a displaced resurrection account, though Pannenberg concedes that it may be an event in Jesus' life, in which case 'we may see it as an anticipatory manifestation of the glorifying that Jesus experienced at his resurrection'.[71] Conclusions about the historicity of the transfiguration are largely the result of presuppositions, since there is no evidence beyond the New Testament accounts. However Dorothy Lee makes two important points about the incident. One is that it does not appear to be a displaced resurrection account since it is 'a very different genre'.[72] She also notes that the reference to the transfiguration in 2 Peter 1:16–18 emphasizes a revelation which is more than anticipatory.[73] The transfiguration accounts challenge Pannenberg's anticipatory Christology since they imply that Jesus was already the glorified divine Son whose identity was hidden but did not need to be realized or constituted.

If Pannenberg's account of Jesus' self-awareness is curtailed in comparison with the presentation of the Synoptics, the contrast with John's Gospel is stronger.[74] In John, Jesus is aware of his identity as the Son (John 5:19 and *passim*) and as Messiah (John 11:25 and *passim*), and his pre-incarnate origin (John 3:12–13; 8:23). He makes strong implicit claims of his own deity (John 8:85; 10:33ff.). This fits comfortably with classical Christology, for which John was an important source. Pannenberg treats John's Gospel as testimony to the reality of the risen Christ, but not as evidence for the historical Jesus. For Pannenberg, the claims which John makes about Jesus' identity could not have been made in the midst of his pre-Easter life, since they were not present in the same way that his human, historical life was present; they were present in anticipation. The question, then, is whether the claims of the Fourth Gospel can be considered an account of the historical Jesus.

Recent biblical scholarship presents varied views of the historical reliability of the Johannine picture of Jesus.[75] Casey argues that John's Gospel is not historically reliable: 'Jesus did not walk this earth presenting himself as the pre-existent Son of God, expounding his relationship with the Father, declaring that he is the Way, the Truth and the Life.'[76] Other scholars argue that John's portrait of Jesus is far more reliable than has been assumed. These scholars recognize that the Johannine presentation is shaped by a post-resurrection view of Jesus and that John's Jesus speaks in the idiom of the evangelist. However, they argue that the gospel is based on the recollections of an eyewitness and its portrait of Jesus, including the high Christology, reflects the historical reality.[77] The arguments of these scholars show that the view, which Pannenberg adopted on the basis of twentieth-century scholarship, cannot be presumed.

The New Testament presents Jesus as claiming to be both the Messiah and the Son, and historical examination cannot easily dismiss that claim. This raises a question over Pannenberg's

Christology. The strength of Pannenberg's position is that he can present Jesus' consistent deference to God as an expression of his filial relationship, and can include this in Jesus' deity. The weakness is that Pannenberg's anticipatory Christology, in which the historical Jesus does not claim these things and in which his path of sonship requires that he not claim them, does not deal satisfactorily with New Testament claims that Jesus was the Son of God before Easter and that he was aware of this.[78]

Pannenberg and Chalcedon

What happens if we look at Pannenberg's Christology from the point of view of classical theology? Remember that Pannenberg's criticism is that the Chalcedonian approach does not adequately allow Jesus' humanity to come into view. His own proposal certainly allows maximal room for the humanity of Jesus by making the historical life of the human Jesus constitutive for his identity as the Son.

Several commentators have wondered if Pannenberg's focus on the historical, human Jesus is adoptionist, that is that he thinks Jesus becomes God's Son during his life.[79] It is not hard to see why they would think this. The view that Jesus did not claim divine sonship during his pre-Easter life and that the resurrection is constitutive for his identity as Son and Messiah would usually indicate an adoptionist Christology. However, Pannenberg explicitly rejects adoptionism and avoids it by his appeal to anticipation.[80] Critics may be unconvinced by his metaphysical proposal, but within Pannenberg's own proposal his Christology is not adoptionist.

The claim that Pannenberg's Christology is adoptionist reflects a feature of his Christology, even though it misunderstands the feature. Pannenberg describes the identity of the divine Son as constituted by the life of the historical, human Jesus and so makes the human Jesus the acting subject in the life of the divine Son. Bradshaw is critical of Pannenberg's *Christology in Jesus – God and Man,* and comments that 'his trinitarian Son lacks an acting subject apart from that of the finite man's consciousness' and suggests that Pannenberg cannot sustain his position unless he posits the pre-existent *Logos*.[81] In *Systematic Theology*, Pannenberg does affirm the pre-existence of the *Logos*. However, the structure of his Christology has not changed from that which Bradshaw criticized since the life of the human, historical Jesus constitutes the identity of the Son.

I would suggest that Pannenberg presents an inverted version of traditional Lutheran Christology. Lutheranism emphasized that in the one Christ the divine and human nature are joined in such a way that there is real exchange of attributes so that the human body of Christ is omnipresent.[82] This is particularly obvious in the view of the Lord's Supper, since it means that the body and blood of Christ are present through Christ's divine nature.[83] Yet it is a general structure of Lutheran Christology as well and is open to the criticism that it leaves Jesus' humanity unexpressed. Dietrich Bonhoeffer, though himself a Lutheran, is critical of this view: 'Lutheran Christology is in the last resort no longer speaking of the real humanity of Christ.'[84]

Pannenberg inverts this since he allows for a very full expression of the humanity of Christ, but makes it difficult to discover the divine Son as an acting subject in the human Jesus. He insists that Jesus is the incarnate Son, but this rests on his human distinction from God which forms his unity with the Father. John Webster suggests that often 'modern Lutheran Christology' does not clearly state that 'divinity *assumed* humanity' with the result that Chalcedonian 'union of the natures' becomes a 'unity'. He insists that the Chalcedonian position of the Son of God assuming humanity underscores that the incarnation is 'free grace' and not needed by God in any sense and that it presents divinity and humanity as 'asymmetrically related'. This asymmetry is that the divine Word is the person in the union and so the work of reconciliation is a divine one accomplished through human nature in which the *Logos* is the acting subject.[85] Pannenberg's Christology is open to Webster's criticism.

The criticism suggested here is a formal one relating to the structure of Pannenberg's Christology. The important test of formal Christology is how it shapes an understanding of redemption. In the next chapter one of the critical questions I want to consider is whether there is a parallel in Pannenberg's thinking about redemption with his Christology. Does the possible lack of 'asymmetry' between the divine and human mean that Pannenberg ends up with the work of Christ as a human work?

Conclusion

Pannenberg's path to Christology 'from below' aims to take Jesus' human life and experience seriously. His appeal to 'anticipation' allows him to view Jesus' human life as the presence of the Son of God, and thus to give full expression to Jesus' human life and also to see him as the presence of God. This approach means that Jesus' submission and obedience are constitutive for the identity of the *Logos*. In these respects, Pannenberg's Christology stands as a challenge to more Chalcedonian approaches, which often fall short of a full appreciation of the historical humanity of Jesus.

However some weaknesses in Pannenberg's Christology have also emerged. It does not deal well with aspects of the New Testament that ascribe to the pre-Easter Jesus the reality and awareness of both divine sonship and a messianic task. Further, because Pannenberg holds that the human Jesus is the acting subject in the identity of the Son, it is not clear that he affirms that reconciliation is a work of the *Logos*.

7.

The Heartbeat of Divine Love: Pannenberg and Reconciliation

Pannenberg's theology is an account of the God who saves. The final sweeping paragraph of *Systematic Theology* begins with a summary of history 'from the beginning of creation by way of reconciliation to the eschatological future of salvation'. Pannenberg's whole work argues that this history is 'the incursion of the eternal future of God to the salvation of creatures' and so 'a manifestation of divine love'. The last climactic sentence of the work declares that the unity and distinction of this movement is 'the heartbeat of divine love' which in a single heartbeat 'encompasses the whole world of creatures'.[1] Pannenberg's concern for history and his view that reality comes from the future are fully integrated with the theological themes of creation, reconciliation and God's identity.

Alongside this grand vision of redemption is the other side of Pannenberg's thought – the requirement that theological claims are based in the evidence of history. How can theology offer a hope of eschatological unity when the reality of historical experience is confusion and fragmentation? The answer for Pannenberg comes from the material we looked at in the last chapter – the historical, human life of Jesus. Pannenberg's primary argument for the claim that all of history is God's reconciling work is that the life of Jesus is a work of salvation which anticipates the future. Conversely, Jesus' life achieves reconciliation because it anticipates the eschatological salvation.

So we turn to consider Pannenberg's account of reconciliation and especially his view of Jesus' death which is central to his account of reconciliation. To begin with, it is important to see how Jesus' death contributes to his identity and how that is linked to redemption. We will then note some of the concerns and questions which shape Pannenberg's exposition of the doctrine of reconciliation and how he integrates the past, present and future to present a trinitarian doctrine of reconciliation. We can then return to the questions from the previous chapter about how Pannenberg understands reconciliation as an act of God the Son.

The Work of Christ and the Cross

In Pannenberg's thought the cross is the climax of the dual movement of distinction-from and unity-with the Father that marked Jesus' life. Jesus' death sealed his self-distinction from the Father: 'as Jesus accepted the death that others inflicted on him as the consequence of his sending to bear witness to the rule of God, he thus sealed the self-distinction from God that he proclaimed'.[2] At the same time it brought unity with the Father: 'only as he let his earthly existence be consumed in service to his mission could Jesus as a creature be one with God'.[3] The cross is also the event which lies at the centre of Pannenberg's account of reconciliation.[4] Understanding the cross as the climactic event that, in anticipation, determines Jesus' identity, as well as the event in which God, in anticipation, reconciles the world, gives Pannenberg's doctrine of reconciliation its distinctive note.

The Cross and Reconciliation: Concerns and Questions

Several concerns lead Pannenberg to relate the theme of reconciliation to the event of the cross. The christological question of the identity of Jesus is one concern. This is intimately related to the claim that the Triune God is reconciler of the world. Pannenberg's goal is to show that God is the one who brings reconciliation through Christ. Second Corinthians 5:19, with its famous statement 'in Christ God was reconciling the world to himself', is the most significant text for him in this regard. Pannenberg seeks to demonstrate that the apostolic authors offer an understanding of the cross which is grounded in 'the special' or distinctive features 'of the event [of Jesus' death] itself'. This argument is demanded by his view that the words of Scripture are authoritative insofar as they witness to the historical reality of the events to which they refer. So he has to show that the apostolic message does come from the event itself.

Pannenberg is also concerned with a series of problems that confront the doctrine of reconciliation. He argues that reconciliation must be an account of the death of Jesus, but that over the course of time Christian thought has both narrowed the meaning of the term 'reconciliation' and understood its relation to Jesus' death in a different sense from the New Testament understanding. The narrowing of the concept involves the loss of the connection between Jesus' death and present participation in the salvation of God. Doctrines of reconciliation, he claims, have become entirely focused on the historical events of the cross and have not included the way believers share in a new relationship with God.

The other shift is that 'in contrast to Paul, for whom God was the subject of the event of reconciliation . . . the idea could arise that God, having been offended by the sin of Adam, had to be reconciled to humanity by the obedience of the Son, or by the sacrificing of his life on the cross'. That is, God becomes the one reconciled rather than the Reconciler. Pannenberg traces this shift through Western theology, arguing that the view was correlated with the doctrine that Christ was mediator of salvation only in his human nature, so that he offered to God on behalf of sinners the satisfaction that was required by God or he received on behalf of sinners the punishment that was due to them. Pannenberg holds that even where the Reformers stressed mediation as a work of the God–human this problem was not overcome.

According to Pannenberg, modern Protestant theology has reclaimed the insight that reconciliation is 'an outworking of the love of God in the face of the opposition of humans who are hostile to God'.[5] However, the same line of thought tended to lose the central place of the cross in God's reconciliation. Pannenberg follows Kähler in asserting that Christ's death is not educative or exemplary but 'a real overcoming of the misery that consists of our having fallen into sin and death and the related estrangement from God'.[6]

Pannenberg is also concerned about a more specific question in interpreting the cross, which is whether the reconciling work on the cross can be described as expiation when contemporary thought can no longer think of Jesus' death in terms of 'sacrifice, expiation, and substitution'.[7] Pannenberg aims to show that the biblical presentation of reconciliation focuses on the cross of Christ, and that the cross can be understood as expiatory, when that term is properly understood. At the same time, he seeks to show how the cross is one part of the Triune God's whole work that brings the creation back to himself.

It is clear then that Pannenberg's thought about reconciliation relates three moments in time: Jesus' life, death and resurrection in the past; the present inclusion of believers into salvation; and the final consummation of salvation. His exposition of the doctrine of reconciliation clarifies how these three relate.

The Cross and Expiation

The most straightforward way to follow Pannenberg's thought about the work of Christ is to begin with his claim that the death of Christ is expiation for sins. If we ask, 'Why is Christ's death an act of expiation?', Pannenberg answers at two levels. On the one hand, he demonstrates that it is *possible* to understand and explain Jesus' death as expiation for sins and that this possibility arises from the historical circumstance, and thus that event is open to the understanding found in the New Testament and later Christian thought. On the other hand, he argues that Jesus' death is actually expiatory when there is reconciliation with God in the life of sinners. The first set of conditions create a possibility; only reconciliation actualizes that.

The possibility of expiation depends on the historical context of Jesus' death, so all of these conditions are related to the first historical 'moments'. There are six elements of the context which Pannenberg identifies.

1. Jesus' ministry as salvation

If Jesus' ministry cannot be understood as salvific then his death cannot be expiatory. Salvation in Christ cannot be merely the projection of human hopes onto a messianic figure.[8] Pannenberg argues that Jesus' message of the kingdom brought the presence of a future salvation that offered the wholeness of life, indicated by the word *shalom* in the Old Testament.[9] Although this was a promise looking to the future, Jesus announced the presence of salvation for those who encountered him.[10]

2. Jesus' message and Paul's message

Most the New Testament teaching about Jesus' death is found in the writings of Paul, not in the teaching of Jesus. So Pannenberg sets out to show that Paul's presentation is consistent with Jesus' ministry and that Paul's emphasis on the cross in reconciliation is a proper understanding of the events of the cross and resurrection. In brief his argument is that when the one who proclaimed the kingdom was crucified because of his message and when his resurrection is an anticipation of the *shalom* of the kingdom, then his death and resurrection had to be understood as related to the promised salvation. Paul could rightly view the salvation that Jesus proclaimed as now accomplished in Jesus' own death and resurrection.[11]

3. Eschatological salvation as rescue from judgement

If Jesus' death is to be understood as expiation it must be understood as relating to divine judgement, since expiation is a term that refers to guilt and penalty. Pannenberg points out that in contemporary Jewish thought eschatological salvation related to 'deliverance in the approaching world judgement'. He concludes that when Jesus spoke of salvation it would have been understood in the same terms. Paul particularly brings the notions of justification and reconciliation to the fore, since they explain how the events of the past bring into the present a reality that lies in the future. Pannenberg's point is that Paul's forensic emphasis is a valid development from Jesus' proclamation.[12]

4. The cross as salvation

It would be possible for Jesus' life and ministry to be one of reconciliation, but for his death to merely be the tragic end to a great life. Similarly, Pannenberg admits that 'not all strata of the primitive Christian tradition view the death of Jesus as a salvation event'.[13] Yet he discerns 'special significance' in the view that Jesus' death was expiatory. Partly this is because Paul's writings make this explicit (2 Cor. 5:21; Rom. 8:3; Gal. 3:13).[14] That, by itself, is not sufficient for Pannenberg. He must also show that Paul offers a valid understanding of the historical event. So Pannenberg points to several aspects of Jesus' ministry and its context which establish the possibility that Jesus' death was expiatory. For one, Jesus' contemporaries would have understood the manner of his death to indicate that he died under God's condemnation as a blasphemer and a lawbreaker. He would have been presumed to face the eschatological judgement that he himself proclaimed.[15] Jesus' innocence is only established by the resurrection in which God vindicates him, against the claims of the Jewish authorities. In Jesus' vindication Israel, through its leaders, is shown to have opposed God and the one he sent. So Israel deserves the judgement that Jesus received. In retrospect, it is possible that Jesus has died in the place of those who executed him, receiving the curse of the law which would finally confront them in the eschatological judgement.[16]

5. *Death for all humanity*

Pannenberg also asks how Jesus' death can be seen as embracing all humanity. Within a Jewish world-view it would be thought that if Jesus died for others, he died for the people of Israel as a whole. Pannenberg argues that the universal scope of Jesus' death was an expansion of a primary relationship with the Jewish people. An important step in the development of this thought is to see that the Roman authorities were involved in his condemnation as well as the Jewish leadership. So just as the leaders of Israel condemned the one who died for them, the leaders of the Gentiles condemned the one who died for them.[17] The context of Jesus' death makes it possible that he died for Jews and Gentiles.

6. Reconciliation as an act of God

Pannenberg devotes considerable attention to how Christ's death can be considered God's act of reconciliation.[18] Here he seeks to show that God is the Reconciler (not the reconciled).[19] As well as discussing the interpretation of 2 Corinthians 5:17, Pannenberg offers a theological argument based on the resurrection. The resurrection, indisputably an act of God, gives the crucifixion atoning force. In it 'God showed himself to be the Victor over sin and death'. So the resurrection establishes that God is the one who acts in reconciliation.[20] The claim that the cross is an act of God toward the world, rather than an act of a human creature toward God, is an important step in establishing Pannenberg's trinitarian account of reconciliation. It is a claim that rests not on the historical nature of the act of Jesus' death in itself, but what it was, anticipated by the resurrection.

This series of conditions of possibility all deal with the past event of Jesus' death, though notice that this understanding of Jesus' death is only possible because of the resurrection, which in turn anticipates eschatological salvation.

Representation: the Actualizing Condition

So far Pannenberg has shown how it is possible for Jesus to die as God's act of reconciliation for the world. Pannenberg finds the idea of Jesus' representative death in Paul's statements that Christ died 'for our sins' and similar expressions (1 Cor. 15:3; Rom. 4:25; 8:22; Gal. 3:13; 2:20; Eph. 5:25; 1 Tim. 2:6; Tit. 2:14; 2 Cor. 5:21). He concludes that Paul has a clear concept of 'a co-human solidarity in which some represent others'.[21] Yet it remains to be shown that Paul's idea of representation can be legitimately applied to Jesus' death. If Jesus' death is to be considered an expiation then it must be the case that he actually acted as a representative and Pannenberg argues that this is the case only when it is shown that others come to be included in it.

Pannenberg states that the cross has achieved reconciliation 'only in anticipation' and that it is the proclamation of the gospel that moves reconciliation 'from anticipation to actualisation'.[22] He points to Paul's appeal for the Corinthians to be reconciled with God as a demonstration that the 'inner telos' of the crucifixion is actual reconciliation. Again, Pannenberg is making use of his temporalized essentialism, asserting that if it turns out that others are included in Jesus' death then, at the time of his death, Jesus was acting as a representative.

The idea that Jesus died as a representative has been rejected in much modern German theology, at least in part due to the influence of Immanuel Kant, who thought representation impossible since one person cannot die for another. Instead Kant reinterprets expiation so that the response of the sinner is the key: the good disposition of a newly righteous individual is exchanged for the previous guilt of that person.[23] Pannenberg sees a similar problem with a form of representation (though his concern is ethical rather than ontological). For Pannenberg, exclusive representation, in which the one represented has no role, is unethical. If Jesus represents us without our agreement then God's action toward us is 'hostile'. God does something to which we give no agreement and is, in effect, against our will. Further, since the problem of sin lies in human enmity to God, a unilateral action on God's side would not bring reconciliation.[24]

Pannenberg's view is made clear in his criticism of Barth's view that the cross is 'self-contained' and that the apostolic preaching must be sharply distinguished from it.[25] Barth claims that the 'conversion of the world to God has . . . taken place in Christ' and explicitly rejects the idea that the call to be reconciled is 'an extension of the atonement in the form of something which man himself can decide'.[26] Pannenberg holds with Barth that the Son is the 'definitive actualizing of our destiny' since the Son is the origin of sonship, which all receive through him. His view differs from Barth, for him Jesus' 'definitiveness leaves room . . . for the individuality of others'.[27]

Rather than exclusive representation, Pannenberg argues that Jesus acted as an inclusive representative. In this view of Jesus' death, 'there takes place in him paradigmatically that which is to be repeated in all the members of humanity that he represents'.[28] Jesus' death was not a straightforward 'exchange' in which he died instead of others since 'those for whom Jesus died must die themselves'. Rather Jesus' death 'preserves them for eternal life in the judgement of God'. So Pannenberg argues that in 2 Corinthians 5 'participation in the obedient suffering and death of Christ that is mediated in baptism and faith . . . is the means whereby believers have reconciliation to God through Christ'.[29] Further support for inclusive representation comes in the fact that it allows an explanation of reconciliation that is not limited to a penal interpretation of the cross. It can interpret the whole course of Christ's life as the new paradigm for humanity, taking up the New Testament descriptions of Jesus as the second Adam, the image of God and the Son of God. In this understanding of the work of Christ 'he is our representative, not as we are now, but as we are to be'. The view of Christ as the representative new Adam is closely related to the incarnation and as such Pannenberg claims it has 'shaped the whole history of Christian soteriology'.[30]

Pannenberg's exposition of the death of Christ as inclusive representative draws from Hegel and Heidegger the idea that death should be understood in relation to finitude.[31] Both Hegel and Heidegger, in very different ways, understand death and the acceptance of death as the point at which the finite relates to the infinite.[32] According to Pannenberg, Jesus' death changes the meaning of death for believers. He writes that those who are represented by Christ now die with the possibility 'in their death . . . of attaining to the hope of participating in the new resurrection life'.[33] This possibility opens up because of the nature of Jesus' own death. In his life, and climactically in his death, Jesus did not assert his individuality or make himself equal to God. Rather he lived in obedient self-distinction from God and accepted his own finitude by submitting to death. 'His death became the seal of his self-distinction and therefore also the proof of unity with God.'[34]

According to Pannenberg, Jesus' death is the reverse of the sin that it overcomes. Sin is enmity to God in wanting to be like him, and means that humans cannot have a place alongside God but must fall victim to death. Jesus accepted the death that others, in their rivalry with God, forced on him. He offered up his 'individuality' and 'particularity' to God and in doing so 'made room' for the particular existence of others. The outcome, according to Pannenberg, is that now others come to the same point through

Jesus' death and through their acceptance of their own death for the sake of God and the kingdom. They anticipate this death in faith and baptism and so accept their finitude before God and share in the hope of the resurrection in Jesus.[35]

So Pannenberg rejects an exclusive representation which sees Jesus acting entirely beyond and outside believers. He affirms an inclusive representation in which Jesus does something apart from believers in his historical action, and in this action opens up for believers the possibility that they could be included in his action. Jesus submits himself to death, accepting finitude, and so finding unity with God. Believers, on the basis of Jesus' action, are able to make the same submission and come to the same unity. Faith and baptism are a present anticipation of submission to God and unity with him in death, so as believers receive reconciliation the representative and expiatory significance of Jesus' death is actualized.

The Triune God as Reconciler

Pannenberg presents a trinitarian account of reconciliation. He presents the work of reconciliation as the work of the Father, as the work of Christ as mediator, and as the work of the Spirit.

Pannenberg refers to the texts that emphasize the giving of the Son by the Father (2 Cor. 5:18–19; Rom. 4:25; 5:10; 8:3,32; John 3:16). He has also shown that Jesus acted in obedience, so that his death is to be understood as the self-giving of the Son (Gal. 2:20; Eph. 5:2,25; Mark 8:31; 9:31; 10:33). This is not to say that Jesus sought death as the goal of his ministry, but rather that since Jesus was raised, his life was the coming of the pre-existent Son of God and so his death was the Son's self-giving. Any apparent tension between the Father giving the Son and the Son's self-giving is resolved by insisting that the Son's self-giving and the Father's giving 'are saying the same thing in different ways' so that 'the obedience of the Son corresponds to the giving up by the Father'.[36]

The work of the Son and the Spirit cohere in similar unity. Traditionally the work of Christ has been described in terms of his 'office' of prophet, priest and king.[37] Pannenberg is critical of the Reformation and post-Reformation approach of the office of Christ for its 'one-sidedly Christological objectivism', which 'did not think through the mutual relation of the work of the ascended Christ and that of the Spirit'.[38] He argues that the historical, human life of Jesus cannot be seen as that of a king, or a priest, or even, strictly, a prophet. He can be seen to occupy the threefold office only in the light of the outcome of resurrection. Here the future horizon comes into focus. Pannenberg explains that 'statements regarding Jesus as the Reconciler who brings salvation to humanity would not be true without their correlate – saved and reconciled humanity'.[39]

Thus the final dimension of the work of the Triune God in reconciliation is the work of the Spirit. In the ministry of the Spirit the creaturely capacity to exist ecstatically, that is with our centre beyond ourselves, is liberated and believers are enabled to live their finitude in distinction from and in unity with God.[40] Pannenberg concludes that 'the Spirit completes our reconciliation with God by enabling us through faith in Jesus Christ to accept our own finite existence before God'.[41] The Spirit will bring about the unity of all things in the eschaton, and participation in Christ by the Spirit now is an anticipation of that unity.[42]

Thinking about Reconciliation with Pannenberg

Pannenberg's account of reconciliation is impressive. As usual he works together a wide range of themes into an exciting synthesis. Surely a fully biblical view of salvation cannot only focus on Jesus' death – it will also need to think about his life, resurrection and return, as well as the work of the Spirit. It is interesting to search theology texts to see how these themes are related. My explorations suggest that in most evangelical theology they rarely are integrated. So many theology books announce the topic of Jesus as Saviour and then only discuss his death. In some it is hard to find even a paragraph which mentions how his 'work' as Saviour relates to other parts of his life. There is often another section which has a discussion of the work of the Spirit in salvation. Sometimes this includes an emphasis on the work of the Spirit bringing believers into union with Christ. That emphasis starts to connect the work of the Spirit with the Son. Yet it fails to address how the work the Son leads to the work of the Spirit, even though Jesus says the two are related (John 16:7). In contrast, Pannenberg's integration of these themes is very careful and gives a model for evangelical theology.

As a result of that careful integration, Pannenberg's account is deeply trinitarian, which helps to show the importance of the doctrine of the Trinity. It is the grammar of the work of God and it is impossible to give a coherent account of the work of God without a doctrine of the Trinity. I suspect that one reason why treatments of reconciliation are so unsatisfying is because they are not thoroughly trinitarian. When you see God at work as Father, Son and Spirit in unity, it is far easier to see how the events of the past in Jesus, the ongoing present work of the inclusion of sinners, and the final redemption of all things are all one work of the Triune God. In all this Pannenberg sets a very high standard to which all theology should aspire.

Much evangelical theology would be highly critical of Pannenberg's doctrine of reconciliation because of the emphasis on inclusive representation. Conservative evangelical theology places great stress on the doctrine of 'substitution', which is a strong version of 'exclusive representation'.[43] It holds that Christ in his death made satisfaction for sins by 'undergoing . . . vicarious punishment to meet the claims on us of God's holy law and wrath'.[44] Substitution involves one party acting in the place of another, with no direct participation by the one who is replaced. Packer argues that while Christ's death is representative, 'setting a pattern of "confession and praise" to be reproduced in our own self-denial and cross-bearing', this can only rest on its primarily substitutionary nature.[45]

Wider theology and streams of thought within evangelicalism have raised questions about the validity of penal substitution.[46] In the last decade many scholars in conservative evangelical theology have forcefully restated the validity of substitution.[47] Yet much of this discussion is irrelevant to considering Pannenberg's position. In the debates substitution and inclusive representation are often set in contrast. Pannenberg sees them as complementary and interdependent. Jesus' historical act of death on behalf of others (substitution) is the necessary condition for reconciliation, but a focus on that without including the present reality of the life of believers and the eschatological culmination must leave us with an 'unactualized' reconciliation. For Pannenberg, we must see what comes about in the end in order to know the nature of Jesus' death. So he affirms the importance of Jesus' death as vicarious penal suffering and indicates that he is not aiming to replace the idea of substitution or representation. Rather he aims to open up to contemporary understanding the classic ideas of representation and substitution by offering an interpretation of them which will help to keep their meaning alive.[48]

Granted that much evangelical discussion would not touch Pannenberg's position and cannot be applied to it I think that the question I raised in the last chapter is important. How does Pannenberg's Christology play out in his account of reconciliation? It seems to me that there are significant New Testament themes that receive no obvious place in Pannenberg's account and that it is likely that they are missing because of the structure of his Christology.

In a traditional Christology, the distinction made between the two natures in the one person is applied to the work of Christ. The Son is understood as working in and through the human nature with which he is united. This conceptual structure enables the traditional view to affirm that the work of Christ is a fully divine and fully human work to which each nature contributes its distinctive element. Pannenberg's Christology abstains from an account of the person of Christ in terms of a hypostatic union of two natures and he is critical of explanations that speak of the Son acting through the human nature. He presents reconciliation as an act of God that brings sinners back into fellowship with him. Yet, for him this work is a human work, which is a divine work on the basis of anticipation. That is, he can claim that 'the human and historical level of the history of Jesus is transparent to the presence of the incarnate Son of God concealed in it' only on the basis that the resurrection establishes Jesus' identity.[49] Similarly, since death is the act in which the human Jesus fully accepts finitude, it is reconciliation when that acceptance of finitude takes place in other lives. The correlate of this account of the work of Christ is that reconciliation is actualized in the response of sinners. Is this reformulated account of the death of Christ an advance over classical views? A close look at the New Testament presentation of reconciliation suggests some strengths in classic formulations which are missing in Pannenberg's approach.

Much of the New Testament presents Christ's death as a finished work, though certainly oriented to the completion of the work of reconciliation in the return of sinners to God. That is the tendency of 2 Corinthians 5, the passage which dominates Pannenberg's thought, where Paul moves from God's reconciling the world to himself in Christ to the ministry of reconciliation (2 Cor. 5:18–21; cf. Tit. 2:14; 1 Pet. 3:18). Pannenberg is right to claim that a view such as Barth's (that the cross and resurrection completed reconciliation in all aspects) is not true to the important New Testament texts. However, recognizing that the response of sinners is part of the New Testament account of reconciliation is not equivalent to saying that the response is that which actualizes the cross as reconciliation. Instead, it is better to say that the work of Christ enables a response on the basis of its achievement.

Many texts emphasize the completeness of reconciliation in the cross and resurrection. The book of Hebrews illustrates the point. In order show this, I am going to consider a few texts, paying close attention to the questions of timing and completeness in the death of Christ. The writer opens his letter describing the Son who sat down at the right hand of God 'having made purification' (Heb. 1:3). The description of Jesus seated at the right hand of God is common in the New Testament. It comes from Psalm 110:1 and is applied to Jesus' ascension by a wide range of New Testament texts. In Hebrews the image is contrasted with the priest who offers purification but must remain standing. The strong implication is that the author of Hebrews understands that Jesus completed the act of purification in his death (and so is seated in his ascension).

Starting from this opening statement, the completeness of the sacrificial work of Christ is a prominent theme in Hebrews. Lindars notes that although the writer must explain how the atonement affects sinners by removing the consciousness of sin, 'nevertheless atonement has certain requirements, and these must be fulfilled in Jesus'.[50] Lindars suggests that one reason for the writer choosing the Day of Atonement as a basis for the presentation of Jesus' death is found in the Jewish understanding that the Day removed the burden of sin for which individual atonement had not been made. He quotes from the Mishnah ('Yoma' 8:8–9), a passage that throws more light on our question. There the Mishnah teaches that repentance effects atonement for lesser transgressions, but that only Yom Kippur deals with graver offences. It also implies that for such grave transgression there is nothing that the sinner can do to appease God, even after the sacrifice.[51] The use of the Day of Atonement to explain Jesus' death highlights the stress on the completeness of atonement. Hebrews also uses the adverb 'once for all' (*ephax*) to describe Jesus' self-offering (Heb. 7:27; 9:12; 10:10). In each case the writer is making the point that, unlike the sacrifices of the earthly tabernacle that had to be repeated, Jesus' offering requires no repetition because it has dealt with sin.

Pannenberg's comment on Hebrews falls short of grasping the theme of the completeness of the work of Christ, suggesting that 'such statements [which speak of Christ' work as complete] anticipate the actual process of the setting aside of humanity's sins'. He appeals to Hebrews 9:28 which in the NRSV states that Christ will come 'not to deal with sin'. The phrase could be translated literally as 'apart from sin' and Pannenberg takes it to mean that Christ will return when sin is finally set aside, that is when reconciliation occurs. However the explanation that Pannenberg himself gives in the footnote, 'in contrast to his first coming, he will no longer have to deal with sin', shows that the phrase does not imply that dealing with sin will be ongoing in the sense of actualizing Christ's atonement until his return. Attridge offers the more straightforward suggestion that 'Christ's second coming will not have the atoning function of the first: it will be apart from sin in its aims and effects'.[52] Attridge's understanding of the text counts against Pannenberg's view. For Pannenberg the return of Christ is the culmination of reconciliation and therefore the full actualization of expiation, yet the text seems to indicate that the return of Christ brings an aspect of salvation that does not entail sin-bearing. Again, Hebrews 10:14 states that 'by a single offering' Jesus 'has perfected' (a perfect verb) for all time those who 'are being sanctified' (a present participle). Attridge comments that the perfect tense with the present substantive participle 'nuances the relationship' between perfection and sanctification showing that Christ's once for all act of sin bearing has continuing results: 'the appropriation of the enduring effects of Christ's act is an ongoing reality'.[53] The pattern of Hebrews of an accomplished work appropriated by believers is not the same as

Pannenberg's suggestion that expiation is actualized in the reconciliation of believers.

Is Our Death Like Jesus' Death?

In Pannenberg's account, Jesus' death is effective because it is the paradigm for the death of believers. Jesus accepts his finitude in humble submission. In reconciliation this acceptance is repeated in other lives. The New Testament shows the similarity of Jesus' death and that of believers. One similarity is that Jesus shares in the fate of all humanity, so Hebrews 2:14 declares that Jesus shared in flesh and blood like those he saves. A second similarity is that believers come to share in what Jesus has won, both in his death and resurrection (Rom. 6:8; Col. 2:20; 3:3). Nevertheless, several New Testament texts also differentiate between the nature of Jesus' death and that of believers. For example, Hebrews states that Jesus tasted death for all and that by his death he destroyed the devil 'who has the power of death' (Heb. 2:14) and freed 'those who all their lives were held in slavery by the fear of death' (Heb. 2:15). That is, Jesus has gone through death as one placed under the power of death so that all those who come after him no longer experience that power. This difference helps to explain why Jesus feared death (Matt. 26:38–9; Mark 14:33; Luke 12:50; 22:40–44; John 12:27; Heb. 5:7) in a way believers do not (Phil. 1:20–23).

The New Testament testifies that for believers death is already defeated, even though they may still die physically (John 5:24; Rom. 5:17; 6:23; 8:38; 1 Cor. 15:55–6; Col. 3:3–4; Heb. 2:9, 14–15; 1 John 3:14). Ian MacFarland highlights this difference, arguing that 'because it has been claimed by Christ, death now becomes the gateway to life'. He develops his argument by an examination of Paul's presentation of baptism as a participation in Jesus' death. The contrast with Pannenberg is interesting. For Pannenberg baptism is the beginning point of a life that anticipates full inclusion into Jesus' obedient death (Rom. 6:5). MacFarland argues that baptism does not look forward to physical death but looks back to Jesus' death. He observes that 'Paul nowhere claims that martyrdom – let alone crucifixion – is necessary or even normative for Christians; moreover his chief interest in Romans 6 is not how we died, but the way we live'.[54] Pannenberg does not regard martyrdom as normative for Christians though he does think that in baptism believers emulate Jesus' (martyr's) death. The view that as sinners are included in reconciliation Jesus' death is actualized as expiation risks reversing the logic of Romans 6. Paul's view is that sinners now live as dead to sin because Jesus 'died to sin, once for all'; not that Jesus died to sin because sinners now die with him.

Grace and Christology

Having praised Pannenberg's doctrine of reconciliation for its careful trinitarian approach it may seem that I have finished with a rather 'picky' critique. Detailed as the point may be, it is worth making since it leads us back to an important theological insight. The issue I am raising is important in Pannenberg's thought. The actualization of expiation in the inclusion of sinners is at the heart of Pannenberg's view of reconciliation. His position is that Christ's death is expiatory because it leads believers into an analogous death.

The same issues recur here as in Pannenberg's Christology. He is insistent that 'God is the acting subject in this expiatory action'.[55] Yet in his account God is the acting subject not in the human, historical action itself, but in anticipation of the response of believers. In contrast, a two-nature Christology, which views Jesus' death as the unique death of the incarnate *Logos*, can view that death as one which is redemptive because of its unique aspects. The traditional conception of the hypostatic union provides a basis for an understanding of the reconciling work of Christ as that of the Son who, given by the Father, graciously takes up humanity and offers himself for sinners. It more clearly articulates the gracious work of God in the work of Christ.

Christology and understandings of redemption always go together. For Christian theology an understanding of Jesus always implies a view of redemption. This is true of classic Christology as much as it is of contemporary approaches. Douglas Fairbairn, in a study of early christological debates, highlights that the real issues at stake were often about redemption.[56] This is quite a relief for anyone who has slogged through the details of those early debates and wondered why they generated such high feeling! The obvious debates about natures and persons are 'a sort of theological shorthand for an entire complex of beliefs regarding grace, salvation, and Christology'. In particular, maintaining an orthodox Christology was important for affirming that salvation comes from God alone.[57]

MacFarland proposes three rules for a doctrine of the atonement: it must not identify, co-ordinate or make superfluous either human or divine activity. Pannenberg's account of the cross risks contravening the first two of these rules. In his account the action of the Son and the human Jesus in the cross are identified (though his eschatological ontology means that he can do so without the compromise of the ontological distinction of God and creation of which MacFarland warns). MacFarland explains that human and divine activity are co-ordinated when it is suggested that one activity completes or complements the other. He insists that 'God and human beings always operate on different planes'.[58] Pannenberg co-ordinates the divine and human actions by making the response of sinners the actualizing condition for the cross to be expiation.

McFarland deals with the place of human response. He contends that this must not be suppressed, but must be conceived as operating on a different plane from that of God's action. He proposes to describe reconciliation in a similar way to Pannenberg: 'God's work of reconciliation may be viewed as a process by which human beings inspired by the Spirit speak back to the Father.' That is, he includes human response in the account of reconciliation. Rather than finding this response directly in the reconciled, MacFarland turns to the *Logos*. He suggests that the economic pattern of the incarnate Word responding to the Father reflects the relations of the ontological Trinity. The Spirit is the one who 'perfects the inner dynamic of the divine life by hearing and responding to the Word spoken by the Father', and in the economy the Spirit enables the incarnate Word to so respond. Thus he concludes that the human response is already established in the life of Christ, and others are then included in this.

Insofar as the inner structure of the divine life is one in which the Word spoken from all eternity by the Father is affirmed in its unity with the

Father by the Holy Spirit, in the incarnation of the Word . . . is the necessary condition of human beings sharing in God's triune communion. The communion is realized first in Jesus . . . thereby opening the way for other human beings to share in that same affirmation through him.[59]

MacFarland can give fuller emphasis than Pannenberg to the completion of reconciliation in the death of Christ because he does not conceive it as an act in which the divine identity of the Son is established, in anticipation, by the human Jesus. By retaining a two-nature account of Christology he can affirm the need for response as fully as Pannenberg does, without viewing the death of Jesus as requiring that response in order to be actualized as reconciliation and expiation. It seems there are some good reasons to retain the Chalcedonian approach, rather than replacing it with Pannenberg's proposal.

8.

The One Who Is All in All: Pannenberg and God

In this chapter we reach the heart of Pannenberg's theological vision. Pannenberg pays careful attention to questions about revelation, anthropology, the historical Jesus and the work of reconciliation, as well as a host of other topics; yet he always leads the discussion back to the reality of God. Although the doctrine of God has received more explicit attention from him in the later part of his career it is not in any sense added merely to round out his theology. Pannenberg's doctrine of God integrates his theological project and has been central to it all along.

Pannenberg's Concerns in the Doctrine of God

As with other areas of theology Pannenberg has concerns with the way the doctrine of God has been developed and expressed and he hopes to help theology reach a better expression of the doctrine.[1]

1. Metaphysics and God

Pannenberg holds that theology needs metaphysics but that traditional metaphysics is no longer viable. Traditional theology and metaphysics stressed God's transcendence and emphasized God's utter separation from creation. Pannenberg thinks that modern thought demands an account of God which shows more carefully that God exists in relations, not only in eternal inner relations but also in relation to the rest of reality. He aims to make his doctrine of God show that 'the events of history in some way bear on the identity of his eternal essence'.[2]

2. Problems in the traditional doctrine of God

Pannenberg identifies three ways in which the traditional doctrine of God seems to be incoherent. First, the trinitarian tradition has never successfully related God's unity and triunity.[3] In order to overcome subordinationism it emphasized that the Father, Son and Spirit are distinct because of their eternal inner relations – a view which could lead to three Gods (tritheism).[4] Later Western discussions assume the unity of God and derive the doctrine of the Trinity from this unity, which risks losing any real distinction in God (modalism).[5]

A second problem is how the inner life of God relates to his presence and work in the world.[6] The terms which are often used for this are the 'immanent Trinity' (God's eternal inner relations) and the 'economic Trinity' (the Father, Son and Spirit at work in the world). These terms were popularized in a famous paper by the Catholic theologian, Karl Rahner, who asserted that 'the economic Trinity is the immanent Trinity'.[7] That is the God present in the world as Father, Son and Spirit exists eternally as the same Father, Son and Spirit. As we will see, this claim (sometimes called Rahner's Rule) can be interpreted in several ways. Pannenberg argues that, after the councils of Nicaea and Constantinople, 'the thought of the eternal and essential Trinity broke loose from its historical moorings and tended to be seen . . . as untouched by the course of history . . . and therefore also inaccessible to all crea-turely knowledge'.[8] That is, the connection between the economic and immanent Trinity was lost. The opposite problem emerged in the twentieth century when the total identification of the economic and immanent Trinity risked the 'absorption of the immanent Trinity in the economic'.[9]

A third problem for trinitarian theology is the question of how to relate the attributes and essence of God. The problem here is how God's infinite unity can have a multiplicity of attributes. If distinctions between the attributes are real, then they have to be distinguished from the divine essence so they do not compromise

God's unity, but then God in his nature is not what he is in his attributes. On the other hand, if the distinctions are only conceptual then God's essence remains undefined.[10] Pannenberg suggests that this question is 'suspended in the history of theology'.[11]

A somewhat different problem for Trinitarian theology is how it relates to human experience. In particular, Pannenberg requires a doctrine of God which shows that God is not a denial of human freedom but is in fact the basis of freedom.[12] His argument is that classical theism fails to account for the indisputable human experience of freedom which is the basis for religious life.[13]

The Doctrine of God and Revelation

Pannenberg is very careful to ground all his theology in revelation and God's revelation takes place in history, particularly in the history of Jesus as an anticipation of God's full revelation in the eschaton. Pannenberg suspects that the traditional doctrine of God loses contact with history and gets lost in speculation so he asserts, 'to find a basis for the doctrine of the Trinity we must begin with the way in which Father, Son and Spirit come on the scene and relate to one another in the event of revelation'.[14]

Pannenberg works from the historical revelation of Jesus and the relationships discovered there. He spends very little time arguing for the historicity of various events. He appeals to a passage such as 1 Corinthians 15:24–5, which cannot be verified historically.[15] This can give an appearance of proof-texting to his doctrine of God. However, every aspect of biblical teaching to which he appeals is a matter of relations of the persons of the Trinity in the economy of salvation, so his study is grounded in history in that sense. Presumably he does not argue for the historicity of the various events because he is concerned primarily with demonstrating the conceptual coherence of his account and its relation to the revelation in Jesus, while the resurrection functions as the anticipatory confirmation.

Pannenberg's concerns about history, relationality and the economic Trinity converge in this discussion. Theological tradition has treated references to the 'generation' of the Son (John 1:14; 3:16; Luke 3:22) and the 'procession' of the Spirit (John 15:26;

20:22) as direct insights into the immanent Trinity.[16] Pannenberg argues that all such texts deal with the economy. The only path to knowledge of God-in-himself is through this historical revelation: 'one can know the inter-trinitarian distinctions and relations, the inner life of God, only through the revelation of the Son, not through the different spheres of the operation of the one God in the world'.[17]

Pannenberg's Reformulated Trinitarianism

How does Pannenberg present a doctrine of God which meets all these demands? In one sense the answer is obvious: he follows the same lines as he did in Christology and presents history and historical revelation as the 'mutual self-distinction' of Father, Son and Spirit which takes place in the 'richly structured nexus of relationship' of trinitarian life.[18] The acts of God that have traditionally been viewed as economic are presented as constitutive for both the distinctions between the persons and of their deity. Olson has called the claim that God's deity is established in his economic lordship, that is that God's being is his rule, 'Pannenberg's Principle'.[19]

Although that principle can be described in quite a straightforward way, its execution is extremely complex. One reason for this is the huge range of theological issues Pannenberg is dealing with as he presents the doctrine of God. The other reason for complexity is indicated by describing the trinitarian life as a 'richly structured nexus'. There is a series of acts which have to be included in Pannenberg's account: the Father sends the Son and hands the kingdom over to the Son and receives it back; the Son obeys the Father and honours him as God; the Spirit confirms, raises and extols the Son; the Father gives the Spirit to the Son; the Spirit sheds abroad the Father's love.[20]

Pannenberg treats these relations as truly mutual, so that the Father–Son relation is constitutive for the Father as well the Son. He extends Athanasius' argument that the Father could not be Father without the Son, asserting that not only is the Father's fatherhood found in relation to the Son, but so is his deity.[21] On Pannenberg's definition, the lordship of the Father, mediated by the Son (Phil.

2:9–11, 1 Cor. 15:24–5), 'goes hand in hand with' deity. To put this another way: God is God because the Son submits to the Father and the Father hands lordship to the Son.[22]

Pannenberg's assertion that the relationship of the Father with the Son constitutes the deity of the Father is a contrast with the more general view that the monarchy of the Father is foundational for the relations of the Trinity.[23] Jenson identifies this as one of Pannenberg's innovations in the doctrine of God.[24] Mostert confirms that this 'is a departure from the classical doctrine of the priority of the Father over the Son and the Spirit'.[25]

For Pannenberg, God's unity is not obvious and must be explicated by theology. This is the reverse of the traditional view that is more likely to consider distinctions in God as problematic. Pannenberg begins his thinking with history which looks fragmented and far from the revelation of a unified Absolute. His philosophical context underscores for him that it is nigh on impossible to provide such an account. He also argues that the New Testament speaks clearly of the Father, the Son and the Spirit, but not so clearly of their unity as one God. The unity of God is the final topic of Pannenberg's doctrine of God since the claim can only be justified at the end of his discussion. This sets the scene for further clarification and exploration of the idea of God's unity in the following volumes of *Systematic Theology* that deal with God's work in creation, redemption and consummation.[26] Father, Son and Spirit are revealed in the history of God's work in the world, but the perfect unity of the three 'is still hidden in the process of history'.[27] This does not mean that we can say nothing about God's unity, but that it must be understood through the economic Trinity and asserted in anticipation as we look toward the consummation of God's work.

The distinctives of Pannenberg's approach can be seen in his treatment of the person of the Spirit, which he approaches via economic relations: the Spirit raised and glorified the Son completing the revelation of the Father.[28] Pannenberg holds that this economic action constitutes the unity of the Spirit with the Father and the Son and differentiates the Spirit who acts as a subject towards both Father and Son.[29] At the same time Pannenberg can identify the divine essence as 'Spirit': the 'unity and perfection of divine life' in which the identity of each person is mediated by relations with the other persons and in this 'self-giving to the others, each of the persons is fully identical with itself'.[30] In this context, Pannenberg makes his suggestion that the Spirit can be conceptualized as a force field. As a field, God's essence is not particular to a subject, but each divine person is a manifestation of the field. 'The idea . . . sees the divine Spirit who unites the three persons as proceeding from the Father, received by the Son, and common to both, so that precisely in this way he is the force field of their fellowship that is distinct from the both.'[31] Because the Spirit is life-giving, God is the living God. So the Spirit is both the essence of God and a person in triune fellowship. Pannenberg then points out that the characteristic work of the Spirit in the world is an expression of his place in the relations within the Trinity. Economically the Spirit is the 'life force that proceeds from God', while immanently the Spirit is the life of God.[32] In Pannenberg's account this parallel is not merely analogical; rather, the Spirit is the immanent life of God because he is the God who brings life to all creation.

In this way Pannenberg develops an account of God's unity which is trinitarian and thoroughly economic. The unity of the Father and Son is constituted by economic acts, which acts constitute the Spirit and are enabled by the Spirit. The work of the Spirit in the world is to overcome differences and create fellowship and life.[33] So Pannenberg insists that theology must 'ascribe to the third Person of the Trinity both the positive relation, in the sense of the fellowship of what is distinct, and also the associated dynamic [of constituting or establishing unity], whether in the trinitarian life of God or in creation'.[34]

Pannenberg's conception of mutual relations must not be confused with 'equivalent' relations, for 'self-distinction' does not mean exactly the same thing for each of the three persons.[35] Monarchy is be ascribed to the Father, while the Son is the 'locus of the monarchy of the Father'.[36] The Spirit is the condition and medium of fellowship between Father and Son.[37] Each of these relations, which refer together to the distinctions, attributes, deity and unity of the persons, is found in the concrete relations of salvation history. Thus Pannenberg presents a doctrine of the Trinity in which the deity, distinctive identity and unity of each of the persons is constituted in and through the others.[38] It is only through the history of reconciliation united in the eschaton that God is constituted in his triune existence. Because that history is anticipatory of the eschaton it is true that God is the Father, Son, and Spirit in perfect unity.

How the Triune God Acts

According to Pannenberg, the conception of God as 'three centres of action' bound in unity by their action is the bridge between God's outward activity and his inner being. God's action on the world and his relation to the world mediate a self-relation for God. He takes this as an instance of a general truth since an action always involves the actor in a relation with that which is acted upon, which means that the object of the action mediates a self-relation for the actor.

Pannenberg considers the goal-directed actions of God in creation and history, identifying two goals of God's action in creation.[39] The first is a complex one, embracing all history: God 'incorporates his creatures into the eternal fellowship of the Son with the Father through the Spirit'. The second is the revelation of God's deity. These goals are reciprocal, since the incorporation of creatures into fellowship with God establishes God's deity and creatures can only be united with the One who is the true Infinite.[40]

Pannenberg insists that God's action in history must not be thought of as that of a finite being whose goals anticipate a future different from the present and who controls the course of events. This model will result in a God who either 'seeks control' or exercises totalitarian rule over a predetermined history.[41] He argues that thinking of God's action in a very different way shows that creatures are free because they participate in God's actions.

Pannenberg views history as trinitarian action in which the monarchy of the Father is mediated by the Son and Spirit, who enable the creatures to share in divine fellowship.[42] In this unity (both divine and creaturely) God's action can be ascribed to the one God (the divine essence), and this unity is the triunity of Father, Son and Spirit. This allows Pannenberg to speak of the attributes of God as both qualities of God's outward actions and constitutive of divine essence, and to affirm that the attributes belong both to the persons and to God's essence. In this account there is no question of whether attributes should be referred to the economy, the divine persons, or the divine essence – they refer to all three.[43] These relations are fully realized as eternal relations, and because Pannenberg's view of eternity is 'simultaneity', he can conceptualize trinitarian relations as 'dynamic' – moving simultaneously in distinction and unity.

Towards the end of his presentation of the doctrine of the Trinity, Pannenberg presents a fairly complete conceptualization of the Triune God. He claims to have shown that theology should 'understand the trinitarian persons, without derivation from a divine essence that differs from them, as centres of action of the one movement which embraces and permeates them all – the movement of the divine Spirit who has his existence only in them'.[44] The appeal to 'self-differentiation' allows Pannenberg to meet all three of his concerns: it makes relations constitutive of essence, it moves toward a new conception of divine unity and is grounded in the event of revelation. Once elucidated, the concept has its own persuasive force within Pannenberg's thought.

Immanent and Economic Trinity

Pannenberg relates his doctrine of God to the discussion of the economic and immanent Trinity initiated by Rahner.[45] Rahner claimed that the God we know in salvation is the true eternal God, though he gives the immanent Trinity an ontological priority over the economic.[46] Pannenberg makes a stronger claim: that 'who God is' rests on the economy of salvation and events in salvation history are 'constitutive' and 'decisive' for God's being.[47] Pannenberg's discussion of the immanent Trinity focuses on the mutual self-distinction of the persons while the discussion of the economic Trinity deals with historical actions and relations.

Pannenberg argues that if the relations of the persons are not determined by history, but are already determined in terms of origin and simply revealed in salvation history, then the doctrine of the Trinity will appeal to static and non-mutual relations as the basis for God's unity and deity. What is more these relations of origin are inaccessible to us because by definition they cannot be revealed in history. Thus, on Pannenberg's telling, if history is removed from the presentation, then the description of the triune life will collapse. On the other hand, if history is not the action of God who is fully involved, then it will no longer be *salvation* history. For only as an expression of real involvement of God with his creation can it be the 'revelation of divine love' which 'will finally lead . . . to participation in his glory'.[48] Remove economic mutual self-distinction of the persons of the Trinity and salvation history is only history, and not even that, for without its final horizon it will no longer be a 'history' but only unrelated events with no rationality.

Pannenberg holds together the immanent and the economic as closely as possible without identifying them in such a way that there is no eternal essence or immanent Trinity. If there were only an economic Trinity then God would come into being in history, but Pannenberg strongly rejects that view.[49] Pannenberg can even state that if God's identity is viewed solely from the viewpoint of the economy, then there is a 'becoming' in God.

> If eternity and time coincide only in the eschatological consummation of history, then from the standpoint of the history of God that moves toward this consummation there is room for becoming in God himself, namely in the relation on the immanent and economic Trinity, and in this frame it is possible to say of God that he himself became something that he previously was not when he became man in his Son.[50]

Yet Pannenberg's doctrine of God is not explained simply from the historical 'frame', and so he does not affirm a divine becoming in history as the full account of God's being. The wider frame is the eschaton since the 'consummation of salvation history' is the 'consummation of the trinitarian life of God' and 'the eschatological consummation is only the locus of the decision that the trinitarian God is always the true God from eternity to eternity'.[51]

Pannenberg's view can be contrasted with how others have developed Rahner's Rule. Rahner himself and Walter Kasper treat the economic as a revelation of the immanent. In contrast, Pannenberg refers to a 'decision' about God's being in history in its consummation. More radical application of Rahner's Rule by Jürgen Moltmann, Eberhard Jüngel and Robert Jenson makes God dependent on history. Olson contrasts Pannenberg with both these approaches.

> Pannenberg is not entirely satisfied with either one of these two inter-pretations . . . what is needed . . . he suggests, is an idea of God which is able to grasp in a single concept two sets of seemingly contradic-tory truths: on the one hand the transcendence of the divine essence and God's eternal self-identity, and on the other hand God's real pres-ence in the world and the debatableness of his reality in the process of history such that only the fulfilment of history finally decides the truth of his reality.[52]

Pannenberg's view is that the eternal God is constituted in the self-distinctions of salvation history.[53] God's essence, determined eschatologically, is both eternal and anticipated in history. In Pannenberg's temporalized essentialism, individual 'moments of existence' form an incomplete series and their 'essence' is 'defined only in anticipation of the completed sequence'.[54] This is true for God as it is for other reality.

> Just as in our understanding of eternity the Easter event is not merely the basis of the knowledge that Jesus of Nazareth even in his earthly form was the eternal Son of God, but also decides that he was this by giving retrospective confirmation, so the deity of the God whom Jesus proclaimed is definitively and irrefutably manifested by the escha-tological consummation of his kingdom and the conflict between atheism and belief is finally settled thereby, with repercussion for all eternity, for talk about God by its very nature implies the concept of eternity.[55]

Pannenberg conceives of God as 'his own future', in a similar way that Thomas Aquinas holds that God is his own being (*Deus est suum esse*). The mutual relations of the trinitarian persons mediate this future because the actions in the economy of salvation have an eschatological orientation and are possessed by God as his own.[56] Hence God possesses history in eternal simultaneity, for 'God is not subject to the march of time', so God's future consti-tutes God's present.[57] Since the trinitarian relations are constituted by the events of salvation history, Pannenberg can describe the economy of salvation moving toward and constituting the future for God and creation. The economy has the same significance for both God and creation, with the crucial distinction that God holds all time together in eternity, so that his future is already present for him[58]

The significance of the future for God and his actions allows Pannenberg to differentiate God from a finite actor. A finite actor anticipates a goal subjectively, but the acting God has no gap between the conception of the goal and achievement, for his eternity brings all time into simultaneity. Pannenberg does not describe God as looking ahead to a future goal; instead he speaks of the opposite: the world in its consummation is 'the mode of time that stands closest to God's eternity', so 'the goal' is in fact 'nearer to God than its commencement', and the action of God is his kingdom breaking in 'from the future'.[59] The future is the point of unity of all reality because in it God's lordship is established.

> The lordship of God will set up righteousness and peace in the world and give human life the totality for which each of us yearns. In the future of the divine rule the life of creation will be renewed for participation in the eternity of God. In it eternity comes together with time. It is the place of eternity itself in time, the place of God in his relation to the world, the starting point of his action in the irruption of his future for his creatures, the source of the mighty workings of the Spirit.[60]

Pannenberg's notion of 'mutual self-distinction' gives a dynamic conception of the Trinity that explains why God's eternity is simultaneity, rather than timelessness.[61] Only because divine eternity is Father, Son, and Spirit in mutual relation, moving together in distinction from one another, and constituted in their own identities through their unity realized in God's life with his creation, can eternity hold all time.[62] This is 'the way in which the divine love declares itself'.[63]

For Pannenberg the mediation of time and eternity through the relation of the immanent and economic Trinity allows for the existence of plurality in the life of God. The God who is realized in the real relations of history cannot be solitary or static. This also provides the basis for the plurality of creatures and their sharing in the eternal glory of God; for if history is in fact the self-realization of God, then from the start creation already shares in the life of God.[64]

God's Attributes

A doctrine of God is not only an account of God's triune being, it must also bear witness to God's attributes and Pannenberg does this in the context of the unity of the immanent and economic Trinity as constitutive of God's eternal essence.[65] He identifies two types of attributes: those that define the word 'God' (arrived at by philosophical reflection on the Infinite) and 'those that are ascribed to God on the basis of his action' (known from revelation).[66] His goal is to show that the two approaches correspond. This correspondence will be another demonstration that the Triune God is the 'true Infinite'. In the discussion of metaphysics Pannenberg sought to show that philosophical reflection runs up against problems for which there are only theological solutions. The discussion of God's attributes works from another angle to show the same harmony of the philosophical and theological. The first group of attributes are formal characteristics that, for Pannenberg, test a doctrine of God. If a doctrine of God cannot show that the God of which it speaks has these attributes, it is inadequate. The other group can be expressed as a single attribute – 'love', which is 'the concrete form of the divine essence'.[67] The Triune God is the true Infinite because he is the God of love.

Definitional Attributes

The infinite God must be omnipresent. Pannenberg defines this as the claim that God 'is present to all things at the place of their existence' because he 'permeates and comprehends all things' (Jer. 23:24). Alongside this understanding Pannenberg sets the need for a certain 'distance' between God and creation in order to allow for creaturely (especially human) freedom. He suggests that in the Scripture God's presence is located in heaven (1 Tim. 6:16; Ps. 103:19; Matt. 6:9 *passim*) in order to show that God allows 'his earthly creatures room to live their own lives'.[68] Yet it is only as God is present that creatures have life and existence (Pss 104:29–30; 139:7; Job 33:4). So as with eternity, omnipresence involves both immanence and transcendence.[69]

The resolution of this tension between God's immanence and transcendence is found in Pannenberg's thought in two important concepts. The first is that God's omnipresence is due to the eschaton, in which the unity of all things will be found in God. Looking toward that future, Pannenberg can argue that even as creatures develop in their own time and space they, in anticipation, have their existence in perfect unity with God. This appeal to the eschaton and anticipation does not, in itself, explain how God can be both immanent and transcendent. To explain this Pannenberg turns to the doctrine of the Trinity, which can 'clarify the unity and tension between transcendence and immanence.[70] Christian faith knows God as the transcendent Father and who is present in the Son and the Spirit in the economy. That is, it is God's acts in the economy, which determine the inner relations of the Triune God and also constitute his omnipresence. Once more it is apparent that Pannenberg's view, that the outworking of God's saving rule in history is constitutive for his identity, provides the framework in which he develops an account of the divine attributes.

Pannenberg holds that divine omnipotence depends on omnipresence and that God's power over all things shows what his presence by the Spirit actually means. He describes God's power as unlimited (Job 42:2; Rom. 1:20; Jer. 32:17; Isa. 45:7–12), but not as 'the abstract idea of unlimited power'. If the immanent Trinity is constituted in the economic, then God's power cannot be opposed to his creatures because the work of God is redemption.[71] Pannenberg finds that this accords with the biblical presentation that even in wrath and judgement God's acts are oriented to the life of his creatures (Jer. 32:26–38). He claims that God acts in freedom, but his action is always that of the Creator who aims 'at the consummation of his creation'.[72]

The theme of divine judgement introduces an ambiguity in Pannenberg's account of omnipotence. God creates independent beings, which are still dependent on his power for existence, and if they turn away from him they fall into nothingness. This negative confirmation of God's power also expresses a kind of impotence, for if it should happen then the Creator's goal is thwarted. Only salvation can fully show his true omnipotence. At one level, Pannenberg resolves this ambiguity, since the eternal Son, in self-distinction from the Father, 'takes the place of the creature and becomes man so as to overcome the assertion of the creature's independence . . . without violating its independence'.[73] Divine love is the mode in which his power is brought to bear on all of creation. What this account does not resolve is how biblical references to divine judgement are to be understood. This question recurs, with greater force, in Pannenberg's exposition of God's love.

Relational Attributes: Love

Pannenberg treats all the relational attributes as 'aspects of the comprehensive statement that God is love'.[74] God's love for the world is the essential content of the history of Jesus, so the economy of salvation is an expression of God's love.[75] Pannenberg's treatment of the Trinity advanced the claim that the Spirit is the essence of God and the love between Father and Son which means that the statement 'God is love' (1 John 4:8,16) is the fullest statement of God's nature.[76]

Love as the essence of the triune life, both immanently and economically, frames Pannenberg's presentation of the attributes of God. God's goodness, grace, mercy, righteousness, faithfulness, patience and wisdom are concrete forms of God's love, expressed by the Spirit. He traces each of these through their biblical presentation, arguing that each attribute is an aspect of God's commitment to his one work in the creation, preservation, redemption and consummation of all his creation.[77]

In this discussion Pannenberg is dealing with a theme often considered under the idea of divine simplicity. This doctrine holds that there are no parts or divisions in God. In terms of God's triune existence each person is fully God not a part of God; in terms of God's attributes they are not distinctions within God but each in absolute perfection is identical with God's being.[78] Pannenberg says little directly about the doctrine of simplicity and his comments are generally negative. He holds it partially responsible for the difficulty of relating attributes to the divine essence because it has implied that any multiplicity in God must be only apparent. Pannenberg's account of the attributes of God as aspects of God's love answers the same concerns but seeks to give the economy a full place in God's being. God in his essence is love, and all his attributes may be understood as economic expressions of that love. Reciprocally, God's act of love in his relation to the world mediates his identity as the God of love. Though the word 'anticipation' is rarely used, the concept pervades the discussion since each of God's attributes is an anticipation of the eschatological embrace of all creation in the love of God.[79]

Pannenberg's insistence that God's attributes are expressions of his love and anticipate the consummation leads him to exclude wrath from the attributes. He does not deny the reality of wrath, but relativizes it as 'a sudden emotional outburst' and an expression of God's holiness against what is unclean.[80] He warns against muting the doctrine of God's wrath in order to meet the mood of modern society. Yet he also affirms the realization of God's purpose to reconcile all things in Christ. He confronts two problems here. For one, if God's redemptive love must extend to all creatures then it seems hard to avoid taking a deterministic view of election. Yet this would compromise human freedom and bring into question whether we see genuine love from God – if he does not grant his creatures freedom. The other problem in affirming that God's love embraces all creatures is that it seems to deny 'the eternal gravity of sin and guilt'.

The first problem is dealt with on the basis of the priority of the future. Because reality comes from the future and not from a prior determination, Pannenberg asserts that it is possible to have a non-deterministic account of providence.[81] For the second issue Pannenberg must explain how the theme of judgement integrates with God's saving love. This too is done by looking to the future when eternity will enter time as a purifying judgement. In this judgement, 'lives necessarily perish of the inner contradictions of their existence', or would do so if God were not the faithful Creator and hence Redeemer, as well as Judge.[82] Elements of lives that have been lived in alienation from and in enmity to God will have no eschatological unity with God and will have to disappear, or at least be transformed. Pannenberg allows that some 'who persist irreconcilably in turning aside from God' may be destroyed since 'nothing may remain when the fire of divine glory has purged away all that is incompatible with God's presence'. This is, however, 'a borderline case'.[83] The predominant emphasis is the work of the Son and the Spirit to purify and unite creation. That is, wrath is not an attribute of God since it is not present in the eschaton. Wrath is the historical manifestation of the God of love who purifies creation to bring all things into unity.

Pannenberg's discussion of the doctrine of God shows why his account cannot include wrath as a divine attribute. God's unity is 'the self-identity of the truth of God which his faithfulness in historical action demonstrates'.[84] Divine unity is realized in reconciliation by love 'which embraces the world and bridges the gulf between God and the world'. God's unity is 'the unity of the true Infinite which transcends the antithesis to what is distinct from it'.[85] This can only be fully shown in the consummation.[86] Pannenberg argues that conceptually this unity is anticipated in the doctrine of the Trinity.[87] Each of the aspects of God's infinity are shown to embrace and redeem the creation, so the Triune God is the true Infinite in whom there is a 'unity that transcends the antithesis' between finite and infinite, without removing that distinction. Such a conception of God allows for judgement as God's purifying love, but cannot affirm wrath as a divine attribute.

How satisfactory is Pannenberg's account of divine wrath? His argument that wrath is an expression of divine love is surely correct. As Hans Boersma argues, 'just as divine hospitality requires at least some violence to make it flourish, so also God's love requires that he become angry when his love is violated'. Boersma views love as the primary attribute of God and states that 'God is love, not wrath' and asserts 'an absolute primacy . . . of hospitality over violence'.[88] Yet Pannenberg goes beyond a statement that love is a primary attribute and wrath secondary and economic when he argues that wrath is not an attribute of God at all. The reason for Pannenberg stating this is apparent: because the divine nature is constituted by the economy, then Pannenberg cannot view wrath as a secondary or economic attribute of God, because no such category may exist.[89]

Boersma recognizes the difficulty of incorporating wrath into an account of the attributes of the God of love and notes the fear that the primacy of love in God may be compromised by a dualism. Despite this difficulty he calls for an approach which allows even this element of Scripture to have a place in a theology: 'fears of such a dualist understanding of God should not tempt us into ignoring the biblical expressions of God's wrath'.[90] Has Pannenberg fallen into such a temptation? Perhaps not, for even when he affirms that 'God constantly turns back to patience with his people', he warns that 'if God's pardoning love is despised, patience can take the form of waiting for the last judgement, for which evildoers heap up their wicked deeds'.[91] Yet if this judgement is to have any outcome other than purification, then, as we have seen, the account of the economy as the expression of God's love and power in reconciliation is compromised.[92]

Mattes highlights the question for Pannenberg when he comments that Pannenberg 'unwind[s] the tensions of certain Lutheran paradoxes'. He refers to the dialectics in Luther's thought between grace and wrath ('gospel' and 'law') in God's relation to the world and asks, 'Can we not agree with Luther . . . that the outworking of God's rule in the cosmos entails perhaps an economy of death?' He suggests that 'if . . . wrath as an alien work can be seen as a legitimate aspect of God's quest to establish the divine rule in the cosmos', then Luther's dialectic 'could be a helpful corrective to Pannenberg's metaphysics'.[93] Luther affirmed God's grace to creation and yet recognized that God acted in judgement and adopted the language of Isaiah to call God's judgement an 'alien work' (Isa. 28:21). For Pannenberg, however, the presence of an alien work in history compromises the way in which history constitutes the identity of God as the triune Infinite of holy love. Mattes points up the problematic element of Pannenberg's thought in this area. The Bible speaks more fully of wrath and judgement than Pannenberg allows and, to the extent that he does affirm them, they introduce an ambiguity into his thought. The recognition of the loss of creatures as a 'borderline' event highlights the ambiguity surrounding these themes.

Learning to Think about God with Pannenberg

Pannenberg's doctrine of God is complex and impressively thorough. As an effort to explore and defend the triune reality of God against philosophical and theological objections it must rank with

Aquinas' *Summa Theologica* and Barth's *Church Dogmatics* as one of the great pieces of thinking on God. As Mostert judges, 'it is likely that he will be recognized as one of the great teachers and defenders of the Christian faith of the twentieth century'.[94] Particularly impressive is Pannenberg's ability to argue defensively at the same time as offering new constructions and new perspectives on the doctrine of God. Pannenberg's doctrine of God is a reminder that the contemplation of God is the highest exercise to which humans are called, and when that contemplation takes the form of a doctrinal exposition of the existence of God, our words and concepts are stretched to breaking point (and beyond).

There is a danger that a discussion like Pannenberg's falls into an arid intellectualism in which we arrange various abstract terms in a pattern that is satisfying for us but has no connection to the reality of God. Acknowledging that danger is not a reason to shrink back from attempting something like Pannenberg's project. Christian theology can teeter on the edge of mysticism, insisting that our ideas about God show more about our ignorant hubris than the knowledge of faith. Faith must speak with humble confidence. If we hold that God is revealed in Christ and in the biblical witness then we are invited to think about his existence and identity. That exercise of thought requires reverence and humility but not absolute silence. In faith we venture some description of God to bear witness to him.

Pannenberg's presentation of the doctrine of God is brilliant. He faces directly the challenges of affirming God in an age which rejects metaphysics and he accepts that the old ways of thinking about God have often failed. He sets out to show that it is possible to think about God who acts in Jesus and the Spirit and at the same time to understand God as the triune Creator and Redeemer who embraces the whole of creation in love. According to Pannenberg this is more than a mere possibility; human life, religious experience and world history will fall into meaningless nonsense if the Triune God is not the true Infinite.

I have already raised some questions about Pannenberg's doctrine of God and I will return to these in a moment. These questions do not add up to a rebuttal of Pannenberg's doctrine of God. There is a great deal in his thought that is stimulating and helps us to think carefully and faithfully about God. Pannenberg contributes to the development of the doctrine of God by advancing the discussion of Rahner's Rule. While the 'rule' has been a major focus in the retrieval of trinitarian thought, its application has tended either to make a hard distinction between reality and revelation or to collapse the two into a divine becoming. Pannenberg presents a view of the Trinity in which the economic and immanent are viewed as one but are not collapsed. He may not have solved all the problems associated with this (I think he has not and suspect that they are not open to a 'solution'). His articulation of these relationships in a careful and coherent way through his appeal to eschatology sets us on a path that needs to be explored.

The close relationship of Pannenberg's doctrine of God to his metaphysical proposal is also a strength, especially since he retains a distinctively Christian witness to God as triune. Pannenberg's position can be set in contrast to postmetaphysical theology which accepts the Heideggerian critique of onto-theology and articulates a theology that acknowledges 'the sense in which our ignorance of God . . . could well signal God's most overwhelming presence'.[95] Pannenberg acknowledges similar challenges for theology but responds very differently. For him, if the idea of God is empty, this must be met with an attempt to understand God in the light of anticipatory revelation. God's absence cannot, by itself, be construed as the mode of God's presence. It is only as God's relation to creation is established in the eschaton that the true meaning of his apparent absence can be understood. Similarly, Pannenberg has no place for a view of the self-revelation of God in which his love is expressed merely through his absence or distance. Pannenberg emphasizes that the self-distinction of God from creation is necessary for reconciliation and revelation; however his version of self-distinction is not a denial of God's presence but is always oriented to the eschatological 'unity-in-distinction' in which God's love is fully known. Pannenberg makes his case convincingly and shows that for theology to eschew metaphysics is not to create a room for God, but to close off the possibility of knowing God.

It is worth reflecting again on how important eschatological ontology is for Pannenberg's doctrine of God. His approach to metaphysics allows him to relate the multiplicity of temporal reality to divine eternity. Multiplicity is found at every point of temporal experience. Pannenberg's philosophical milieu presents him with the question of how the one infinite God can truly be the source and goal of such a diverse reality. His answer is to understand all history as the work of a mutually self-differentiating Triune God. In this way he can see all diversity as the work of the one God who exists always in unity and distinction. In the face of obvious diversity and little apparent unity, Pannenberg's claim would seem unfounded, except that he appeals to the eschaton as the point at which true unity-in-distinction is found. At the same time he claims that we must see that essence, both creaturely and divine, grounded in the eschaton, has been present all along. All reality in its diversity is already, in anticipation, bound in unity-in-distinction in the love of God. This is Pannenberg's Christian ontology – proclaiming the love of God for all creation, revealed in Christ, completed in the Spirit, consummated in the eschatological and eternal life of Father, Son and Spirit. In order to show this, Pannenberg must argue that all reality is an expression of God's loving commitment to his creation.[96]

Postmetaphysical theology conceives of divine love 'exercised primordially through the paternal distance wherein separation alone allows for filial relation'.[97] That is, the absence of God is an act of divine love, granting freedom to creatures. For this view the continued search for a final description of 'reality' is always limiting and only the acceptance of the Christian destruction of metaphysics frees us from moralism for love.[98]

Pannenberg agrees that self-distinction of God from creation is necessary for creation to be itself and to develop in freedom. However his version of self-distinction is not a denial of God's presence but is always oriented to the full eschatological embrace of God's love. Pannenberg's claim is that present historical reality may seem to exist in the apparent absence of God, but that the entry of eternity into time in the eschaton brings all reality into the glorious presence of God, and it is from this consummation of reality that all things have their identity in God. So Pannenberg's account is not one of absence alone, but one in which God's absence is his act of self-distinction which, in the eschaton, is sublated into a relation of unity-in-distinction of God and creation. This chapter has shown that Pannenberg's claim about the eschatological unity of creation and God is complementary to his claim that God's identity is established in the economy of reconciliation.

Now to return to what seems to be the key weakness in Pannenberg's doctrine of God, the ambivalence created by the idea of God's wrath. The ambivalence comes because he holds history and God's being in a close and reciprocal relation. Thus, if some creatures are lost in judgement, it is hard to conceive all history as the anticipation of the holy love of God. If history is the anticipation of God's love, then it cannot have in it 'an economy of death', at most the loss of creatures must be considered 'borderline' cases. Yet even borderline cases highlight the ambiguity in Pannenberg's thought for if some creatures on the border fall into non-existence then we have to wonder if God is the Creator–Consummator of all and so a question is placed on God's identity.

Why does this concern matter? One reason is that the Bible testifies to judgement as part of God's work. Yes, it is an 'alien' task – but it is his task all the same (Isa. 28:21; 1 Chr. 14:11; Rom. 12:19; Heb. 10:26–36). Additionally, some reflection on the theme will show that wrath and judgement are not incidental to God's ways. If the reality of sin and evil is acknowledged in all its horror, then we must hope for a God who responds to these in wrath and judgement. At the centre of the biblical message lies the declaration that God has received into himself the wrath and judgement deserved by his creatures. On that basis we have a real hope in the face of evil. But the judgement of the world in the cross of Jesus does not exhaust the biblical presentation of the theme; the threat of hell remains.

Every approach to Christian theology finds the theme of hell and judgement difficult (if there is no difficulty then the theology falls short of being truly Christian!). That the God who speaks and acts in the Lord Jesus to show grace and truth also condemns is a terrible mystery. It is no criticism of Pannenberg that he does not easily accommodate it. The problem for Pannenberg is twofold. He has so bound the identity of God to the eschatological outcome that any final condemnation leaves God himself compromised. The effect of this is that Pannenberg mutes the biblical witness to God's judgement and removes wrath from any account of God's attributes. Yet, in the face of evil we need a God whose holy love is truly expressed in wrath. The other side of the problem for Pannenberg is that his commitment to coherence in theology means that he cannot resort to the approach I suggested above – that we must simply say that there is a terrible mystery that the God of grace also condemns. Pannenberg's method closes off that option; he must strive to give a fully coherent account of the relationship between God's eternal love and the outcome of the economy.

Conclusion

Theology has no conclusion or, rather, it is not the place of the theologian to provide the conclusion. Pannenberg reminds us that the final revelation is the embrace of God's love for his creation when God will be all in all. Until then Christians continue the task of seeking to understand and demonstrate the claims of the faith.

> Only by this eschatological consummation of the world does God definitively prove himself to be the true God and Creator of his creatures and also give definitive proof of the truth of his revelation in Jesus Christ. Development of this theme in Christian doctrine has in view such a self-demonstration of God, but it does so only by way of conjectures and hypotheses that always show themselves to be in need of correction . . . The definitive truth of God is herein grasped and therefore present – in an eternal present – but only in a provisional form, so that we must not take it to be the definitive truth.[1]

In the same vein, the aim of this conclusion is not to present a verdict on Pannenberg's theology. While theology thrives on vigorous disagreement, the final day will bring the true determination of the value of all theological contributions. Then the foundation, materials and craftwork of all theology will be revealed (1 Cor. 3:10–14). I have set out in this book to introduce Pannenberg's work and to allow him to lead us into doing some theology. So the end of this book is not the place to make a full assessment of Pannenberg's work. I will not rehearse the concerns and questions I raised in earlier chapters, though I will return to one key issue below. Most of this brief conclusion will focus on summarizing some of the key lessons for theology from Pannenberg.

Learning from Pannenberg

Pannenberg is a theologian's theologian. His detailed, technically precise work rests on a base of thorough research in a wide range of fields. His engagement with complex philosophical questions adds a further degree of difficulty to his work. This raises the question of whether learning from Pannenberg's theology will inevitably commit us to similarly complex, detailed theology. I do not think it has to. He is responding to a particular context, that of the German university, in which he is seeking to present theology as a scientific discipline. In different contexts theology can and should take different forms. So we can learn from Pannenberg without imitating the form of his work.

I have already noted several of the lessons Pannenberg offers for evangelical theology. He shows how theology must take a very wide vision. If God is the Creator and Redeemer of the cosmos, then knowledge of God will engage with knowledge of every other area of life. Pannenberg stresses that if God is God, nothing in reality can be understood in depth apart from him and, conversely, that thinking about everything is part of how theology tests its own claims about God. To be sure, there are dangers in striving for a correlation of theology with other areas of study. Karl Barth warned vigorously against these dangers as he declared the failure of natural theology.[2] Pannenberg holds that Barth's position leads to an artificial isolation of theology from the rest of knowledge, and this inevitably reduces theology to a subjectivist and authoritarian exercise. His criticism of Barth is very sharp: 'Barth's apparently so lofty objectivity about God and God's word turns out to rest on no more than the irrational subjectivity of a venture of faith with no justification outside itself.'[3] I am not so convinced that we should turn to other disciplines to secure a rational justification of theology (and we have seen that Pannenberg seeks to retain a primacy for immediate theological concerns). Even if we do not follow Pannenberg in the precise role he gives to non-theological disciplines nor in the details of his interaction with other disciplines, his point that theology must engage is well made.

The mixture of confidence and caution in Pannenberg's thought is admirable. Because he recognizes that God reveals himself as the one who determines all reality he holds that theology refers to an objective reality and can be tested for its truth. Because that reve-lation is eschatological and is now anticipated, theology cannot claim to present directly full knowledge of God. While I consider Pannenberg overly cautious about the truth of present revelation, his point about theology is important. Humility is an important virtue for the theologian and one we should develop. Evangel-ical theology is far more likely to fail by overreaching itself and claiming to know more of God than it can, rather than it is to be too cautious.

The careful attention Pannenberg pays to the history of theology is instructive. He shows that contemporary theology can and should learn from the past. We are part of a long tradition of discussion and we cannot pretend to be starting over again. Nothing is gained by such a pretence, rather we benefit by paying attention to the debates and discussions of the past. Pannenberg does not consider himself constrained to reproduce the conclu-sions of the past, but he seeks to develop his view in relationship to the great tradition.

I hope that this study of Pannenberg has demonstrated the value of extended interaction with a great theologian. It is tempting to take quotes from great thinkers as theological deco-ration. It is far more productive to think long and hard about the position of one person, trying to understand and respond to it at depth. Pannenberg questions my assumptions and challenges me to present a carefully argued position. He highlights themes in theology which I may not focus on otherwise and raises ques-tions I have not considered. It takes time and effort expended on a single thinker to benefit in this way; the gain is worth the work.

Pannenberg highlights some important elements in the content of theology. He shows us that theology must have God at its heart. It is not simply a list of teachings from the Bible, but a map which requires proper proportions. Evangelical theology, at times, marginalizes the most important topics of theology. This can be through a focus on conversion and the life of faith (distinc-tive emphases of evangelicalism) or an emphasis on 'practical concerns' or a concern with areas of controversy. Each of these has a place in theology, but it should not be the main place. Theology must keep its focus on God and view all things in relation to him. Pannenberg's theology is a challenge to do this consistently.

Pannenberg's discussion of God seeks to develop from the historical work of God in the economy of redemption, so he grounds Christian knowledge of God in Jesus Christ. While I think that his Christology from below is not ultimately successful, I affirm his commitment to relate the doctrine of God to the risen Christ. If evangelical theologians will not adopt Pannenberg's Christology and doctrine of God, then we should accept the challenge to develop as rich and careful an account of God as possible in relation to a more thoroughly biblical Christology.

Pannenberg demonstrates the need to integrate eschatology into all theology and the value of doing so. Biblical studies rediscovered eschatology in the twentieth century, and this rediscovery eventually began to have an impact on systematic theology.[4] Schwarz observes that Pannenberg was one of the first important twentieth-century theologians who recognizes the significance of a cosmic eschatology and to include this in his thinking.[5] Pannenberg remains a crucial resource in the ongoing discussion. He demonstrates the need to stress that present reality is not a complete reality and to understand it in the light of its consummation and he shows that doctrinal positions can be rethought in fruitful ways from the perspective of eschatology.

Theology and Philosophy Once More

One issue that recurs in discussions of Pannenberg is the question of whether he is too rationalistic or too indebted to philosophy. I have argued that the claim about 'rationalism' is too nebulous to sustain and that an overemphasis on philosophy is not so obvious a problem in his thought as some critics imagine. His work engages in philosophical discussions and his metaphysical proposal is central to his project. That proposal is, however, grounded in revelation in Christ and is developed in close interaction with theological concerns. Chapter 5 showed good reasons to accept Shults' claim that in Pannenberg's thought 'the "from above" (systematic) move has material primacy and . . . asymmetric control over the "from below" (fundamental) move'.[6] At the same time I noted that the full test of Pannenberg's proposal (and of Shults' claim) comes in an examination of Pannenberg's exposition of explicitly theological themes.

The result of that test, in the following chapters, was that the primary role of systematic concerns is not always apparent. Because Pannenberg conceives of the future as the locus of the realization of full identity, he is able to incorporate the historicism of Dilthey and Heidegger and still offer a unified account of reality. However, the 'ontological weight' of the future introduces a distorting factor into some of his theological formulations. Pannenberg's view of the relationship of the present and the future (developed to deal with philosophical challenges) gives rise to unsatisfactory features in his discussion of Christology, doctrine of redemption and doctrine of God.

Olthuis judges that 'for Pannenberg it is finally the internal dynamics of his system that speaks the decisive voice and dictates his use of Scripture'.[7] Schwöbel suggests the same thing when he argues that Pannenberg's description of God as the true Infinite is not drawn from biblical material but is 'required' by the claim of a 'non-thematic awareness of the Infinite' which is at the heart of his religious epistemology. Schwöbel traces problems in Pannenberg's thought back through his epistemology to its roots in his concerns with fundamental theology. He concludes that Pannenberg's treatment of God as the true Infinite illustrates that 'if the theologian employs non-theological considerations as foundational principles for theology the categories developed from the perspective of reason . . . have a determinative effect for the conceptions of faith from the perspective of faith'.[8] After surveying Pannenberg's work closely we can conclude that these concerns are to some extent justified.

There are points in Pannenberg's project in which his commitment to answer the philosophical challenge of the end of metaphysics and his subsequent use of his temporalized essentialism gain a certain amount of control over his systematic exposition. In Christology this seems to be the key reason that he makes the divine identity of Jesus dependent on his human historical life. In the doctrine of reconciliation the stress on the future means that the work of Christ is actualized in the repentance of sinners. The doctrine of God, the completion of God's own divinity in the eschaton, bars Pannenberg from giving an account of God's wrath. In each case I have argued that there is a weakness in Pannenberg's theology which flows from his temporalized essentialism. In turn, his metaphysic is developed in order to respond to philosophical challenges. My assessment, then, is that at points Pannenberg is not able to maintain the priority of theological concerns. The close dialogue with philosophy along with a very strong demand for coherence in his thought seem to generate these problems.

Such an observation does not deny the many achievements of his project. Like all theological reflection, Pannenberg's project is anticipatory, and speaks doxologically of God and all things in relation to him. Christian theology benefits from Pannenberg's work, and the problematic elements in his thought are invitations to develop his ideas in new ways or to show how his concerns can be answered with alternative approaches. As Pannenberg's thought produces such responses it underscores the importance of his own contribution to the project of 'constructive thought' which seeks to 'exemplify how the God of the Bible can be understood as creator and Lord of all reality'.[9]

Bibliography

Works by Pannenberg

Books

Anthropology in Theological Perspective [ATP] (trans. M.J. O'Connell; Edinburgh: T&T Clark, 1999). A translation of *Anthropologie in theologischer Perspektive* (Göttingen: Vandenhoeck & Ruprecht, 1983).

Basic Questions in Theology [BQT] (trans. G.H. Kehm, 3 vols; London: SCM, 1970–72). A translation of *Grundfragen systematischer Theologie* (Göttingen: Vandenhoeck & Ruprecht, 1967).

Erwägungen zu einer Theologie der Natur (ed. W. Pannenberg and A.M. Klaus Müller; Gütersloh: Gerd Mohn, 1970).

The Historicity of Nature: Essays on Science and Theology (ed. Niels Henrik Gregersen; Philadelphia: Templeton Press, 2007).

An Introduction to Systematic Theology [IST] (Grand Rapids: Eerdmans, 1991).

Jesus – God and Man [JGM] (trans. L.L. Wilkins and D.A. Priebe; Philadelphia: Westminster, 2nd English edn, 1977). A translation of *Grundzüge der Christologie* (Gütersloh: Gerd Mohn, 5th edn, 1976).

Metaphysics and the Idea of God [MIG] (trans. Philip Clayton; Grand Rapids: Eerdmans, 1990). A translation of *Metaphysik und Gottesgedanke* (Göttingen: Vandenhoeck & Ruprecht, 1988).

Revelation as History [RaH] (ed. W. Pannenberg; trans. D. Granskou; London: Macmillan, 1968). A translation of *Offenbarung als Geschichte* (Göttingen: Vandenhoeck & Ruprecht, 1961).

Systematic Theology [ST] (trans. Geoffrey Bromiley, 3 vols; Grand Rapids/Edinburgh: Eerdmans/T&T Clark, 1991–7). A translation of *Systematische Theologie*, Band 1–3 (Göttingen: Vandenhoeck & Ruprecht, 1988–93).

Theologie und Philosophie: ihr Verhältnis im Lichte ihrer gemeinsamen Geschichte (Gottingen: Vandenhoeck & Ruprecht, 1996).

Theology and the Philosophy of Science [TPS] (trans. F. McDonagh; London: Darton, Longman & Todd, 1976). A translation of *Wissenschaftstheorie und Theologie* (Frankfurt am Main: Suhrkamp, 1973).

Towards a Theology of Nature: Essays on Science and Faith [TTN] (ed. Ted Peters; Louisville/Philadelphia: Westminster/John Knox, 1993).

Chapters and articles

'Analogy and Doxology', *BQT* 1, p. 238.

'Anthropology and the Question of God'. *BQT* 2, pp. 80–98.

'An Autobiographical Sketch'. Pages 11–18 in *The Theology of Wolfhart Pannenberg* (ed. C.E. Braaten and P. Clayton; Minneapolis: Augsburg; 1988).

'Can Christianity Do without an Eschatology?'. Pages 25–34 in *The Christian Hope* (ed. G.B. Caird et al.; London: SPCK, 1970).

'Christian Theology and Philosophical Criticism'. *BQT* 3, p. 127.

'The Christian Visions of God: The New Discussion on the Trinitarian Doctrine'. *Asbury Theological Journal* 46/2 (Fall 1991): pp. 27–36.

'Constructive and Critical Functions of Christian Eschatology'. *Harvard Theological Review* 77 (1984): pp. 119–39.

'The Crisis in the Scripture Principle'. *BQT* 1, pp. 3–6.

'Dogmatic Theses on the Doctrine of Revelation'. Pages 123–58 in *RaH*.

'Eternity, Time and the Trinitarian God'. Pages 62–70 in *Trinity, Time, and Church: A Response to the Theology of Robert W. Jenson* (ed. Colin Gunton; Grand Rapids/Cambridge, UK: Eerdmans, 2000).

'Eternity, Time, and Space'. *Zygon: Journal of Religion & Science* 40/1 (March 2005): pp. 97–106.

'Faith and Reason'. *BQT* 2, pp. 50–57.

'Feminine Language about God?'. *Asbury Theological Journal* 48 (Fall 1993): pp. 27–9.

'The God of Hope'. *BQT* 2, pp. 34–49.

'God's Presence in History'. *Christian Century* 98 (11 March 1981): pp. 260–63.

'Hermeneutic and Universal History'. *BQT* 1, pp. 96–136.

'An Intellectual Pilgrimage'. *Dialog* 45/2 (2006): pp. 184–91.

'Introduction'. *RaH*, pp. 3–21.

'Kerygma and History', *BQT* 1, pp. 83, 85.

'On Historical and Theological Hermeneutic'. *BQT* 1, pp.137–81.

'On the Inspiration of Scripture'. *Theology Today* 54/2 (1997): pp. 212–15.

'Problems between Science and Theology in the Course of Their Modern History'. *Zygon* 41/1 (March 2006): pp. 105–11.

'Providence, God and Eschatology'. Page 271, note 16 in *The Historicity of Nature: Essays on Science and Theology* (ed. N.H. Gregersen; West Conshohocken: Templeton Foundation, 2008).

'The Question of God'. *BQT* 2, pp. 201–33.

'The Religions from the Perspective of Christian Theology and the Self-Interpretation of Christianity in Relation to the Non-Christian Religions'. *Modern Theology* 9/3 (July 1993): pp. 285–97.

'A Response to My American Friends'. Pages 313–36 in *The Theology of Wolfhart Pannenberg* (ed. Carl Braaten and Philip Clayton; Minneapolis: Augsburg, 1988).

'A Response to the Discussion'. Pages 221–76 in *Theology as History* (ed. James M. Robinson and John B. Cobb Jr; New York: Harper & Row, 1962).

'Revelation in Early Christianity'. Pages 76–85 in *Christian Authority: Essays in Honour of Henry Chadwick* (ed. G.R. Evans; Oxford: Clarendon Press, 1988).

'The Significance of Christianity in the Philosophy of Hegel'. *BQT* 3, pp. 144–77.

'Speaking about God in the Face of Atheist Criticism'. *BQT* 3, pp. 80–115.

'Theological Questions for Scientists'. Page 37–49 in *Beginning with the End: God, Science and Wolfhart Pannenberg* (ed. C.R. Albright and J. Haugen; Chicago: Open Court, 1997).

'Theology of Creation and Natural Science'. *Asbury Theological Journal* 50/1 (Spring 1995): pp. 5–15.

'Types of Atheism and Their Theological Significance'. *BQT* 2, pp.194–5.

'What Is a Dogmatic Statement?', *BQT* 1, pp. 209–10.
'What is Truth?', *BQT* 2, pp. 12–16.

Works by Others

Allen, Diogenes. *Philosophy for Understanding Theology* (Louisville: Westminster John Knox, 1985).

Allison, C.F. *The Cruelty of Heresy* (SPCK, 1994).

Allison, H.E. 'Kant's Transcendental Idealism'. In *A Companion to Kant* (ed. G. Bird; Malden: Blackwell, 2006).

Anderson, James N. *Paradox in Christian Theology: An Analysis of Its Presence, Character, and Epistemic Status* (London: Paternoster, 2007).

Anderson, Paul N. 'Beyond the Shade of the Oak Tree: The Recent Growth of Johannine Studies'. *Expository Times*, 119 (2008): pp. 365–73.

Anderson, Paul N. *The Fourth Gospel and the Quest for Jesus: Modern Foundations Reconsidered*. Library of New Testament Studies, 321; Library of Historical Jesus Studies (London/New York: T&T Clark/Continuum, 2006).

Aristotle. *Aristotle in Twenty-Three Volumes*. Volume 17. *The Metaphysics*. Books 1–9 (trans. H. Tredennick; London: Heinemann, 1975).

Attridge, Harold W. *The Epistle to the Hebrews: A Commentary on the Epistle to the Hebrews* (ed. H. Koester; Philadelphia: Fortress Press, 1989).

Audi, Robert, ed. *The Cambridge Dictionary of Philosophy* (Cambridge: Cambridge University Press, 1999).

Augustine. *Confessions* (trans. H. Chadwick; Oxford: Oxford University Press, 1991).

Avis, Paul, ed. *Divine Revelation* (London: Darton, Longman & Todd, 1997)

Avis, Paul. *Faith in the Fires of Criticism* (London: Darton, Longman & Todd, 1995).

Baghramian, Maria. *Relativism* (Abingdon: Routledge, 2004).

Barth, Karl. *Church Dogmatics* (trans. Geoffrey W. Bromiley and Thomas F. Torrance, 12 vols; Edinburgh: T&T Clark, 1936–77). A translation of *Die kirchliche Dogmatik* (Zurich: EVZ, 1932–70).

Bartholomew, C. 'Introduction'. In *Behind the Text: History and Biblical Interpretation* (ed. C.S. Evans, M. Healy and M. Rae; Grand Rapids: Zondervan, 2003).

Bartlett, A. *Cross Purposes: The Violent Grammar of Christian Atonement* (Valley Forge: Trinity, 2001).

Barton, John. *The Nature of Biblical Criticism* (Louisville: Westminster/John Knox, 2007).

Bartsch, Hans Werner, ed. *Kerygma and Myth, Rudolf Bultmann and Five Critics* (trans. Reginald H. Fuller; London: SPCK, 1953) http://www.religion-online.org/showbook.asp?title=4 31 (accessed 13 July 2012).

Bauckham, Richard. *Jesus and the Eyewitnesses: The Gospels as Eyewitness Testimony* (Grand Rapids: Eerdmans, 2006).

Bauckham, Richard. 'Jürgen Moltmann'. *In The Modern Theologians: An Introduction to Christian Theology since 1918* (ed. D.F. Ford and R. Muers; Oxford: Blackwell, 3rd edn, 2005).

Bauckham, Richard. *Moltmann: Messianic Theology in the Making* (London: Marshall Pickering, 1987).

Bavinck, Herman, *Reformed Dogmatics* (ed. J. Bolt; trans. J. Vriend; 4 vols; Grand Rapids: Baker Academic, 2008). A translation of *Gereformeerde Dogmatiek* (Kampen: Kok, 1928).

Beiser, Frederick C. ed. *The Cambridge Companion to Hegel* (Cambridge: Cambridge University Press, 1993).

Beiser, Frederick C. *The Romantic Imperative: The Concept of Early German Romanticism* (Harvard: Harvard University Press, 2003).

Benner, Drayton C. 'Immanuel Kant's Demythologization of Christian Theories of Atonement in Religion within the Limits of Reason Alone'. *Evangelical Quarterly* 79/2 (2007): pp. 99–111.

Berkouwer, G.C. *The Person of Christ* (trans J.H. Kok; Grand Rapids: Eerdmans, 1977). A translation of De Persoon Van Christus: Dogmatische Studien (Kampen: Kok, 1952).

Berkouwer, G.C. *The Providence of God* (trans. Lewis B. Smedes; Grand Rapids: Eerdmans, 1974). A translation of *De Voorverziening Gods* (Kampen: Kok, 1950).

Biddy, W.S. 'Review of Wolfhart Pannenberg on Human Linguisticality and the Word of God', *Ars Disputandi* 5 (2005) (accessed 10 July 2012).

Bird, Graham, ed. *A Companion to Kant* (Malden: Blackwell, 2006).

Bird, Michael F. *Are You the One who is to Come?: The Historical Jesus and the Messianic Question* (Grand Rapids: Baker Academic, 2009).

Blomberg, Craig L. *The Historical Reliability of John's Gospel: Issues and Commentary* (Downers Grove: InterVarsity Press, 2001).

Bockmuehl, Markus, ed. *The Cambridge Companion to Jesus* (Cambridge: Cambridge University Press, 2001).

Boersma, H. *Violence, Hospitality and the Cross* (Grand Rapids: Baker Academic, 2004).

Bonhoeffer, Dietrich. *Christology* (trans. J. Bowden. London: Collins, 1966). A translation of lectures given in Berlin in 1933 found in *Gesammelte Schriften* Bd. 3. *Theologie-Gemeinde: Vorlesungen, Briefe, Gesprache, 1927–1944* (Munchen: Christian Kaiser, 1960).

Borg, Marcus J. *Conflict, Holiness, and Politics in the Teachings of Jesus* (Harrisburg: Trinity Press, rev. edn, 1998).

Bornkamm, Gunther. *Jesus of Nazareth* (New York: Harper & Row, 1960).

Braaten, Carl and Philip Clayton, eds. *The Theology of Wolfhart Pannenberg: Twelve American Critiques with an Autobiographical Essay and Response* (Minneapolis: Augsburg; 1988).

Bradshaw, Timothy. *Pannenberg: A Guide for the Perplexed* (London/ New York: T&T Clark, 2009).

Bradshaw, Timothy. *Trinity and Ontology: A Comparative Study of the Theologies of Karl Barth and Wolfhart Pannenberg* (Edinburgh: Rutherford House Books, 1988).

Broadhead, Edwin K. 'The Fourth Gospel and the Synoptic Saying Source: The Relation Reconsidered'. Pages 291–320 in *Jesus in the Johannine Tradition* (ed. Robert T. Fortna and Tom Thatcher; Louisville: Westminster John Knox, 2001).

Brondos, D.A. *Paul on the Cross: Reconstructing the Apostle's Story of Redemption* (Minneapolis: Fortress, 2006).

Brown, Colin. *Jesus in European Thought 1778–1860* (Grand Rapids: Baker, 1988).

Bultmann, Rudolph. *Faith and Understanding* (ed. R.W. Funk; trans. Louise Pettibone; London: SCM Press, 1969). A translation of *Glauben und Verstehen* (Tübingen: J.C.B. Mohr, 1964).

Bultmann, Rudolph. *The Gospel of John: A Commentary* (trans G.R. Beasley-Murray, R.W.N. Hoare and J.K. Riches; Oxford: Blackwell,

1971). A translation of *Die drei Johannesbriefe* (Gottingen: Vanden-hoeck & Ruprecht, 1967).

Bultmann, Rudolph. 'The New Testament and Mythology'. In *Kerygma and Myth, Rudolf Bultmann and Five Critics* (London: SPCK, 1953), cited from http://www.religion-online.org/showbook.asp?title=431 (accessed 13 July 2012).

Bunnin, Nicholas and Jiyuan Yu, eds. *The Blackwell Dictionary of Western Philosophy* (Malden: Blackwell, 2004).

Burbidge, John W. 'Hegel's Conception of Logic'. In *The Cambridge Companion to Hegel* (ed. F.C. Beiser; Cambridge: Cambridge University Press, 1993).

Butchvarov, Panayot. 'Metaphyics'. In *The Cambridge Dictionary of Philosophy* (ed. R. Audi; Cambridge: Cambridge University Press, 2nd edn, 1999).

Byrne, James M. 'Bultmann and Tillich'. In *The Blackwell Companion to Modern Theology* (ed. G. Jones; Malden/Oxford: Blackwell, 2004).

Cahill, Joseph P. 'The Theological Significance of Rudolph Bult-mann'. *Theological Studies* 38/2 (June 1977): pp. 231–74.

Carel, Havi. 'Temporal Finitude and Finitude of Possibility: The Double Meaning of Death in Being and Time'. *International Journal of Philosophical Studies* 15/4 (December 2007): pp 541–56.

Carl, H.F. 'Only the Father Knows: Historical and Evangelical Responses to Jesus' Eschatological Ignorance in Mark 13:32'. *Journal of Biblical Studies* 1/3 (July–September 2001). http://journalofbiblicalstudies.org/issue3.html (accessed 30 July 2009, no longer available).

Carlson, Thomas A. 'Postmetaphysical Theology'. Page 58–72 in *The Cambridge Companion to Postmodern Theology* (ed. Kevin J. Vanhoozer; Cambridge: Cambridge University Press, 2003).

Casey, Maurice. *Is John's Gospel True?* (London: Routledge, 1996).

Casey, Maurice. *The Solution to the 'Son of Man' Problem* (London: Continuum, 2007).

Cecilia, Avelina. 'The Axiological Dimension of the Human Being'. Pages 23–33 in *Morality within the Life and Social World: Interdisciplinary Phenomenology of the Authentic Life in the 'Moral Sense'* (ed. A. Tymieniecka; Dordrecht: D. Reidel, 1987).

Chalke, Steve and A. Mann. *The Lost Message of Jesus* (Grand Rapids: Zondervan, 2003).

Charlesworth, James H. *The Historical Jesus: An Essential Guide* (Nashville: Abingdon Press, 2008).

Clayton, P. 'Anticipation and Theological Method'. In *The Theology of Wolfhart Pannenberg* (ed. Carl Braaten and Philip Clayton; Minneapolis: Augsburg, 1988).

Clayton, Philip. 'Science, Meaning, and Metaphysics: A Tribute to Wolfhart Pannenberg', *Interdisciplinary Science Reviews* 28 (December 2003): pp. 237–8.

Cobb, J. 'Pannenberg and Process Theology'. In *The Theology of Wolfhart Pannenberg* (ed. Carl Braaten and Philip Clayton; Minneapolis: Augsburg, 1988).

Denzinger, Henri ed. *Enchiridion symbolorum: definitionum et declarationum de rebus fidei et morum* (rev. Iohannes Bapt. Umberg. Editio 18–20. Friberg: Herder & Co., 1932).

Denzinger, H. and K. Rahner, eds. *Sources of Catholic Dogma* (St. Louis and London: Herder, 1957).

Dilthey, Wilhelm. *W. Dilthey Selected Writings* (ed. and trans. H.P. Rickman; Cambridge: Cambridge University Press, 1976). A translation of *Gesammelte Schriften V: Die geistige Welt. Einleitung in die Philosophie des Lebens* (Stuttgart, Leipzig and Berlin: Teubner, 1927).

Drickamer, John M. 'Higher Criticism and the Incarnation in the Thought of I.A. Dorner'. *Concordia Theological Quarterly* 43/3 (July 1979): pp. 197–206.

Dulles, A. 'Pannenberg on Revelation and Faith'. In *The Theology of Wolfhart Pannenberg* (ed. Carl Braaten and Philip Clayton; Minneapolis: Augsburg, 1988).

Dunn, James D.G. *Jesus Remembered* (Grand Rapids: Eerdmans, 2003).

Dunn, James D.G. Review of *The Pre-existent Son: Recovering the Christologies of Matthew, Mark, and Luke* by Simon Gathercole. *Review of Biblical Literature* (April 2007). http://www.bookreviews.org (accessed 5 August 2012).

Dunn, James D.G. and S. McKnight, eds. *The Historical Jesus in Recent Research* (Winona Lake: Eisenbrauns, 2005).

Ebeling, G. *God and Word* (Philadelphia: Fortress, 1967).

Edgar, W. 'Justification and Violence: Reflections on Atonement and Contemporary Apologetics'. Pages 131–51 in *Justified In Christ: God's Plan for Us in Justification* (ed. K. Scott Oliphint; Fearn: Mentor, 2007).

Eilers, Kent. *Faithful to Save: Pannenberg on God's Reconciling Action* (London: T&T Clark, 2011).

Ensor, P.W. 'The Johannine Sayings of Jesus and the Question of Authenticity'. Pages 14–33 in *Challenging Perspectives on the Gospel of John* (ed. John Lierman, Tübingen: Mohr Siebeck, 2006).

Erickson, Millard J. *Christian Theology* (Grand Rapids: Baker, 1998, rev. edn).

Evans, C. Stephen, M. Healy and Murray Rae, eds. *Behind the Text: History and Biblical Interpretation* (Grand Rapids: Zondervan, 2003).

Evans, C. Stephen. 'The Historical Reliability of John's Gospel: From What Perspective Should it be Assessed?'. Pages 91–119 in *Gospel of John and Christian Theology* (ed. Richard Bauckham and Carl Mosser; Grand Rapids: Eerdmans, 2008).

Evans, Craig A. 'Assessing Progress in the Third Quest of the Historical Jesus'. *Journal for the Study of the Historical Jesus* 4/1 (January 2006): pp. 35–54.

Fairbairn, D. *Grace and Christology in the Early Church* (Oxford: Oxford University Press, 2003).

Fergusson, David. 'Eschatology'. Pages 226–44 in *The Cambridge Companion to Christian Doctrine* (ed. Colin E. Gunton; Cambridge: Cambridge University Press, 1997).

Feuerbach, Ludwig. *The Essence of Christianity* (New York: Colin Blanchard, 1855). A translation of *Das Wesen des Christentums* (Leipzig: O. Wigand, 1841).

Finlan, S. *Problems with the Atonement: The Origins of, and Controversy about, the Atonement Doctrine* (Collegeville: Liturgical, 2005).

Ford, David F. with Rachel Muers, eds. *The Modern Theologians: An Introduction to Christian Theology since 1918* (Oxford: Blackwell, 2005, 3rd combined edn).

Ford, Lewis S. 'The Nature of the Power of the Future'. In *The Theology of Wolfhart Pannenberg* (ed. Carl Braaten and Philip Clayton; Minneapolis: Augsburg, 1988).

Foster, P. *Review of The Pre-existent Son: Recovering the Christologies of Matthew, Mark, and Luke* by Simon Gathercole. *Expository Times* 118/7 (April 2007): pp. 357–8.

France, R.T. *Jesus and the Old Testament: His Application of Old Testament Passages to Himself and His Mission* (London: Tyndale, 1971).

Freedman, David Noel, Gary A. Herion, David F. Graf, John D. Pleins and Astrid B. Beck eds. *The Anchor Bible Dictionary* (6 vols; New York: Doubleday, 1992).

Frei, Hans. *Types of Christian Theology* (ed. G. Hunsiunger and W. Placher; New Haven: Yale, 1992).

Friedrich, G. *Die Verkündigung des Todes Jesu im Neuen Testament* (Neukirchen-Vluyn: Neukirchener Verlag, 1982).

Funk, Robert W. ed. *The Acts of Jesus: What Did Jesus Really Do? The Search for the Authentic Deeds of Jesus* (San Francisco: HarperCollins, 1998).

Galloway, A.D. 'Theology Today'. Pages 345–51 in *The History of Christian Theology*. Vol. 1. *The Science of Theology* (ed. G.R. Evans, Alister E. McGrath and Allan D. Galloway; Basingstoke/Grand Rapids: Marshall Pickering/Eerdmans, 1986).

Gathercole, Simon. 'The Cross and Substitutionary Atonement', *Southern Baptist Journal of Theology* 11/2 (Summer 2007): pp. 64–73.

Gathercole, Simon. *The Pre-existent Son: Recovering the Christologies of Matthew, Mark and Luke* (Grand Rapids: Eerdmans, 2006).

Goldingay, J. 'Biblical Narrative and Systematic Theology'. Pages 123–42 in *Between Two Horizons: Spanning New Testament Studies and Systematic Theology* (ed. J.B. Green and M. Turner; Grand Rapids: Eerdmans, 2000).

Green, Joel B. and M.D. Baker. *Recovering the Scandal of the Cross: Atonement in New Testament and Contemporary Contexts* (Downers Grove: InterVarsity Press, 2000).

Green, Joel B. and Max Turner, eds. *Between Two Horizons: Spanning New Testament Studies and Systematic Theology* (Grand Rapids: Eerdmans, 2000).

Green, J.B., S. McKnight and I.H. Marshall, eds. *Dictionary of Jesus and the Gospels* (Downers Grove: InterVarsity Press, 1992).

Gregory of Nazianzus, *To Cledonius the Priest Against Apollinarius.* (Ep. CI.) . Pages 440–43, in *A Select Library of the Nicene and Post-Nicene Fathers of the Christian Church*, 2nd series, vol. 7. *S. Cyril of Jerusalem, S. Gregory Nazianzen* (trans. and ed. Philip Schaff and Henry Wace; New York: Christian Literature Publishing Co., 1893) http://www.ccel.org/ccel/schaff/npnf 207.html (accessed 30 September 2009).

Grenz, Stanley J. *Reason for Hope: The Systematic Theology of Wolfhart Pannenberg* (Grand Rapids: Eerdmans, 2nd edn, 2005).

Grenz, Stanley J. 'Wolfhart Pannenberg's Quest for Ultimate Truth'. *Christian Century* (14–21 September 1991): pp. 795–8.

Grubbs, N.C. and C.S. Drumm. 'What Does Theology Have to Do with the Bible? A Call for the Expansion of the Doctrine of Inspiration', *Journal of Evangelical Theological Society* 53/1 (March 2010): pp. 65–72.

Guigon, C. 'Heidegger'. In *The Cambridge Dictionary of Philosophy* (ed. R. Audi; Cambridge: Cambridge University Press, 2nd edn, 1999).

Guignon, Charles B. ed. *Cambridge Companion to Heidegger* (Cambridge: Cambridge University Press, 1993).

Gumerlock, F.X. 'Mark 13:32 and Christ's Supposed Ignorance: Four Patristic Solutions'. *Trinity Journal* 28 (2007): pp. 205–13.

Gundry, S.N. and A.F. Johnson. *Tensions in Contemporary Theology* (Chicago: Moody Press, 1976).

Gunton, Colin E. *Yesterday and Today: a Study of Continuities in Christology* (Grand Rapids: Eerdmans, 1997, 2nd edn).

Gutenson, Charles. 'Can Belief in the Christian God be Properly Basic? A Pannenbergian Perspective on Plantinga and Basic Beliefs', *Christian Scholars Review* 29/1 (Fall 1999): pp. 49–72.

Gutenson, Charles. *Reconsidering the Doctrine of God* (New York/ London; T&T Clark, 2005).

Guyer, Paul, ed. *The Cambridge Companion to Kant* (Cambridge: Cambridge University Press, 1992).

Hallanger, Nathan J. 'Wolfhart Pannenberg'. Pages 394–407 in *The Blackwell Companion to the Theologians* (ed. I.S. Markham; 2 vols; West Sussex: Wiley-Blackwell, 2009).

Hare, J.E. *The Moral Gap: Kantian Ethics, Human Limits, and God's Assistance* (Oxford: Clarendon Press, 1997).

Hart, T. 'Revelation'. In *The Cambridge Companion to Karl Barth* (ed. J. Webster; Cambridge: Cambridge University Press, 2000).

Hefner, P. 'The Role of Science in Pannenberg's Theological Thinking'. In *Beginning with the End: God, Science and Wolfhart Pannenberg* (ed. C. Rausch and J. Haugen; Chicago: OpenCourt; 1997).

Heidegger, Martin. *Being and Time* (trans. J. Macquarrie and E. Robinson; London: SCM Press, 1962). A translation of *Sein und Zeit* (Tubingen: Niemayer, 1927).

Heim, S.M. *Saved from Sacrifice: A Theology of the Cross* (Grand Rapids: Eerdmans, 2006).

Hengel, Martin. *Studies in Early Christology* (Edinburgh: T&T Clark, 1995).

Hill, Charles E, Roger R. Nicole and Frank. A. James. *The Glory of the Atonement* (Downers Grove: InterVarsity Press, 2004).

Hill, W.J. 'The Historicity of God'. *Theological Studies* 45 (1984): pp. 320–33.

Hinton, Rory A.A. 'Pannenberg's *Systematic Theology*, Vol 1: A Symposium III. Pannenberg on the Truth of Christian Discourse: A Logical Response'. *Calvin Theological Journal* 27 (1997): pp. 312–18.

Hodge, Charles. *Systematic Theology* (3 vols; New York : Charles Scribner, 1872).

Hood, J.B. 'The Cross in the New Testament: Two Theses in Conversation with Recent Literature (2000–2007)'. *Westminster Theological Journal* 71 (2009): pp. 281–95.

Howard, Thomas A. *Protestant Theology and the Making of the Modern German University* (Oxford: Oxford University Press, 2006).

Ingraffia, Brian. *Postmodern Theory and Biblical Theology* (Cambridge: Cambridge University Press, 1995).

Jeffery, S., A. Sach and M. Ovey, *Pierced for Our Transgressions* (Leicester: Inter-Varsity Press, 2007).

Jenson, R. 'Jesus in the Trinity: Wolfhart Pannenberg's Christology and the Doctrine of the Trinity'. In *The Theology of Wolfhart Pannenberg* (ed. Carl Braaten and Philip Clayton; Minneapolis: Augsburg, 1988).

Jenson, Robert W. Review of *Systematic Theology*: Volume 2 by Wolfhart Pannenberg. *First Things* 53 (May 1995): pp. 60–62.

Jersak, B. and M. Hardin, eds. *Stricken by God? Nonviolent Identification and the Victory of Christ* (Grand Rapids: Eerdmans, 2007).

Jones, Gareth, ed. *The Blackwell Companion to Modern Theology* (Malden/Oxford: Blackwell, 2004).

Jüngel, Eberhard. *God as the Mystery of the World* (trans. Darrell Guder; Grand Rapids: Eerdmans, 1983). Translation of *Gott als Geheimnis der Welt* (Tübingen: Mohr, 1977).

Kähler, M. *Die Wissenschaft der christlichen Lehre* (Leipzig: Deichert, 2nd edn, 1893).

Kant, Immanuel. *Religion within the Limits of Reason Alone* (trans. and ed. T.M. Greene and H.H. Hudson; New York: Harper & Row, 1960).

Kimel, A.F. ed. *Speaking the Christian God* (Grand Rapids: Eerdmans, 1992).

Krauth, Charles P. *Conservative Reformation and its Theology* (Philadelphia: J.B. Lippincott, 1872).

Labute, Todd S. 'The Ontological Motif Anticipation in the Theology of Wolfhart Pannenberg'. *Journal of Evangelical Theological Society* 37/2 (June 1994): pp. 275–82.

Lee, Dorothy A. *Transfiguration* (London; New York: Continuum, 2004).

Letham, Robert. *The Trinity* (Phillipsburg: P&R, 2005).

Lichtenberger, Frédéric. *History of German Theology in the Nineteenth Century* (ed. W. Hastie; Edinburgh: T&T Clark, 1889).

Liefeld, W.L. 'Transfiguration'. In *Dictionary of Jesus and the Gospels* (ed. J.B. Green and S. McKnight; Downers Grove: InterVarsity Press, 1992).

Lincoln, Andrew T. ' "We Know that His Testimony is True": Johannine Truth Claims and Historicity'. Pages 179–98 in *John, Jesus, and History*, Vol. 1: *Critical Appraisals of Critical Views* (ed. Paul N. Anderson, Felix Just and Tom Thatcher; Atlanta: Society of Biblical Literature, 2007).

Lindars, Barnabus. *The Theology of the Letter to the Hebrews* (Cambridge: Cambridge University Press, 1991).

Lindsay, Mark. 'Barth'. In *The Blackwell Companion to Modern Theology* (ed. G. Jones; Malden/Oxford: Blackwell, 2004).

Lösel, Steffen. 'Wolfhart Pannenberg's Response to the Challenge of Religious Pluralism: The Anticipation of Divine Absoluteness?'. *Journal of Ecumenical Studies* 34/4 (Fall 1997): pp. 499–519.

Löwith, Karl. *From Hegel to Nietzsche: The Revolution in Nineteenth-Century Thought* (trans. David E. Green; New York: Holt, Rinehart & Winston, 1964). Translation of *Von Hegel bis Nietzsche* (Zürich: Europa, 1941).

Makkreel, Rudolf A. *Dilthey: Philosopher of the Human Studies* (Princeton: Princeton University Press, 1975).

Marshall, Christopher D. *Beyond Retribution: A New Testament Vision for Justice, Crime and Punishment* (Grand Rapids/Cambridge UK: Eerdmans; Auckland/Sydney: Lime Grove, 2001).

Marshall, I. Howard. *Aspects of the Atonement* (Place: Paternoster, 2008).

Matera. F.J., Review of *The Pre-existent Son: Recovering the Christologies of Matthew, Mark, and Luke* by Simon Gathercole. *Review of Biblical Literature* 04/2007 http://www.bookreviews.org (accessed 5 August 2012).

Mattes, Mark. 'Pannenberg's Achievement: An Analysis and Assessment of his "Systematic Theology"'. *Currents in Theology and Mission* 26 (Feb 1999): pp. 51–60.

Mayerhofer, Bernd, 'Karl Löwith', Goethe-Institut, http://www.goethe.de/ges/phi/prt/en7944393.htm (accessed 20 June 2012).

McClean, J.A. *Anticipation in the Thought of Wolfhart Pannenberg* (2010), accessible at http://repository.mcd.edu.au/540/'.

McFarland, Ian. 'Christ, Spirit and Atonement'. *International Journal of Systematic Theology* 3/1 (March 2001): pp. 83–93.

McGrath, Alistair E. *The Making of Modern German Christology* (Oxford: Basil Blackwell, 1986).

McKenzie, David. *Wolfhart Pannenberg and Religious Philosophy* (Lanham: University Press of America, 1980).

McKim, Donald K. ed. *Dictionary of Major Biblical Interpreters* (Downers Grove: InterVarsity Press, 2nd edn, 2007).

McKnight, Scott. *A Community Called Atonement* (Nashville, TN: Abingdon Press, 2007).

Melanchthon, Philip. 'Loci Communes'. Pages 18–152 in *Melanchthon and Bucer* (ed. W. Pauck, trans. L.J. Satre; Philadelphia: Westminster, 1969).

Meyer, Ben F. 'Appointed Deed, Appointed Doer: Jesus and the Scriptures'. Pages 155–76 in *Authenticating the Activities of Jesus* (ed. B. Chilton and C.A. Evans; Boston: Brill, 2002).

Molnar, Paul D. *Incarnation and Resurrection: Toward a Contemporary Understanding* (Grand Rapids: Eerdmans, 2007).

Molnar, Paul D. 'Some Problems with Pannenberg's Solution to Barth's "Faith Subjectivism"'. *Scottish Journal of Theology* 48/3 (1995): pp. 315–39.

Morgan, R. 'Bornkamm, Günther'. In *Dictionary of Major Biblical Interpreters* (ed. D.K. McKim; Downers Grove: InterVarsity Press, 2nd edn, 2007).

Mostert, Christiaan. 'From Eschatology to Trinity: Pannenberg's Doctrine of God'. *Pacifica* 10 (February 1997): pp. 70–83.

Mostert, Christiaan. *God and the Future* (Edinburgh/London/New York: T&T Clark/Continuum, 2002).

Myers, Benjamin. 'The Difference Totality Makes: Reconsidering Pannenberg's Eschatological Ontology'. *NZSTR* 49/2 (November 2007).

Myers, Benjamin. 'Faith as Self-Understanding: Towards a Post-Barthian Appreciation of Rudolf Bultmann'. *International Journal for Systematic Theology* 10/1 (January 2008): pp. 21–35.

Nickelsburg, G.W.E. 'Son of Man'. In *The Anchor Bible Dictionary* (ed. David N. Freedman et al.; 6 vols; New York: Doubleday, 1992).

Nietzsche, Friedrich. *Die Geburt der Tragödie aus dem Geiste der Musik* (Leipzig: E.W. Fritzsch, 1872).

Nietzsche, Friedrich. *Joyful Wisdom* (intro. Kurt F. Reinhardt, trans. Thomas Common, poetry Paul V. Cohn and Maude D. Petre; New York: Frederick Ungar, 1960). Translation of *Fröhliche Wissenschaft* (Leipzig: E.W. Fritzsch, rev. edn, 1887).

O'Leary, Joseph S. Questioning Back: *The Overcoming of Metaphysics in Christian Tradition* (Minneapolis: Winston Press, 1985).

Olive, Don. *Wolfhart Pannenberg* (Waco: Word, 1973).

Olson, R.E. 'The Human Self-realization of God: Hegelian Elements in Pannenberg's Christology', *Perspectives in Religious Studies* 13/3 (Fall 1986).

Olson, Roger. 'Trinity and Eschatology: The Historical Being of God in Jürgen Moltmann and Wolfhart Pannenberg'. *Scottish Journal of Theology* 36 (1983): pp. 213–27.

Olson, Roger. 'Wolfhart Pannenberg's Doctrine of the Trinity'. *Scottish Journal of Theology* 43 (1990): pp. 175–206.

Olson, Roger. *Review of Metaphysics and the Idea of God* by Wolfhart Pannenberg. *Journal of Religion* 72/2 (1992): pp. 285–6.

Olthuis, James H. 'Pannenberg's Systematic Theology, Vol 1: A Symposium IV. God as True Infinite: Concerns about Wolfhart Pannenberg's Systematic Theology, Vol 1'. *Calvin Theological Journal* 27 (1997): pp. 318–25.

Oord, Thomas. J. 'Future Perfect: A Conversation with Wolfhart Pannenberg', in *Books and Culture*, 2001. HYPERLINK "http://www.booksandculture.com/articles/2001/sepoct/6.18.html"http://www.booksandculture.com/articles/2001/sepoct/6.18.html (accessed 20 June 2012).

Packer, James I. 'What Did the Cross Achieve? The Logic of Penal Substitution' *Tyndale Bulletin* 25 (1974): pp. 3–45

Paget, J.C. 'Quests for the Historical Jesus'. In *The Cambridge Companion to Jesus* (ed. M. Bockmuehl; Cambridge: Cambridge University Press, 2001).

Pailin, David A. *Review of Metaphysics and the Idea of God* by Wolfhart Pannenberg. *Theology* 44 (May–June 1991): pp. 208–9.

Pattison, George. *Review of Metaphysics and the Idea of God* by Wolfhart Pannenberg, *Expository Times* 102/8 (May 1991).

Pelikan, Jaroslav. *The Christian Tradition: A History of the Development of Doctrine* (5 vols; Chicago: University of Chicago Press, 1971–89).

Peters, Ted. 'The Systematic Theology of Wolfhart Pannenberg'. *Dialog* 37/2 (Spring 1988): pp. 123–33.

Peterson, David. ed. *Where Wrath and Mercy Meet: Proclaiming the Atonement Today* (Carlisle: Paternoster, 2001)

Pfleiderer, Otto. *The Development of Theology in Germany since Kant: And its Progress in Great Britain since 1825* (London: Sonnenschein, 1890).

Pike, Nelson. *God and Timelessness* (London: Routledge & Kegan Paul, 1970).

Pojman, Louis P. 'Relativism'. In *The Cambridge Dictionary of Philosophy* (ed. R. Audi; Cambridge: Cambridge University Press, 2nd edn, 1999).

Polk, David P. 'The All-Determining God and the Peril of Determinism', in *The Theology of Wolfhart Pannenberg* (ed. Carl Braaten and Philip Clayton; Minneapolis: Augsburg, 1988).

Polkinghorne, John. *Faith, Science and Understanding* (London: SPCK: 2000).

Rahner, Karl. *Theological Investigations*. Vol. 4 *More Recent Writings* (trans. K. Smyth; London: Darton, Longman & Todd, 1966).

Rahner, Karl. *Theological Investigations*. Vol. 5 *Later Writings* (trans. Karl-Heinz Kruger; New York: Crossroad, 1983).

Rahner, Karl. *The Trinity* (trans. J. Donceel; London, Burns & Oates, 1970). Translation of 'Der dreifaltige Gott als transzendenter Urgrund der Heilsgeschichte'. Pages 317–401 in *Mysterium Salutis Band* 2, (Einsiedeln: Benziger, 1967).

Reymond, Robert L. *A New Systematic Theology of the Christian Faith* (Nashville: Nelson, 1998).

Richter, Cornelia. 'The Productive Power of Reason: Voices on Rationality and Religion – A Sketch of the Development of the Enlightenment and its Aftermath'. Pages 23–38 in *Faith in the Enlightenment? The Critique of the Enlightenment Revisited* (ed. L. Boeve, J. Schrijvers, W. Stoker and Hendrik M. Vroom; Amsterdam: Rodopi, 2006).

Rise, Svein. *The Christology of Wolfhart Pannenberg* (Lewiston, Queenston, Lampeter: Mellen University Press, 1997).

Rothe, R. Offenbarung, I, *Theologische Studien und Kritiken* 31 (1858): pp. 3–49.

Rothgangel, Martin. *Naturwissenschaft und Theologie: wissenschaftstheoretische Gesichtspunkte im Horizont religionspädagogischer Überlegungen* (Göttingen: Vandenhoeck & Ruprecht, 1999).

Scaer, D.P. 'Theology of Hope'. In *Tensions in Contemporary Theology* (ed. S.N. Gundry and Alan F. Johnson; Chicago: Moody Press; 1976).

Schacht, Richard. 'Nietzsche, Friedrich Wilhelm'. Page 615 in *The Cambridge Dictionary of Philosophy* (ed. R. Audi; Cambridge: Cambridge University Press, 2nd edn, 1999).

Schleiermacher, Friedrich D.E. *The Christian Faith* (ed. H.R. Mackintosh and J.S. Stewart; Edinburgh: T&T Clark, 1960). A translation of *Der christliche Glaube nach den Grundsätzen der evangelischen Kirche im Zusammenhange dargestellt* (2 vols; Berlin: G. Reimer1884).

Schleiermacher, Friedrich D.E. *On Religion: Speeches to its Cultured Despisers* (ed. Richard Crouter; Cambridge: Cambridge University Press, 1988). A translation of *Über die Religion: Reden an die Gebildeten unter ihren Verächtern* (Leipzig : Fritz Eckhardt, 1st edn, 1799).

Schwarz, Hans. *Eschatology* (Grand Rapids: Eerdmans, 2000).

Schwarz, Hans. *Method and Context as Problems for Contemporary Theology: Doing Theology in an Alien World* (Lewiston: Edwin Mellen Press, 1991).

Schwarz, Hans. *Theology in a Global Context: The Last Two Hundred Years* (Grand Rapids: Eerdmans, 2005).

Schwöbel, Christoph. 'Last Things First? The Century of Eschatology in Retrospect'. Pages 217–41 in *The Future as God's Gift: Explorations in Christian Eschatology* (ed. D. Fergusson and M. Sarot, Edinburgh: T&T Claark, 2000).

Schwöbel, Christoph. 'Rational Theology in Trinitarian Perspective: Wolfhart Pannenberg's "Systematic Theology"'. *Journal of Theological Studies* NS 47/2 (October 1996): pp. 498–527.

Schwöbel, Christoph. 'Wolfhart Pannenberg'. Pages 129–46 in *The Modern Theologians: An Introduction to Christian Theology since 1918* (ed. D.F. Ford and R. Muers; Oxford: Blackwell, 3rd edn, 2005).

Shelton, R.L. *Cross and Covenant: Interpreting the Atonement for 21st Century Mission* (Carlisle: Paternoster, 2006).

Shults, F. Leron. 'A Theology of Everything? Evaluating Pannenberg's Interdisciplinary Method – Review Essay'. *Christian Scholar's Review* 29/1 (1998): pp. 155–63.

Shults, F. Leron. *The Postfoundationalist Task of Theology: Wolfhart Pannenberg and the New Theological Rationality* (Grand Rapids: Eerdmans, 1999).

Shults, L. 'Foundationalism'. Page 335 in *Encyclopedia of Science and Religion* (ed. J. van Huyssteen; New York: Macmillan Reference, 2nd edn, 2003).

Shults, L. 'Nonfoundationalism'. Page 624 in *Encyclopedia of Science and Religion* (ed. J. van Huyssteen; New York: Macmillan Reference, 2nd edn, 2003).

Sölle, Dorothy. *Christ the Representative* (trans. D. Lewis; London: SCM Press, 1967).

Stott, John. *The Cross of Christ* (Leicester: Inter-Varsity Press, 1986).

Streett, D.R. *Review of The Pre-existent Son: Recovering the Christologies of Matthew, Mark, and Luke* by Simon Gathercole. *Criswell Theological Review* 4/2 (Spring 2007): pp. 115–17.

Sturch, Richard. *The Word and the Christ: An Essay in Analytic Christology* (Oxford: Clarendon Press, 1991).

Taylor, Iain. *Pannenberg on the Triune God* (London: T&T Clark, 2007).

Thiselton, Anthony C. *The Hermeneutics of Doctrine* (Grand Rapids: Eerdmans, 2007).

Thompson, J. *Modern Trinitarian Perspectives* (New York and Oxford: Oxford University Press, 1994).

Thornhill, Christopher. 'Utopian Emancipation: Bloch'. Pages 480–88 in *The Edinburgh Encyclopedia of Continental Philosophy* (ed. S. Glendinning; London: Routledge, 1999).

Tidball D., D. Hilborn and J. Thacker, eds. *The Atonement Debate: Papers from the London Symposium on the Theology of the Atonement* (Grand Rapids: Zondervan, 2008).

Trelstad, M. ed. *Cross Examinations: Readings on the Meaning of the Cross Today* (Minneapolis: Fortress, 2006).

Trueman, Carl R. *John Owen: Reformed Catholic, Renaissance Man* (Aldershot: Ashgate, 2007).

Tuckett, C.M. 'Messianic Secret'. In *The Anchor Bible Dictionary* (ed. David N. Freedman et al.; 6 vols; New York: Doubleday, 1992).

Tupper, E.F. *The Theology of Wolfhart Pannenberg* (Philadelphia: Westminster, 1973).

Van Huyssteen, J. Wentzel, ed. *Encyclopedia of Science and Religion* (New York: Macmillan Reference, 2nd edn, 2003).

Vanhoozer, Kevin J. *The Drama of Doctrine: A Canonical-linguistic Approach to Christian Theology* (Louisville: Westminster John Knox Press, 2005).

Vanhoozer, Kevin J. *First Theology: God, Scripture and Hermeneutic* (Downers Grove: InterVarsity Press, 2002).

Vanhoozer, Kevin J. *Remythologizing Theology: Divine Action, Passion, and Authorship* (Cambridge: Cambridge University Press, 2010).

Vattimo, G. 'The Christian Message and the Dissolution of Metaphysics'. In *The Blackwell Companion to Postmodern Theology* (ed. G. Ward; Malden: Blackwell, 2001, 2005).

Wallis, R.T. *Neoplatonism* (London: Duckworth, 1972).

Warfield, B.B. 'The Human Development of Jesus'. Pages 157–66 in *Selected Shorter Writings of Benjamin B. Warfield.* Vol 1. (ed. J. E. Meeter; Nutley: Presbyterian and Reformed, 1970).

Wartofsky, Marx W. *Feuerbach* (Cambridge, Cambridge University Press, 1977).

Watson, David F. *Honor Among Christians: The Cultural Key to the Messianic Secret* (Minneapolis: Fortress, 2010).

Watts, G.J. *Revelation and the Spirit: A Comparative Study of the Relationship between the Doctrine of Revelation and Pneumatology in the Theology of Eberhard Jüngel and Wolfhart Pannenberg* (Milton Keynes: Paternoster, 2005).

Waxman, W. 'Kant's Debt to the British Empiricists'. In *A Companion to Kant* (ed. G. Bird; Malden: Blackwell, 2006).

Weaver J.D. *The Nonviolent Atonement* (Grand Rapids/Cambridge: Eerdmans, 2001).

Webb, Robert L. Review of The Pre-existent Son: Recovering the Christologies of Mathew, Mark, and Luke by Simon Gathercole *Journal for the Study of the Historical Jesus* 5/2 (July 2007) p. 215.

Webber, O. *Grundlagen der Dogmatik Band II* (Neukirchen: Verlag der Buchhandlung des Erziehungsvereins, 1962).

Webster, J. 'Introduction: Systematic Theology'. In *The Oxford Handbook of Systematic Theology* (ed. J. Webster, K. Tanner and I. Torrance; Oxford: Oxford University Press, 2007).

Webster, John. 'Incarnation'. In *The Blackwell Companion to Modern Theology* (ed. G. Jones; Oxford: Blackwell, 2004).

Webster, John. B., Kathryn Tanner and Iain Torrance, eds. *The Oxford Handbook of Systematic Theology* (Oxford: Oxford University Press, 2007).

Weinandy, Thomas. *In the Likeness of Sinful Flesh: An Essay on the Humanity of Christ* (Edinburgh: T&T Clark, 1993).

Westhelle, V. *The Scandalous God: The Use and Abuse of the Cross* (Minneapolis: Fortress, 2006).

Whitehead, Alfred North. *Adventures of Ideas* (New York: Free Press, 1967, originally published 1933).

Williams, G.J. 'Penal Substitution: A Response to Recent Criticism'. *Journal of the Evangelical Theological Society* 50/1 (March 2007): pp. 71–86.

Witherington, Ben. *Jesus, Paul and the End of the World* (Downers Grove; InterVarsity Press, 1992).

Wolin, Richard. *Heidegger's Children: Hannah Arendt, Karl Löwith, Hans Jonas, and Herbert Marcuse* (Princeton: Princeton University Press, 2001).

Wong, Kam Ming. *Wolfhart Pannenberg on Human Destiny* (Aldershot: Ashgate, 2008).

Wood, A.W. 'Rational Theology, Moral Faith, and Religion'. In *The Cambridge Companion to Kant* (ed. P. Guyer; Cambridge: Cambridge University Press, 1992).

Work, Telford. *Living and Active: Scripture in the Economy of Salvation* (Grand Rapids: Eerdmans, 2002).

Worthing, Mark. *Foundation and Functions of Theology as Universal Science* (Frankfurt am Main: Peter Lang; 1996).

Wrathall, Mark A. 'Introduction: Metaphysics and Onto-theology'. Pages 1–6 in *Religion After Metaphysics* (ed. M.A. Wrathal; Cambridge: Cambridge University Press, 2003).

Wrede, William. *The Messianic Secret* (trans. J.C.G. Grieg; Cambridge: James Clarke, 1971). A translation of *Das Messiasgeheimnis in den Evangelien: Zugleich ein Beitrag zum Verständnis des Markusevangeliums* (Göttingen: Vandenhoeck & Ruprecht, 1901).

Wright, N.T. *Jesus and the Victory of God* (London: SPCK, 1999).

Wright, N.T. *New Testament and the People of God* (London: SPCK, 1992).

Wyman, W.E. 'Revelation and the Doctrine of Faith: Historical Revelation within the Limits of Historical Consciousness', *Journal of Religion* 78/1 (January, 1998): pp. 41–51.

Endnotes

Introduction

[1] C. Mostert, *God and the Future* (Edinburgh/London/New York: T&T Clark/Continuum, 2002); S.J. Grenz, *Reason for Hope: The Systematic Theology of Wolfhart Pannenberg* (Grand Rapids: Eerdmans, 2nd edn, 2005); T. Bradshaw, *Pannenberg: A Guide for the Perplexed* (London: T&T Clark, 2009); C. Schwöbel, 'Wolfhart Pannenberg', in *The Modern Theologians: An Introduction to Christian Theology since 1918* (ed. D.F. Ford and R. Muers; Oxford: Blackwell, 3rd edn, 2005), pp. 129–46; N.J. Hallanger, 'Wolfhart Pannenberg' in *The Blackwell Companion to the Theologians* (ed. I.S. Markham, 2 vols; West Sussex: Wiley-Blackwell, 2009), 2:394–407.

[2] J.A. McClean, *Anticipation in the Thought of Wolfhart Pannenberg* (2010), accessible at http://repository.mcd.edu.au/540/'.

[3] Wolfhart Pannenberg, 'Feminine Language about God?', *AsTJ* 48 (Fall, 1993): pp. 27–9.

[4] See A.F. Kimel, ed., *Speaking the Christian God* (Grand Rapids: Eerdmans, 1992).

1. God, History and Hope: Introducing Pannenberg

[1] See W. Pannenberg, 'God's Presence in History', *ChrCent* 98 (11 March 1981): pp. 260–63; W. Pannenberg, 'An Autobiographical Sketch', in *The Theology of Wolfhart Pannenberg* (ed. C.E. Braaten and P. Clayton; Minneapolis: Augsburg; 1988), pp. 11–8; W. Pannenberg, 'An Intellectual Pilgrimage', *Dialog* 45/2 (2006): pp. 184–91; Schwöbel, 'Wolfhart Pannenberg', pp. 129–46; Hallanger, 'Wolfhart Pannenberg', pp. 394–407.

2 F. Nietzsche, *Die Geburt der Tragödie aus dem Geiste der Musik* (Leipzig: E.W. Fritzsch, 1872).

3 Pannenberg, 'Intellectual Pilgrimage', p. 184; W. Pannenberg, *Systematic Theology* (3 vols. Grand Rapids/Edinburgh: Eerdmans/T&T Clark, 1991–7); 1:152–5 and 2:232–6 refer to Nietzsche.

4 Paul Avis, *Faith in the Fires of Criticism* (London: Darton, Longman & Todd, 1995), p. 37.

5 Richard Schacht, 'Nietzsche, Friedrich Wilhelm', in *The Cambridge Dictionary of Philosophy* (ed. R. Audi; Cambridge: CUP, 2nd edn, 1999), p. 615; see also Brian Ingraffia, *Postmodern Theory and Biblical Theology* (Cambridge: CUP, 1995), pp. 19–32.

6 F. Nietzsche, *Joyful Wisdom* (trans. Thomas Common; New York: Frederick Ungar, 1960), p. 152.

7 W. Pannenberg, 'Types of Atheism and Their Theological Significance', in *Basic Questions in Theology* (3 vols.; London: SCM, 1971), 2:194–5.

8 Pannenberg, 'God's Presence', p. 260.

9 Pannenberg, 'God's Presence', p. 261.

10 T.J. Oord, 'Future Perfect: A Conversation with Wolfhart Pannenberg', in *Books and Culture*, 2001, "http://www.booksandculture.com/articles/2001/sepoct/6.18.html"http://www.booksandculture.com/articles/2001/sepoct/6.18.html (accessed 20 June 2012).

11 W. Pannenberg, 'Hermeneutic and Universal History', *BQT* 1:96–136; 'On Historical and Theological Hermeneutic', *BQT* 1:137–81; 'Types of Atheism and their Theological Significance', *BQT* 2:186–200; 'The Question of God', *BQT* 2:201–33; 'The God of Hope', *BQT* 2:34–49; 'Anthropology and the Question of God', *BQT* 2:80–98; 'Speaking about God in the Face of Atheist Criticism', *BQT* 3:80–115; 'The Significance of Christianity in the Philosophy of Hegel', *BQT* 3:144–77; *ST* 1:83–95; *Theology and the Philosophy of Science* (London: Darton, Longman & Todd, 1976), pp. 29–224; *Metaphysics and the Idea of God* (Grand Rapids: Eerdmans; 1990), pp. 3–109; *Theologie und Philosophie: ihr Verhältnis im Lichte ihrer gemeinsamen Geschichte* (Gottingen: Vandenhoeck & Ruprecht, 1996).

12 Pannenberg, 'God's Presence', p. 261. See also D. Olive, *Wolfhart Pannenberg* (Waco: Word; 1973), pp. 23–5. On the influence of Löwith see R. Wolin, *Heidegger's Children: Hannah Arendt, Karl Löwith, Hans Jonas, and Herbert Marcuse* (Princeton: Princeton University Press, 2001), pp. 71–100.

13 See C. Guigon, 'Heidegger', *CDP*, pp. 370–73.

14 C. Gutenson, *Reconsidering the Doctrine of God* (New York/London; T&T Clark; 2005), p. 30.

15 B. Mayerhofer, 'Karl Löwith', Goethe-Institut, http://www.goethe. de/ges/phi/prt/en7944393.htm (accessed 20 June 2012).

16 For a brief overview of the kerygmatic dimension of the thought of Bultmann and Barth see James M. Byrne, 'Bultmann and Tillich', in *The Blackwell Companion to Modern Theology* (ed. G. Jones; Malden / Oxford: Blackwell, 2004), pp. 374–6; Mark Lindsay, 'Barth' in *Blackwell Companion to Modern Theology*, pp. 338–40.

17 W. Pannenberg, 'Dogmatic Theses on the Doctrine of Revelation' in *Revelation as History* (ed. W. Pannenberg; London: Macmillan; 1968), pp. 123–58.

18 *RaH*, p. 139.

19 See R. Bauckham, 'Jürgen Moltmann', in *The Modern Theologians: An Introduction to Christian Theology since 1918* (ed. D.F. Ford and R. Muers; Oxford: Blackwell, 3rd edn, 2005), pp. 147–8.

20 C. Thornhill, 'Utopian Emancipation: Bloch' in *The Edinburgh Encyclopedia of Continental Philosophy* (ed. S. Glendinning; London: Routledge, 1999), p. 480.

21 R. Bauckham, *Moltmann: Messianic Theology in the Making* (London: Marshall Pickering, 1987) shows the influence of Bloch on Moltmann.

22 E.F. Tupper, *The Theology of Wolfhart Pannenberg* (Philadelphia: Westminster, 1973), p. 26; Mostert, *God and the Future*, p. 91; cf. W. Pannenberg, 'Providence, God and Eschatology', in *The Historicity of Nature: Essays on Science and Theology* (ed. N.H. Gregersen; West Conshohocken: Templeton Foundation, 2008), p. 271, n. 16.

23 Oord, 'Future Perfect'.

24 A.N. Whitehead, *Adventures of Ideas* (New York: The Free Press: 1967, originally published 1933), pp. 167–8.

25 W. Pannenberg, *Jesus – God and Man* (trans. L.L. Wilkins and D.A. Priebe; Philadelphia: Westminster, 1977, 2nd English edn).

26 J.C. Paget, 'Quests for the Historical Jesus', in *The Cambridge Companion to Jesus* (ed. M. Bockmuehl; Cambridge: CUP, 2001), pp. 146–8.

27 G. Bornkamm, *Jesus of Nazareth* (New York: Harper & Row, 1960) and see R. Morgan, 'Bornkamm, Günther', in *Dictionary of Major Biblical Interpreters* (ed. D.K. McKim; Downers Grove: IVP, 2nd edn, 2007), p. 211.

28 Bornkamm, *Jesus of Nazareth*, p. 172.

29 Bornkamm, *Jesus of Nazareth*, pp. 169–70.

30 Bornkamm, *Jesus of Nazareth*, p. 178.

31 *JGM*, p. 58.

32 *JGM*, p. 66.

33 He asserts that 'only by his resurrection . . . did Christ attain to the dignity of the Kyrios . . . Only thus was he appointed the Son of God in power . . . Only in the light of the resurrection is he the pre-existent Son. Only as the risen Lord is he always the living Lord of his community', *ST* 2:283.

34 *JGM*, p. 137.

35 T.A. Howard, *Protestant Theology and the Making of the Modern German University* (Oxford: OUP, 2006), p. 131, see pp. 130–210 for a discussion of the organization of the Berlin University and the impact of Wissenschaftsideologie.

36 *TPS*, p. 273.

37 *TPS*, pp. 299–300, original emphasis.

38 His position is that statements are to be judged not substantiated if and only if: 1) though intended as based in Israelite-Christian faith they 'cannot be shown to express implication of biblical traditions'; 2) 'they have no connection with reality as a whole which is cashable in terms of present experience' as assessed by current philosophical enquiry; 3) 'they are incapable of being integrated with the appropriate area of experience or no attempt is made to integrate them'; 4) 'their explanatory force is inadequate to the stage reached in theological discussion', *TPS*, p. 345.

39 'The obligation of covering the entire field of systematic theology in my academic lectures brought to my attention not only new facts and perspectives, but also complete fields of learning that I had scarcely noticed before. They helped to put my theological project in a broader and more differentiated context.' Pannenberg, 'God's Presence', p. 263.

2. Thinking about Everything: Themes in Pannenberg's Thought

1 J.S. O'Leary, *Questioning Back: The Overcoming of Metaphysics in Christian Tradition* (Minneapolis: Winston Press, 1985), pp. 6–7, comments that metaphysics is 'a slippery term, commonly used in a vast variety of senses, and people who talk of "overcoming metaphysics" are likely

to find that the phrase assumes different connotations from context to context, connotations which have a way of changing places quickly and unnoticed unless subject to vigilant reflexive control'.

[2] Panayot Butchvarov, 'Metaphyics', *CDP*, p. 563.

[3] *MIG*, p. 20.

[4] *ST* 1:71.

[5] H. Frei, *Types of Christian Theology* (New Haven: Yale UP), p. 3.

[6] *MIG*, pp. 11–2 'the connection between Christian faith and Hellenistic thought in general – and the connection between the God of the Bible and the god of the philosophers in particular – does not represent a foreign infiltration into the original Christian message, but rather belongs to its very foundations'. Mostert, *God and the Future*, pp. 62–8 shows the way in which a concern for an 'ontology of the whole' means that Pannenberg 'regards theology and philosophy as close partners'.

[7] Pannenberg, 'Faith and Reason', *BQT* 2:50–57.

[8] Pannenberg, 'Christian Theology and Philosophical Criticism', *BQT* 3:127.

[9] See 'philosophical anthropology' in *The Blackwell Dictionary of Western Philosophy* (ed. N. Bunnin and J. Yu; Malden: Blackwell, 2004), p. 519 and A. Cecilia, 'The Axiological Dimension of the Human Being', *Morality within the Life and Social World: Interdisciplinary Phenomenology of the Authentic Life in the 'Moral Sense'* (ed. A. Tymieniecka; Dordrecht: D. Reidel, 1987), pp. 27–30.

[10] W. Pannenberg, *Anthropology in Theological Perspective* (Philadelphia: Westminster, 1985; Repr. Edinburgh: T&T Clark, 1999).

[11] *TPS*, p. 126.

[12] *ATP*, p. 16.

[13] L. Feuerbach, *The Essence of Christianity* (New York: Colin Blanchard, 1855); see M.W. Wartofsky, *Feuerbach* (Cambridge, Cambridge University Press, 1977), p. 197.

[14] Feuerbach, *Essence*, pp. 48, 340–45, and see Avis, *Faith*, pp. 20–22.

[15] W. Pannenberg, 'Anthropology and the Question of God' in *BQT* 3:86–7.

[16] 'Anthropology and the Question of God', p. 93.

[17] K.M. Wong, *Wolfhart Pannenberg on Human Destiny* (Aldershot: Ashgate, 2008), pp. 59–61.

[18] See also P. Hefner, 'The Role of Science in Pannenberg's Theological Thinking' in *Beginning with the End: God, Science and Wolfhart Pannenberg* (ed. C.R. Albright and J. Haugen; Chicago: OpenCourt; 1997), pp. 266–86.

19 'Theological Questions for Scientists', in *BWE*, p. 37. See his summary discussion in W. Pannenberg, 'Problems Between Science and Theology in the Course of Their Modern History', *Zygon* 41/1 (March 2006): pp. 105–11.

20 W. Pannenberg, *Towards a Theology of Nature: Essays on Science and Faith* (ed. Ted Peters; Louisville/Philadelphia: Westminster/John Knox, 1993), p. 74.

21 M. Rothgangel, *Naturwissenschaft und Theologie: wissenschaftstheoretische Gesichtspunkte im Horizont religionspädagogischer Überlegungen* (Göttingen: Vandenhoeck & Ruprecht, 1999), p. 172 and P. Clayton 'Science, Meaning, and Metaphysics: A Tribute to Wolfhart Pannenberg', *ISR* 28 (December 2003): pp. 237–8.

22 *Erwägungen zu einer Theologie der Natur* (ed. W. Pannenberg and A.M. Klaus Müller; Gütersloh: Gerd Mohn, 1970).

23 TTN, see note 59 above; W. Pannenberg, *The Historicity of Nature: Essays on Science and Theology* (ed. Niels Henrik Gregersen; Philadelphia: Templeton Press, 2007).

24 *ST* 2:115–36, quote from p. 127.

25 'Theological Questions for Scientists', p. 40 and see p. 48; see also W. Pannenberg, 'Theology of Creation and Natural Science', *ATJ* 50/1 (Spring 1995): pp. 5–15.

26 e.g. *ST* 1:119–87 and see also W. Pannenberg, 'The Religions from the Perspective of Christian Theology and the Self-Interpretation of Christianity in Relation to the Non-Christian Religions', *Modern Theology* 9/3 (1993 July): pp. 285–97.

27 Pannenberg, 'The Religions', p. 285.

28 *ST* 1:157.

29 *TPS*, pp. 327.

30 *TPS*, pp. 358–71; *ATP*, pp. 473–84; *ST* 2:119–88.

31 *ST* 1:127.

32 Pannenberg, 'The Religions', p. 297.

33 Grenz, *Reason for Hope*, p. 48; cf. K. Eilers, *Faithful to Save: Pannenberg on God's Reconciling Action* (London: T&T Clark, 2011), pp. 10–11.

34 Pannenberg, 'Intellectual Pilgrimage', p. 187.

35 Grenz, *Reason for Hope*, pp. 296–7, notes that commitment to Scripture and classic Christian thought in Pannenberg's thought is a constraint which 'often becomes a stumbling block to the avant-garde in both church and society'.

36 Pannenberg, 'God's Presence', p. 263.

37 Pannenberg himself acknowledges the long-term work of developing his thought into a systematic whole in Pannenberg, 'An Autobiographical Sketch', in *TWP*, p. 16.

38 Schwöbel, 'Wolfhart Pannenberg', p. 145, and see survey (pp. 130–35).

39 C. Gutenson, *Reconsidering the Doctrine of God* (New York/London; T&T Clark, 2005), p. 8.

40 S. Rise, *The Christology of Wolfhart Pannenberg* (Lewiston, Queenston, Lampeter: Mellen University Press, 1997), p. 29; I. Taylor, *Pannenberg on the Triune God* (London: T&T Clark, 2007), pp. 5–6.

41 *ST* 1:249–57.

42 See *ST* 2:446; cf. *JGM*, pp. 212–25.

43 Mostert, *God and the Future*, pp. 128–31.

44 Contra Robert W. Jenson, *Review of Systematic Theology: Volume 2*, in *First Things* 53 (May 1995): p. 62.

45 Eilers, *Faithful to Save*, p. 5.

3. Thinking about God: Pannenberg and Systematic Theology

1 Vincent, *The Commonitory*, II.6, *NPNF*, 132, http://www.ccel.org/ccel/schaff/npnf211.iii.iii.html (accessed 29 September 2009).

2 *ST* 1:11, pp. 15–6.

3 Grenz, *Reason for Hope*, p. 42.

4 Grenz, *Reason for Hope*, pp. 290–95.

5 J.H. Olthuis, 'Pannenberg's Systematic Theology, Vol 1: A Symposium IV. God as true Infinite: Concerns about Wolfhart Pannenberg's Systematic Theology, Vol 1', *CTJ* 27 (1997): p. 320 expresses this concern.

6 See L. Shults, 'Foundationalism', in *Encyclopedia of Science and Religion* (ed. J. van Huyssteen; New York: Macmillan Reference, 2nd edn, 2003), p. 335.

7 L. Shults, 'Nonfoundationalism', in Van Huyssteen, *Encyclopedia*, p. 624.

8 F.L. Shults, *The Postfoundationalist Task of Theology: Wolfhart Pannenberg and the New Theological Rationality* (Grand Rapids: Eerdmans, 1999), pp. 206–8.

9 Shults, *Postfoundationalist Task*, pp. 2–11. Bradshaw, *Pannenberg*, pp.177–8, agrees that despite accusations that Pannenberg is too

committed to modernity, Shults is correct to view him as postfoundationalist.

10 C. Schwöbel, 'Rational Theology in Trinitarian Perspective: Wolfhart Pannenberg's "Systematic Theology"', *JTS* 47/2 (October 1996): p. 499.

11 P. Clayton, 'Anticipation and Theological Method', in *TWP*, p. 125.

12 Schwöbel, 'Rational Theology', p. 499.

13 M. Worthing, *Foundation and Functions of Theology as Universal Science* (Frankfurt am Main: Peter Lang, 1996), pp. 66–8; see H. Schwarz, *Method and Context as Problems for Contemporary Theology: Doing Theology in an Alien World* (Lewiston: Edwin Mellen Press, 1991), pp. 14–15.

14 Bradshaw, *Pannenberg*, pp. 177–8.

15 T. Peters, 'The Systematic Theology of Wolfhart Pannenberg', *Dialog* 37/2 (Spring 1988): p. 127.

16 *ST* 1:336.

17 H. Frei, *Types of Christian Theology* (ed. G. Hunsinger and W. Placher; New Haven: Yale University Press, 1994).

18 Frei, *Types of Christian Theology*, pp. 28, 46.

19 Frei, *Types of Christian Theology*, p. 3.

20 Frei, *Types of Christian Theology*, pp. 30–34, 82.

21 *ST* 1:xii.

22 *MIG* , p. 42; cf. *ST* 1:95.

23 P. Molnar, 'Some Problems with Pannenberg's Solution to Barth's "Faith Subjectivism"', *SJT* 48/3 (1995): p. 324, offers a one-sided reading of Pannenberg when he claims that Pannenberg grounds truth in 'the locus of those limits which can be established on the basis of human knowledge and experience'. He notes Pannenberg's concern for correlation with philosophy (and all human knowledge) but fails to appreciate Pannenberg's sublation of this into theology.

24 Pannenberg, 'Analogy and Doxology', *BQT* 1:238, see also 'What Is a Dogmatic Statement?', *BQT* 1:209–10 and *ST* 1:55–6.

25 P. Melanchthon, 'Loci Communes' in *Melanchthon and Bucer* (ed. W. Pauck, Philadelphia: Westminster, 1969), p. 22.

26 J. Webster, 'Introduction: Systematic Theology', in *The Oxford Handbook of Systematic Theology* (ed. J. Webster, K. Tanner and I. Torrance; Oxford: OUP, 2007), p. 6.

27 W. Pannenberg, *An Introduction to Systematic Theology* (Grand Rapids: Eerdmans, 1991), p. 18.

28 *IST*, pp. 8–18.

29 *IST*, p. 5.

30 K. Vanhoozer, *The Drama of Doctrine: A Canonical-linguistic Approach to Christian Theology* (Louisville: Westminster John Knox, 2005), pp. 243–63.

31 See C.R. Trueman, *John Owen: Reformed Catholic, Renaissance Man* (Aldershot: Ashgate, 2007).

32 See J. Anderson, *Paradox in Christian Theology: An Analysis of Its Presence, Character, and Epistemic Status* (London: Paternoster Press, 2007), for a very important discussion of the need to recognize the 'rational affirmation of paradoxical theology' in *Christianity* (p. 214).

33 J. Goldingay, 'Biblical Narrative and Systematic Theology,' in *Between Two Horizons: Spanning New Testament Studies and Systematic Theology* (ed. J.B. Green and M. Turner; Grand Rapids: Eerdmans, 2000), p. 138.

34 Webster, 'Introduction', p. 7.

35 *IST*, p. 19.

4. Jesus, History and God: Pannenberg and Revelation

1 Paul Avis, 'Foreword' in *Divine Revelation* (London: Darton, Longman & Todd, 1997), p. vii.

2 Pannenberg, 'Dogmatic Theses', *RaH*, pp. 123–58.

3 Pannenberg, 'What is a Dogmatic Statement?', *BQT* 1:193.

4 For an introduction to biblical criticism and a vigorous defence of it as Christian interpretation of Scripture, see J. Barton, *The Nature of Biblical Criticism* (Louisville: Westminster/John Knox, 2007).

5 See W. Waxman, 'Kant's Debt to the British Empiricists', in *A Companion to Kant* (ed. G. Bird; Malden: Blackwell, 2006), pp. 93–4, 103–6.

6 H.E. Allison, 'Kant's Transcendental Idealism', in *Companion to Kant*, pp. 111–23.

7 A.W. Wood, 'Rational Theology, Moral Faith, and Religion', in *Cambridge Companion to Kant* (ed. P. Guyer; Cambridge: CUP, 1992), pp. 412–3.

8 The best way to describe the intellectual developments of the late seventeenth, eighteenth and early nineteenth centuries is a matter of dispute. See C. Richter, 'The Productive Power of Reason: Voices on Rationality and Religion – A Sketch of the Development of the Enlightenment and its Aftermath' in *Faith in the Enlightenment? The Critique of the Enlightenment Revisited* (ed. L. Boeve, J. Schrijvers, W. Stoker and Hendrik M. Vroom; Amsterdam: Rodopi, 2006), pp. 23–38.

9 This is not to claim a total break between the Enlightenment and Romanticism; see F.C. Beiser, *The Romantic Imperative: The Concept of Early German Romanticism* (Harvard: Harvard University Press, 2003), pp. 56–9.

10 F. Schleiermacher, *On Religion: Speeches to its Cultured Despisers* (ed. Richard Crouter; Cambridge: CUP, 1988), p. 22.

11 F. Schleiermacher, *The Christian Faith* (ed. H.R. Mackintosh and J.S. Stewart; Edinburgh: T&T Clark, 1960), 1:26. For further discussion of Schleiermacher's view of revelation, see W.E. Wyman, 'Revelation and the Doctrine of Faith: Historical Revelation within the Limits of Historical Consciousness', *JR* 78/1 (January 1998): pp. 41–51.

12 *ST* 1:224.

13 *ST* 1:223 and 'Introduction', *RaH*, pp. 3–5.

14 See *ST* 1:224–6, 239–40, 249.

15 See H. Schwarz, *Theology in a Global Context: The Last Two Hundred Years* (Grand Rapids: Eerdmans, 2005), pp. 41–3, on Rothe; O. Pfleiderer, *The Development of Theology in Germany since Kant: And its Progress in Great Britain since 1825* (London: Sonnenschein, 1890), pp. 148–9, describes Rothe's thought as 'a Christian system of philosophy to which the supernaturalism of the Bible, the theosophy of Schelling and Oetinger, and the theology of Schleiermacher have been made to contribute'; F. Lichtenberger, *History of German Theology in the Nineteenth Century* (ed. W. Hastie; Edinburgh: T&T Clark, 1889), pp. 492–526.

16 See T. Bradshaw, *Trinity and Ontology: A Comparative Study of the Theologies of Karl Barth and Wolfhart Pannenberg* (Edinburgh: Rutherford House, 1988), p. 15.

17 *ST* 1:223.

18 'Introduction', *RaH*, pp. 17–8.

19 *ST* 1:225.

20 See 'Introduction', RaH, p. 12, for Pannenberg's hostility to a Gnostic view of revelation. Bradshaw, *Pannenberg*, p. 33, explains that in Pannenberg's view 'the modern personalistic idea of the Word as a "Thou" directly engaging the hearer is more like the Gnostic than Israelite understanding of revelation in history'.

21 See K. Barth, *Church Dogmatics* Volume 1. *The Doctrine of the Word of God.* Part 1 (ed. G.W. Bromiley and T.F. Torrance; Edinburgh: T&T Clark, 2nd edn, 1975), pp. 88–124.

22 See Barth, *CD* I/1, pp. 227–47 and T. Hart, 'Revelation', in *The Cambridge Companion to Karl Barth* (ed. J. Webster; Cambridge: CUP, 2000), pp. 45–7.

23 Barth, *CD* I/1, p. 228.

24 Hart, 'Revelation', p. 48.

25 Hart, 'Revelation', pp. 50–51.

26 J.P. Cahill, 'The Theological Significance of Rudolph Bultmann', *Theological Studies* 38/2 (Jun 1977): pp. 235–6.

27 R. Bultmann, *Jesus and the Word* (London: Ivor Nicholson & Watson, 1935), p. 14 quoted in H. Schwarz, Theology, p. 276.

28 R. Bultmann, *Faith and Understanding* (ed. R.W. Funk; London: SCM Press, 1969), p. 316.

29 B. Myers, 'Faith as Self-Understanding: Towards a Post-Barthian Appreciation of Rudolf Bultmann', *IJST* 10/1 (January 2008): p. 29, quoting from R. Bultmann, *Jesus Christ and Mythology* (New York: Charles Scribner's Sons, 1958), p. 36.

30 R. Bultmann, 'The New Testament and Mythology', in *Kerygma and Myth, Rudolf Bultmann and Five Critics* (London: SPCK, 1953), cited from http://www.religion-online.org/showbook.asp?title=431 (accessed 13 July 2012).

31 *ST* 1:43–4, 227–8. See also Peters, 'Systematic Theology', *Dialog* 37/2 (Spring 1988): pp. 124–5.

32 Wolfhart Pannenberg, 'Kerygma and History', *BQT* 1:83, 85.

33 Pannenberg, 'God's Presence in History', *CC* 98 (11 March 1981): pp. 260–63.

34 *ST* 1:5, 189.

35 *ST* 1:2.

36 Myers, 'Faith', pp. 29–32.

37 'Introduction', *RaH*, pp. 8–13; cf. *ST* 1:198–214.

38 *CD* I/1, p. 169. The reference in *RaH* to *CD* I/1, p. 369 is incorrect.

39 'Dogmatic Theses', pp. 149–52. Gnosticism was an early church heresy which offered a knowledge of God only as a secret available to initiates.

40 *ST* 1:248–56, and see n. 154.

41 'Introduction', *RaH*, p. 4.

42 'Introduction', *RaH*, p. 7. Both Bradshaw and Watts recognize that Pannenberg accepts that self-disclosure is the proper understanding of revelation; Bradshaw, *Pannenberg*, p. 32; G.J. Watts, *Revelation and the Spirit: A Comparative Study of the Relationship between the Doctrine of Revelation and Pneumatology in the Theology of Eberhard Jüngel and Wolfhart Pannenberg* (Milton Keynes: Paternoster, 2005), p. 78.

43 See his general comments regarding Moses' experience which is the most intimate encounter with God in the Old Testament, *ST* 2:203.

44 'Dogmatic Theses', p. 131.

45 *ST* 1:229.

46 *ST* 1:193–5.

47 *ST* 3:603.

48 W. Pannenberg, 'Eternity, Time, and the Trinitarian God', in *Trinity, Time, and Church: A Response to the Theology of Robert W. Jenson* (ed. C.E. Gunton; Grand Rapids/Cambridge, UK: Eerdmans, 2000), p. 70; *ST* 3:606–7.

49 See 'The Crisis in the Scripture Principle', in *BQT* 1:3–6 and *ST* 1:218–9 and A. Dulles, 'Pannenberg on Revelation and Faith', *TWP*, pp. 171–6.

50 *ST* 1:229.

51 'Dogmatic Theses', p. 125.

52 *ST* 1:206–7, and see 'Introduction', *RaH*, pp. 8–16 and *ST* 1:203–6.

53 *ST* 1:243–4.

54 See *ST* 1:214 for comments on 'the debatability of the reality of God'.

55 *ST* 1:185–6.

56 See *ST* 2:115–46 for Pannenberg's discussion of the place of humanity in the sequence of forms and the connections between creation and eschatology.

57 *ST* 1:199–213, and see Grenz, *Reason for Hope*, p. 32.

58 Bradshaw, *Trinity*, p. 290, comments that although Pannenberg holds that every aspect of reality is related to God's reality and so 'shot through with God', he also holds that 'noetically the only access to this fact is via Jesus' life'. This confirms the following analysis of Pannenberg's christological focus in revelation. *ST* 1:257, concludes the chapter on revelation, claiming that all theology is 'to be seen and developed as an explication of the self-revelation of God in Jesus Christ'; see also Watts, *Revelation*, pp. 84–8.

59 See Bradshaw, *Trinity*, pp. 152–6 on the centrality of the resurrection of Jesus in Pannenberg's doctrine of revelation.

60 *ST* 1:247.

61 *ST* 1:326, 334.

62 *ST* 2:342–3, 'the Easter event means directly that God himself justified the condemned and executed Jesus . . . by the Spirit'.

63 *ST* 2:345.

64 *ST* 1:212–3.

65 *ST* 1:212–4, 246–7 quote from p. 247. Pannenberg also allows that 'materially this thought is present already in what John says about the incarnation'.

⁶⁶ *JGM*, p. 66.

⁶⁷ *ST* 1:224ff., 249, referring to R. Rothe, *Offenbarung*, I, *TSK* 31 (1858), pp. 3–49. See Grenz, *Reason for Hope*, pp. 34–5, for a discussion of Pannenberg's assessment of Rothe.

⁶⁸ *ST* 1:255–56; Eberhard Jüngel, *God as the Mystery of the World* (Grand Rapids: Eerdmans, 1983), p. 13.

⁶⁹ The place of word in the doctrine of revelation is an area in which Pannenberg's theology has very clearly developed. In the 'Dogmatic Theses' he argues that 'the word of the kerygma is not its own revelatory event in any isolated fashion, but is an aspect of the event of revelation in that it reports the eschatological event' ('Dogmatic Theses', p. 155). In *ST* his basic claim has not changed, but he does allow for a fuller inclusion of 'word' in the theology of revelation.

⁷⁰ *ST* 1:250, n. 158, claims that this is not a different view from that of *RaH*, but that there it was dealt with 'too cursorily' which allowed misunderstanding, and it needs a 'stronger profile'.

⁷¹ *ST* 1:249–50.

⁷² 'Dogmatic Theses', pp. 153–5.

⁷³ *ST* 1:251–2 including n. 163. 'Dogmatic Theses', pp. 154–5, discussing Thesis 7, says, 'the *kerygma* is not by itself a revelatory speech by virtue of its formal characteristic, that is, as a challenge or call. The *kerygma* is to be understood solely on the basis of its content', contra Bultmann for whom the word of God is 'address without legitimation'.

⁷⁴ *ST* 1:252 quoting G. Ebeling, *Gott und Wort* (Tübingen: J.C.B. Mohr, 1966), pp. 50–58.

⁷⁵ See G. Ebeling, *God and Word* (Philadelphia: Fortress, 1967), pp. 24–32 and the discussion in W.S. Biddy, 'Review of Wolfhart Pannenberg on Human Linguisticality and the Word of God', *AD* 5 (2005), §§20–23. www.arsdisputandi.org/publish/articles/000219/article.pdf (accessed 10 July 2012).

⁷⁶ *ATP*, pp. 316–84.

⁷⁷ *ST* 1:253–4. The gospel report 'makes the history of Jesus Christ a present event to those who hear it, since it has as its content the manifestation of the future of God'.

⁷⁸ *ST* 1:255. Pannenberg argues that in the Bible, God's word is 'subject to divine freedom' and is related to historical salvation, not prehistorical order (which would be mythical). God's word in the Bible is also wisdom which 'views the order of the world . . . in terms of the regularity of occurrence'. Wisdom and history converge in the Bible

'so that in place of the mythical word which is the basis of the world we now have the thought of the revelation of the divine plan for history, the divine "mystery"' (pp. 254–5).

79 *ST* 1:257.

80 *JGM*, pp. 67–73; cf. the comment in *ST* 1:224, 'The unity of the content of Scripture (res scripturae) which, for Luther, was intimately related to the clarity of Scripture, is hardly visible any longer among the differentiation of the witnesses'; Pannenberg's acceptance of the Enlightenment account of rationality, though qualified, means that in his view critical assessments of the Bible will largely be accepted. *ST* 3:146–7 states: 'the Enlightenment replaced the need to rely on the authority of traditions for knowledge of the past with the new historical scholarship and its principle of critical reconstruction' with the result that 'if . . . Christian theology clings to the authoritative form of establishing its teaching . . . then in a way that was not true in earlier centuries it comes into basic conflict with reason'. See also 'Crisis', pp. 1–14.

81 *ST* 2:463–4. Wolfhart Pannenberg, 'On the Inspiration of Scripture', *ThTo* 54/2 (1997), p. 215 gives a more recent statement, 'The sequence of argument has to proceed . . . starting from the apostolic gospel . . . [so] the doctrine of scriptural inspiration does not yield a formal guarantee of the truth of each and every single biblical sentence before one has concerned oneself with any of the contents of Scripture'.

82 'What is a Dogmatic Statement?', *BQT* 1:195–7.

83 *ST* 1:231.

84 Pannenberg develops his doctrine of revelation in *ST* 1 without assuming biblical authority and that volume does not establish a positive doctrine of Scripture. He returns to the question of Scripture in *ST* 2. For comments about the position of the doctrine of Scripture in between soteriology and ecclesiology see 'Inspiration', p. 214; cf. 'Crisis', p. 11.

85 *ST* 2:459.

86 *ST* 2:464.

87 *ST* 2:463. *TPS*, p. 379, sets biblical studies the task of 'historical procedure . . . set within a theologically oriented history of religions which would be theology of religions'. In this setting 'the phenomena of the history of Judaeo-Christian religion themselves and their own context in that history [of religions] . . . requires them to be interpreted as the self-manifestation of the divine power

over everything'. In this process the questions arise of 'whether and how far the religious conceptions documented in these texts were adequate to the experience of the reality of their period, how far therefore they were able to describe the divine activity they claimed to have taken place as a manifestation of the all-determining reality'.

88 *TPS*, p. 375, treats questions of canon as truly secondary and views historical theology and biblical exegesis as part of the same discipline; *ST* 2 places greater stress on the significance of canon.

89 See Bradshaw, *Trinity*, p. 137; C. Mostert, 'From Eschatology to Trinity: Pannenberg's Doctrine of God', *Pacifica* 10 (February 1997): pp. 71–2.

90 Grenz, *Reason for Hope*, pp. 31–2, cf. Bradshaw, *Trinity*, p. 150.

91 S. Lösel, 'Wolfhart Pannenberg's Response to the Challenge of Religious Pluralism: The Anticipation of Divine Absoluteness?', *JES* 34/4 (Fall 1997): pp. 508–509, shows that Pannenberg uses the notion of 'anticipation' to mediate between his view of 'the open-ended character of divine self-revelation in the history of religions' and 'the Christian conviction that God is revealed in a definite and unsurpassable way in Jesus'.

92 D.P. Scaer, 'Theology of Hope', in *Tensions in Contemporary Theology* (ed. S.N. Gundry and Alan F. Johnson; Chicago: Moody Press; 1976), p. 225.

93 Molnar, 'Some Problems', pp. 333–7, quoting from *ST* 1:253–4.

94 Two works which do this well in evangelical thought about revelation are K.J. Vanhoozer, *First Theology: God, Scripture and Hermeneutic* (Downers Grove: IVP, 2002) and T. Work, *Living and Active: Scripture in the Economy of Salvation* (Grand Rapids: Eerdmans, 2002).

95 *ST* 2:463–4.

96 *ST* 1:231–2, n. 104, indicates Pannenberg's rejection of a 'mere history of political and economic facts'.

97 Grenz, *Reason for Hope*, p. 48, notes that Pannenberg has been criticized for 'minimizing the Bible as divine revelation'. Grenz defends him arguing that Pannenberg emphasizes the importance of showing the historical truth of biblical texts and that he 'includes lengthy and illuminating discussions of biblical materials throughout the dogmatics'. Despite Grenz's defences, I maintain that Pannenberg does not pay sufficient attention to the texts themselves, their literary features and thought forms.

[98] See C. Bartholomew, 'Introduction', in *Behind the Text: History and Biblical Interpretation* (ed. C.S. Evans, M. Healy and M. Rae; Grand Rapids: Zondervan, 2003), pp. 6–8.

[99] 'Inspiration', p. 213.

[100] See N.C. Grubbs and C.S. Drumm, 'What Does Theology Have to Do with the Bible? A Call for the Expansion of the Doctrine of Inspiration', *JETS* 53/1 (March 2010): pp. 65–72 for a survey of evangelical accounts of the doctrine of inspiration.

[101] Grenz, *Reason for Hope*, p. 182, observes that Pannenberg offers a doctrine of redemption which is pneumatological and includes an ecclesiology grounded in apostolic preaching. He suggests that, since the apostolic preaching is recorded in Scripture, Pannenberg's doctrine of redemption 'raises again the question of biblical inspiration' and that 'Pannenberg may be providing . . . a new foundation for such a doctrine', cf. comments on pp. 47–9. Gutenson, *Reconsidering*, pp. 47–50, comments that a fuller doctrine of Scripture could be developed on the basis of a 'possible argument that might be presented in a manner consistent with Pannenberg's broader set of concerns, one that Pannenberg should find acceptable'.

[102] R.T. France, *Jesus and the Old Testament: His Application of Old Testament Passages to Himself and His Mission* (London: Tyndale, 1971), pp. 259–63, records approximately 140 distinct quotations of or allusions to the Hebrew Bible attributed to Jesus in the Synoptic Gospels.

[103] Ben F. Meyer, 'Appointed Deed, Appointed Doer: Jesus and the Scriptures', in *Authenticating the Activities of Jesus* (ed. B. Chilton and C.A. Evans; Boston: Brill, 2002), p. 170. See also M.J. Borg, *Conflict, Holiness, and Politics in the Teachings of Jesus* (Harrisburg: Trinity Press; rev. edn, 1998), pp. 85, 721; N.T. Wright, *The New Testament and the People of God* (London: SPCK, 1992), pp. 216–43; N.T. Wright, *Jesus and the Victory of God* (London: SPCK, 1996), pp. 198–442.

[104] 'Hermeneutic and Universal History', *BQT* 1:96. Gutenson, *Reconsidering*, p. 49, comments at the conclusion of his presentation of an alternative view of Scripture developed from Pannenberg's thought, 'we need not argue that one can set aside the hypothetical nature of theology or the need to inquire systematically into the truth of the doctrinal claims of the Christian faith'. He also summarizes Pannenberg's questioning of Scripture and doctrine (p. 22).

5. How the Future Makes the Past: Pannenberg and Metaphysics

[1] e.g. 'What is Truth?' *BQT* 2:12–16.

[2] *ST* 3:444–5; 'Speaking about God', pp. 108–10; *ATP*, p. 506. See also Grenz, *Reason for Hope*, pp. 140–41.

[3] *ST* 2:218–31, 258–60 and Grenz, *Reason for Hope*, pp. 133–4.

[4] 'Speaking about God', p. 110; see also Mostert, *God and the Future*, pp. 97–9.

[5] 'Speaking about God', p. 107, and see Mostert, *God and the Future*, p. 57.

[6] *ATP*, p. 485; and see Mostert, *God and the Future*, pp. 70–74.

[7] *ATP*, pp. 502, 514–5.

[8] *TPS*, p. 137. Shults, *Postfoundationalist Task*, p. 70, describes the distinction as follows: 'explanation aims for universal, transcontextual understanding, and understanding derives from particular contextualized explanations'.

[9] *TPS*, pp. 154.

[10] See *MIG*, p. 22.

[11] John W. Burbidge, 'Hegel's Conception of Logic' in *The Cambridge Companion to Hegel* (ed. F.C. Beiser; Cambridge: CUP, 1993), p. 93.

[12] Mostert, *God and the Future*, p. 69.

[13] *TPS*, p. 68; cf. *ATP*, p. 515.

[14] *MIG*, p. vii.

[15] *MIG*, p. 22.

[16] *MIG*, p. 42.

[17] *MIG*, pp. 24–5.

[18] In this he appeals to Schleiermacher, *MIG*, p. 25; more surprisingly, he also appeals to Descartes, *MIG*, pp. 27–8.

[19] Here Pannenberg acknowledges Fitche's objection to such an idea, *MIG*, p. 34.

[20] *MIG*, pp. 35–6.

[21] *MIG*, p. 37.

[22] *MIG*, pp. 39–41.

[23] *MIG*, pp. 43–6. Pannenberg traces this view in the thinking of Fitche and Hegel after Kant.

[24] *MIG*, p. 46.

[25] *MIG*, pp. 47–53, quote from p. 53. The details of this developmental argument are presented more fully in *ATP*, pp. 179–224.

²⁶ *MIG*, p. 56.

²⁷ *MIG*, p. 61.

²⁸ *MIG*, p. 62.

²⁹ *MIG*, p. 66.

³⁰ *MIG*, p. 68.

³¹ *MIG*, p. 72. See also the fuller examination of process thought in pp. 113–29.

³² *MIG*, pp. 71–5.

³³ For a fuller explanation of Plotinus, see D. Allen, *Philosophy for Understanding Theology* (Atlanta: Westminster John Knox Press, 1985), pp. 46–63 and R.T. Wallis, *Neoplatonism* (London: Duckworth, 1972).

³⁴ *MIG*, pp. 77–8, quotes Plotinus, *Enneads* (trans. A.H Armstrong; Cambridge: Harvard University Press, 1967), 3.7.11, 343, 'Instead of the completed infinite and whole, [there is only] the moment after moment into the infinite; instead of the unitary whole, [only] the partial and always merely future whole.'

³⁵ Augustine, *Confessions* (Oxford: Oxford University Press; 1991), XI.xx (26), p. 235, 'What is by now evident and clear is that neither future nor past exists, and it is inexact language to speak of three times – past, present and future. Perhaps it would be more exact to say: there are three times, a present of things past, a present of things present and a present of things to come. In the soul there are these three aspects of time, and I do not see them anywhere else.'

³⁶ *MIG*, pp. 79–82.

³⁷ M. Heidegger, *Being and Time* (London: SCM; 1962), p. 307.

³⁸ *MIG*, pp. 83–6.

³⁹ *MIG*, p. 77.

⁴⁰ *MIG*, pp. 86–7.

⁴¹ *MIG*, p. 88.

⁴² *ST* 2:303, n. 92.

⁴³ Rudolf A. Makkreel, *Dilthey: Philosopher of the Human Studies* (Princeton: Princeton University Press, 1975), p. 345.

⁴⁴ *MIG*, p. 94.

⁴⁵ *MIG*, pp. 95–6. T.S. Labute, 'The Ontological Motif of Anticipation in the Theology of Wolfhart Pannenberg', *JETS* 37/2 (June 1994): p. 277, observes that 'the ideas that are being proposed by Pannenberg are not to be understood as merely on an epistemological basis . . . he is proposing an ontology that is future oriented'.

⁴⁶ *MIG*, p. 97.

47 'On Historical and Theological Hermeneutic', p. 181. See comments of Clayton, 'Anticipation', p. 129, and Mostert, *God and the Future*, pp. 112–6.

48 Lösel, 'Wolfhart Pannenberg's Response', p. 515; Molnar, 'Some Problems', p. 323.

49 *MIG*, pp. 104–5; cf. W. Pannenberg, *Theology and the Kingdom of God* (ed. R.J. Neuhaus; Philadelphia: Westminster; 1969), p. 65.

50 *MIG*, p. 107.

51 *MIG*, pp. 107–8, 125–9. Pannenberg notes that an obvious objection to his view is that natural sciences describe reality as moving from the past not the future (p. 108). In *MIG* he suggests how field theory may allow this, but does not present there. The argument can be found in *ST* 2:79–84.

52 *MIG*, p. 109.

53 *MIG*, p. 109.

54 *ST* 1:401–10, and Pannenberg, 'Eternity, Time, and the Trinitarian God', pp. 62–70.

55 'Eternity, Time, and the Trinitarian God', p. 63, comments on Augustine; *ST* 1:405, comments on Nelson Pike, *God and Timelessness* (London: Routledge & Kegan Paul, 1970).

56 See 'Eternity, Time, and the Trinitarian God', p. 67, for discussion; cf. *ST* 1:331.

57 *ST* 1:401–8; cf. 'Eternity, Time, and the Trinitarian God', pp. 63–5. Pannenberg notes that even Plato sought to express some positive relation between time and eternity. Mostert, *God and the Future*, pp. 106–9, comments on the importance for Pannenberg's thought of God's involvement in time and his assessment of Augustine and Plotinus.

58 'Eternity, Time, and the Trinitarian God', p. 65.

59 'Eternity, Time, and the Trinitarian God', p. 54.

60 'Eternity, Time, and the Trinitarian God', pp. 66–7.

61 *ST* 1:410.

62 Clayton, 'Anticipation', p. 129, in 1988, commented that Pannenberg had not offered an explicit definition of 'anticipation'. Even in *MIG* (which Clayton translated) there is no full definition. The words Pannenberg uses for this idea are Antizipation and Vorgriff which are both translated as 'anticipation' in most English translations. He also uses the adjective antizipatorischen and the verb antizipieren. Occasionally he uses the noun Prolepse (prolepsis) and the adjective

proleptisch (proleptic) as synonyms for 'anticipation' and 'anticipatory'. The phrases 'the retroactive power of the future' and 'irruption from the future' express the same thought from a different perspective.

[63] See also Mostert, *God and the Future*, p. 116.

[64] *TKG*, pp. 56, 61.

[65] *MIG*, p. 88.

[66] Aristotle, *Aristotle in Twenty-three Volumes*. Volume 17. *The Metaphysics. Books 1–9* (trans. H. Tredennick; (London: Heinemann, 1975), VIII.vi.5, 425.

[67] *MIG*, p. 106.

[68] Louis P. Pojman, 'Relativism', *CDP*, p. 790. See further Maria Baghramian, *Relativism* (Abingdon: Routledge, 2004), p. 6.

[69] Allan D. Galloway, 'Theology Today', in *The History of Christian Theology* Volume 1 *The Science of Theology* (ed. G.R. Evans, Alister E. McGrath and Allan D. Galloway; Marshall Pickering: Basingstoke, 1986), p. 347, comments that 'this viewpoint lays the foundation for the reintegration of the historical and existential with the metaphysical and essential'.

[70] Roger Olson, 'Wolfhart Pannenberg's Doctrine of the Trinity', *SJT* 43 (1990): p. 203.

[71] William J. Hill, 'The Historicity of God', *TS* 45 (1984): p. 323; and J. Polkinghorne, *Faith, Science and Understanding* (London: SPCK: 2000), pp. 167–8, observes that while it is possible to solve physics equations in such a way that 'effects propagate from the future into the past', in fact the universe always runs the other way, and he asserts 'it is perfectly possible to combine ordinary notions of causality . . . with the belief that the determinative divine purposes will be fulfilled'.

[72] D. McKenzie, *Wolfhart Pannenberg and Religious Philosophy* (Lanham: University Press of America, 1980), p. 129.

[73] David A. Pailin, review of *Metaphysics and the Idea of God* by Wolfhart Pannenberg, *Theology* 44 (May–June, 1991): p. 209.

[74] George Pattison, review of *Metaphysics and the Idea of God* by Wolfhart Pannenberg, *ExpTim* 102/8 (May 1991): p. 2.

[75] Mostert, *God and the Future*, p. 125.

[76] Clayton, 'Translator's Preface', *MIG*, p. viii.

[77] Clayton, 'Anticipation', pp. 136–42; Lewis S. Ford, 'The Nature of the Power of the Future', in *TWP*, pp. 85–90; David P. Polk, 'The All-Determining God and the Peril of Determinism', in *TWP*, pp. 152–68.

78 Polk, 'All-Determining God', p. 163, from L.B. Gilkey, 'Pannenberg's Basic Questions in Theology: A Review Article', *Perspective* 14 (1973): p. 53.

79 Mostert, *God and the Future*, pp. 97–104.

80 *ST* 3:462.

81 Clayton, 'Anticipation', in *TWP*, pp. 136–42; R. Olson, review of *Metaphysics and the Idea of God* in *JR* 72/2 (1992): p. 286.

82 Olson, review of *MIG*, p. 286. This is in contrast to R. Olson, 'Trinity and Eschatology: The Historical Being of God in Jürgen Moltmann and Wolfhart Pannenberg', *SJT* 36 (1983): pp. 222–3, where he expresses the view that Pannenberg's metaphysical suggestions made his position 'a more viable doctrine of the immanent and economic Trinity' than Moltmann; and that Pannenberg's view of the relationship between present and future is 'the key to making this reciprocal causality [between God's historical being and his transcendence] ontologically feasible'. Olson, 'Pannenberg's Doctrine of the Trinity', pp. 201–6 returns to a greater appreciation of Pannenberg, suggesting that *ST* sheds some light on his 'understanding of this enigmatic power of the future', though still holding that for some the enigma will only be deepened and that the 'eschatological ontology' retains an ambiguity.

83 Mostert, *God and the Future*, p. 125.

84 Mostert, *God and the Future*, p. 235.

6. Jesus, God and History: Pannenberg and Christology

1 *JGM*, p. 33. *ST* 2:278, defines 'Christology from above' as any view that takes 'the whole *NT* witness to Christ from the standpoint of [the] sending of the pre-existent Son into the world'. See Bradshaw, *Pannenberg*, pp. 68–70, for a further discussion of Pannenberg's 'Christology from below'.

2 *ST* 2:287.

3 An example of the first is Isaak A. Dorner (1809–84); see *ST* 2:279 and J.M. Drickamer, 'Higher Criticism and the Incarnation in The Thought of I.A. Dorner', *CTQ* 43.3 (July 1979): pp. 97–206. The second approach includes Schleiermacher and Wilhelm Herrmann (1846–1922); see *ST* 2:281.

4 *JGM*, p. 34.

5 *ST* 2:325; *JGM*, pp. 34–5.

6 *JGM*, p. 158.

7 *JGM*, p. 35.

8 *ST* 2:278–323 discusses the relationship between general anthropology and Christology.

9 *ST* 2:301; see Bradshaw, *Pannenberg*, pp. 96–8 and Grenz, *Reason for Hope*, pp. 160–61, for further discussion of Pannenberg's assessment of Chalcedon.

10 *ST* 2:384; cf. *JGM*, pp. 291–2.

11 *JGM*, pp. 405–6.

12 *ST* 2:288–9.

13 *JGM*, p. 134.

14 *ST* 2:328–34, quote from p. 334.

15 *ST* 2:334.

16 *ST* 2:335–43, quotes from p. 343; see *JGM*, pp. 66–73.

17 See R. Letham, *The Trinity* (Phillipsburg: P&R, 2005), pp. 392–404, for a discussion.

18 See J. Thompson, *Modern Trinitarian Perspectives* (New York and Oxford: OUP, 1994), pp. 47–9.

19 *ST* 1:263.

20 *ST* 1:309.

21 *ST* 1:264–5.

22 *ST* 2:372–3.

23 *ST* 2:377.

24 *ST* 2:313.

25 *JGM*, p. 157. ST 2:302–3 explains that 'the particular identity of [Jesus'] person is related to the course of his history . . . only in the light of this outcome may we say . . . that the child Jesus who was born of Mary was the Messiah and the Son of God . . . rightly the christology of the early church found the uniqueness of Jesus in his divine sonship'.

26 *ST* 2:63.

27 I.A. Dorner, *System der christlichen Glaubenslehre* (Berlin: Verlag von Wilhelm Hertz, 1886), 2:431, quoted in Drickamer, 'Higher Criticism', p. 202.

28 Drickamer, p. 204f. Ironically, Dorner's view of Jesus after his resurrection and ascension seems to be almost Eutychian, a view that Christ has only one (divine) nature.

29 *JGM*, p. 307.

30 *ST* 2:319; cf. pp. 367–71. *JGM*, p. 141, argues similarly that 'if Jesus as a person is "the Son of God", as becomes clear retroactively from

his resurrection, then he has always been the Son of God' (emphasis added); and see *JGM*, pp. 152–8.

[31] *ST* 2:301–3.

[32] *ST* 2:389. Bradshaw, *Trinity*, p. 157, points out that Pannenberg focuses on the 'Father–Jesus relation rather than the Word–Jesus relation'.

[33] *ST* 2:391–2.

[34] *ST* 2:389, n. 188, describes his solution as a variation of Leontius' model of enhypostatic union; cf. *JGM*, pp. 337–44.

[35] See *ST* 1:319–27.

[36] *ST* 1:383–4.

[37] See Jenson for an illuminating and appreciative discussion of this aspect of Pannenberg's Christology; R. Jenson, 'Jesus in the Trinity: Wolfhart Pannenberg's Christology and the Doctrine of the Trinity', in *TWP*, pp. 192–5.

[38] *ST* 2:347–63.

[39] *ST* 2:344.

[40] *ST* 2:345.

[41] *ST* 2:283ff. Mostert, *God and the Future*, p. 43, shows that 'the resurrection of Jesus is of foundational importance in Pannenberg's theology'; see full discussion (pp. 43–54).

[42] *JGM*, p. 137. The first quote is from O. Webber, *Grundlagen der Dogmatik* Band II (Neukirchen: Verlag der Buchhandlung des Erziehungsvereins, 1962), p. 102, which Pannenberg accepts and expands.

[43] P. Molnar, *Incarnation and Resurrection: Toward a Contemporary Understanding* (Grand Rapids: Eerdmans, 2007), p. 261. See Grenz, *Reason for Hope*, pp. 179–200 for a review of the major criticisms of Pannenberg's Christology and a thoughtful defence of it against many of the criticisms. A.C. Thiselton, *The Hermeneutics of Doctrine* (Grand Rapids: Eerdmans, 2007), pp. 410–13, offers a very appreciative assessment of Pannenberg's Christology.

[44] T. Weinandy, *In the Likeness of Sinful Flesh: An Essay on the Humanity of Christ* (Edinburgh: T&T Clark, 1993), p. 3.

[45] *JGM*, p. 33, n. 24.

[46] G.C. Berkouwer, *The Person of Christ* (trans. J.H. Kok; Grand Rapids: Eerdmans, 1977), p. 212.

[47] *Sources of Catholic Dogma* (ed. H. Denzinger and K. Rahner, St. Louis and London: Herder, 1957), pp. 2183–5

[48] The summary of approaches is largely taken from H.F. Carl, 'Only the Father Knows: Historical and Evangelical Responses to Jesus' Escha-

tological Ignorance in Mark 13:32', *JBS* 1/3 (July–September 2001), http://journalofbiblicalstudies.org/issue3.html (accessed July 30, 2009, no longer available).

49 B.B. Warfield, 'The Human Development of Jesus', in *Selected Shorter Writings of Benjamin B. Warfield*, Vol 1. (ed. J.E. Meeter; Nutley: Presbyterian and Reformed, 1970), p. 164, states that the question of Jesus' knowledge is 'a topic very much under discussion nowadays'.

50 Warfield, 'Human Development', p. 164, 'there is mystery enough attaching to the conception; but the glory of the Incarnation is that it presents to our adoring gaze, not a humanized God or a deified man, but a true God-man'.

51 Thomas Aquinas, *Summa Theologica*, III.15.3 resp.; III.10.2 ad.1. takes a similar approach.

52 Scotus, *Opus Oxoniense* (Ordinatio), 1.3, dist. 14, q.2, n. 20. quoted in R. Sturch, *The Word and the Christ: An Essay in Analytic Christology* (Oxford: Clarendon Press, 1991), p. 25.

53 Carl, 'Only the Father Knows', pp. 5, 18–19. See F.X. Gumerlock, 'Mark 13:32 and Christ's Supposed Ignorance: Four Patristic Solutions', *TrinJ* 28 (2007): p. 213.

54 *JGM*, p. 333. K. Rahner, *Theological Investigations* (trans. Karl-Heinz Kruger; New York: Crossroad, 1983), 5:202, states that 'a philosophy of the person and of the freedom of a finite being, a philosophy of history and of decisions, could undoubtedly show with comparative ease that the fact of challenge, of going into the open, of confiding oneself to the incalculable, of the obscurity of origin and the veiled nature of the end – in short, of a certain kind of ignorance – are all necessary factors in the very nature of self-realization of the finite person in the historical decisions of freedom'.

55 W. Wrede, *The Messianic Secret* (Cambridge: James Clarke, 1971, 1st pub. 1901).

56 D.F. Watson, *Honor Among Christians: The Cultural Key to the Messianic Secret* (Minneapolis: Fortress, 2010), pp. 3–12.

57 C.M. Tuckett, 'Messianic Secret', in *The Anchor Bible Dictionary* (ed. David N. Freedman et al.; 6 vols; New York: Doubleday, 1992), 4:797.

58 H. Bavinck, *Reformed Dogmatics*, Vol. 3, Sin and Salvation in Christ (ed. John Bolt; Grand Rapids: Baker Academic, 2006), pp. 406–10.

59 *ST* 2:389; cf. *ST* 2:372–3; cf. *JGM*, pp. 324–37.

60 *ST* 2:364, 391.

61 *ST* 2:312–4, refers to Ferdinand Hahn, *The Titles of Jesus in Christology: Their History in Early Christianity* (London: Lutterworth, 1969); E.P. Sanders, *Jesus and Judaism* (London: SCM Press, 1985) and D.R. Catchpole, 'The Answer of Jesus to Caiaphas (Matt. xxvi, 64)', *NTS* 17 (1971): pp. 213–26.

62 e.g. R.W. Funk, ed., *The Acts of Jesus: What Did Jesus Really Do? The Search for the Authentic Deeds of Jesus* (San Francisco: Harper Collins, 1998); G.W.E. Nickelsburg, 'Son of Man', *ABD* 6:149 and M. Casey, *The Solution to the 'Son of Man' Problem* (London: Continuum, 2007), argue that Jesus' use of 'son of man' was not a messianic title but simply a term of self-reference.

63 B. Witherington, *Jesus, Paul and the End of the World* (Downers Grove; IVP, 1992), p. 170 and see whole discussion (pp. 170–77). His focus is on finding what Jesus expected for 'the coming of the Son of Man'.

64 M.F. Bird, *Are You the One who is to Come?: The Historical Jesus and the Messianic Question* (Grand Rapids: Baker Academic, 2009), p. 65.

65 Wright, *Jesus and the Victory of God*, p. 539, comes to a similar conclusion.

66 'Many commentators and exegetes do not even raise the possibility of seeing pre-existence in the Gospels of Matthew, Mark and Luke', S. Gathercole, *The Pre-existent Son: Recovering the Christologies of Matthew, Mark and Luke* (Grand Rapids: Eerdmans, 2006), p. 5.

67 Gathercole, *Pre-existent Son*, p. 87.

68 Positive reviews include P. Foster, *ExpTim* 118.7 (April 2007): pp. 357–8; D.R. Streett, *CTR* 4/2 (Spr. 2007): pp. 115–17; F.J. Matera, *RBL* 04/2007, http://www.bookreviews.org (accessed 13 December 2007); Robert L. Webb, *JSHJ* 5/2 (July 2007), p. 215. The strongly negative review is from J.D.G. Dunn, *RBL* 04/2007, http://www.bookreviews.org (accessed 13 December 2007).

69 See Alister E. McGrath, *The Making of Modern German Christology* (Oxford: Basil Blackwell; 1986), pp. 160–80, who sets Pannenberg clearly in his New Quest context.

70 Craig A. Evans, 'Assessing Progress in the Third Quest of the Historical Jesus', *JSHJ* 4/1 (January 2006): pp. 43–4, 47 and 49–54. J.H. Charlesworth, *The Historical Jesus: An Essential Guide* (Nashville: Abingdon Press, 2008), pp. 8–12 outlines the era of 'Jesus Research', as he prefers to call the Third Quest. His own conclusion on the evidence is cautious: 'There is evidence that Jesus may have had a messianic consciousness' (p. 110). Martin Hengel, *Studies in Early Christology*

(Edinburgh: T&T Clark, 1995), p. 72, concludes that Jesus 'proved by the methods of historical-critical research . . . conducted himself with that . . . 'apocalyptic' right to usher in God's reign over Israel . . . and as the 'Anointed of God'. See J.D.G. Dunn and S. McKnight, eds, *The Historical Jesus in Recent Research* (Winona Lake: Eisenbrauns, 2005), for a wide range of views on the study of the Historical Jesus edited from a Third Quest perspective.

[71] *ST* 3:626.

[72] Dorothy. A. Lee, *Transfiguration* (London and New York: Continuum, 2004), p. 4. Wright, Jesus and the Victory of God, p. 650, acknowledges the questions about the historicity of the transfiguration, but argues that it fits well into his paradigm of understanding Jesus. See W.L. Liefeld, 'Transfiguration', in *Dictionary of Jesus and the Gospels* (ed. J.B. Green, S. McKnight and I.H. Marshall; Downers Grove: IVP, 1992), pp. 834–41, for a discussion of the historicity of the transfiguration.

[73] Lee, *Transfiguration*, p. 95, and see pp. 125–6.

[74] I will refer to 'the Fourth Gospel' as 'John's Gospel' and the author and the narrator as 'John' while recognizing that some of the scholars I am quoting would not accept these identifications.

[75] See Paul Anderson, 'Beyond the Shade of the Oak Tree: The Recent Growth of Johannine Studies', *ExpTim* 119 (2008): pp. 370–71, for a survey of recent discussion of the historicity of the Fourth Gospel which demonstrates that the matter is far from settled.

[76] M. Casey, *Is John's Gospel True?* (London: Routledge, 1996), p. 62; cf. A.T. Lincoln, ' "We Know that His Testimony is True": Johannine Truth Claims and Historicity', in *John, Jesus, and History*, Vol. 1: *Critical Appraisals of Critical Views* (ed. Paul N. Anderson, Felix Just and Tom Thatcher; Atlanta: SBL, 2007), p. 187. E.K. Broadhead, 'The Fourth Gospel and the Synoptic Saying Source: The Relation Reconsidered', in *Jesus in the Johannine Tradition* (ed. Robert T. Fortna and Tom Thatcher; Louisville: Westminster John Knox, 2001), pp. 291–320 and James D.G. Dunn, *Jesus Remembered* (Grand Rapids: Eerdmans, 2003), pp. 165–7, express similar views.

[77] C.L. Blomberg, *The Historical Reliability of John's Gospel: Issues and Commentary* (Downers Grove: IVP, 2001); P.N. Anderson, *The Fourth Gospel and the Quest for Jesus: Modern Foundations Reconsidered* (London and New York: T&T Clark/Continuum, 2006); R. Bauckham, *Jesus and the Eyewitnesses: The Gospels as Eyewitness Testimony* (Grand Rapids: Eerdmans, 2006), pp. 358–471; P.W. Ensor, 'The Johannine Sayings of

Jesus and the Question of Authenticity' in *Challenging Perspectives on the Gospel of John* (ed. J. Lierman; Tübingen: Mohr Siebeck, 2006), pp. 14–33.

[78] *Work, Living and Active*, p. 186, makes similar observations about the difference between Pannenberg's Christology and the New Testament presentation.

[79] e.g. C. Gunton, *Yesterday and Today: A Study of Continuities in Christology* (Grand Rapids: Eerdmans, 2nd edn, 1997), pp. 18–24; R.E. Olson, 'The Human Self-realization of God: Hegelian Elements in Pannenberg's Christology', *PRSt* 13/3 (Fall 1986): p. 221. On adoptionism see J. Pelikan, *The Christian Tradition: A History of the Development of Doctrine*. Vol. 1 *The Emergence of the Catholic Tradition* (Chicago: University of Chicago Press, 1971–89), pp. 175–6.

[80] *ST* 2:367, 371, 377. Olson, 'Pannenberg's Doctrine of the Trinity', p. 188, comments that it would be 'easy to label [Pannenberg's] account of Jesus' sonship "adoptionistic" . . . were it not for Pannenberg's insistence that there is a reciprocal relationship between the Son and the Father by which the Father also receives his divinity from Jesus the Son'.

[81] Bradshaw, *Trinity*, pp. 291–3.

[82] C.P. Krauth, *Conservative Reformation and its Theology* (Philadelphia: J.B. Lippincott, 1872), p. 459, explains the traditional Lutheran view: 'The body of Christ which, in its own nature, is determinately in heaven, and is thus present nowhere else, nor will be thus present on earth till His second coming, has also another presence, diverse from the determinate, yet no less true. It is present through that Divine nature into whose personality it has been received, and with which it has formed an inseparable union . . . As the divine nature, without extension, expansion, or locality, has a presence which is no less true than the local presence, from which it is wholly diverse, so does it render present the human, which is now in one personality with it, renders it present without extension, expansion, or locality for, as is the presence which the divine has, so must be the presence of the human which it makes.'

[83] See Pelikan, *Christian Tradition*, 4:355–9.

[84] Dietrich Bonhoeffer, *Christology* (trans. J. Bowden; London: Collins, 1966), pp. 93–5.

[85] John Webster, 'Incarnation', in *The Blackwell Companion to Modern Theology* (ed. G. Jones, Oxford: Blackwell, 2004), p. 224.

7. The Heartbeat of Divine Love: Pannenberg and Reconciliation

[1] *ST* 3:646.

[2] *ST* 2:434.

[3] *ST* 2:375.

[4] *ST* 2:406.

[5] *ST* 2:407.

[6] *ST* 2:410.

[7] *ST* 2:421 refers to G. Friedrich, *Die Verkündigung des Todes Jesu im Neuen Testament* (Neukirchen-Vluyn: Neukirchener Verlag, 1982), who concludes that explanations of the cross have to be drawn from contemporary ideas.

[8] *ST* 2:397.

[9] *ST* 2:397–8. *JGM*, pp. 225–32, offers a longer version of this argument with explicit interaction with New Testament scholarship.

[10] This claim is argued in *JGM* and is an assumption of the argument in *ST*, which is expressed in phrases such as 'the proleptic presence of the salvation of divine rule in the message and work of Jesus', *ST* 2:402. *JGM*, pp. 227–8, argues that 'Jesus directly granted eschatological salvation'. Salvation is 'fulfilment of openness for God', and 'it is already present to those who long for the nearness of God proclaimed by Jesus; it has already come to those who hear and accept Jesus' messages of the imminent Kingdom of God'.

[11] *ST* 2:400.

[12] *ST* 2:400.

[13] *ST* 2:416, refers to the Q document and the work of Friedrich, *Verkündigung*, 14–21.

[14] *ST* 2:418.

[15] *ST* 2:423, cf. *JGM*, pp. 354–64.

[16] *ST* 2:425–6.

[17] *ST* 2:426.

[18] *ST* 2:437.

[19] *ST* 2:403, 407.

[20] *ST* 2:412.

[21] *ST* 2:419, 423.

[22] *ST* 2:413.

[23] See I. Kant, *Religion within the Limits of Reason Alone* (trans. and ed. T.M. Greene and H.H. Hudson (New York: Harper & Row, 1960),

pp. 67–70. See D.C. Benner, 'Immanuel Kant's Demythologization of Christian Theories of Atonement in Religion within the Limits of Reason Alone', *EvQ* 79/2 (2007), pp. 99–111, and J.E. Hare, *The Moral Gap: Kantian Ethics, Human Limits, and God's Assistance* (Oxford: Clarendon Press, 1997), pp. 56–7, for convincing arguments that Kant entirely individualizes his account of atonement, despite his references to Jesus.

24 *ST* 2:415.

25 *ST* 2:412–13. See Barth, *CD* IV/1, p. 76.

26 Barth, *CD* IV/1, p. 76. *CD* IV/1, p. 222 says, 'What took place is that the Son of God fulfilled the righteous judgement on us human beings by himself taking our place as a human being and in our place undergoing the judgement under which we had passed.' Pannenberg seems to overstate his case against Barth who does not exclude human response. In his exposition of 2 Cor. 5 Barth writes, 'we must insist at once that the initiative and the decisive action in the happening described as atonement are both with God (as in John 3:16). This is not to say that man's part is only passive: we will see later that there is a proper place for his activity, and what this activity is' (p. 74). Barth's concession at this point, though more than Pannenberg allows for in his account of Barth, does not meet Pannenberg's demand for inclusive representation.

27 *ST* 2:433. Pannenberg does not view Sölle's temporary representation as a sufficient description. In this conception Jesus no longer has a representative role once others come to share his position with him. ST 2:432, and see Dorothy Sölle, *Christ the Representative* (trans. D. Lewis; London: SCM Press, 1967), p. 146.

28 *ST* 2:430. *ST* 2:450, states that Jesus vicariously reconciles 'in exemplary fashion' in his 'acceptance of death [as] the extreme consequence of the self-distinction of the Son from the Father'. Pannenberg agrees with Kähler that Christ's death is a 'sponsoring representation' which is 'orientated to future reception, so that the dedication of our own will to obedience to God is not superfluous but is for the first time made possible'. *ST* 2:414–15; the phrase 'sponsoring representation' is from M. Kähler, *Die Wissenschaft der christlichen Lehre* (Leipzig: Deichert, 2nd edn, 1893), §428.

29 *ST* 2:420.

30 *ST* 2:430–31.

31 *ST* 2:429–30, 435–6, explicitly notes some of the intellectual sources of Pannenberg's concept of inclusive representation.

32 There has been considerable debate about Heidegger's account of death. H. Carel, 'Temporal Finitude and Finitude of Possibility: The Double Meaning of Death in Being and Time', *IJPS* 15/4 (December 2007): p. 548, outlines various analyses and criticisms of Heidegger's view of death. He argues that for Heidegger death marks both 'finitude of possibility' and 'temporal finitude' and that 'because death could come at any moment, the radical contingency of each individual life becomes apparent, and to acknowledge this is to acknowledge finitude'. Pannenberg draws on Heidegger's view that death and awareness of death mark Dasein as finite and so underlines the contingency of Dasein.

33 *ST* 2:427.

34 *ST* 2:433.

35 *ST* 2:433–4.

36 *ST* 2:439.

37 *ST* 2:446.

38 *ST* 2:448. This is only partly true. Calvin's treatment of the threefold office is rich in references to the ongoing work of Christ by the Spirit, J. Calvin, *Institutes of the Christian Religion* (ed. J.T. McNeill; Philadelphia: Westminster, 1960), II.xv.1–6, pp. 494–503. Bavinck, *Reformed Dogmatics*, 3:475–82, who summarizes much of 'older Protestant dogmatics', has a section in his consideration of Christ's state of exaltation which deals with the threefold office. He discusses the work of the Spirit in the continuing work of Christ as prophet and king, and gives a brief reference to the Spirit and Christ's ongoing priesthood. Where both differ from Pannenberg is that they do not include the ongoing work of reconciliation as part of the expiatory work, and so retain the objectivism of which he is critical.

39 *ST* 2:443.

40 Pannenberg uses the term 'ecstatic' to denote the way in which the Spirit takes believers outside themselves to be 'in Christ' and to 'participate in the filial relationship of Jesus with the Father'. In both *ATP*, p. 525 and *ST* 2:196–7, 'ecstatic' describes how humans should live in relation to others and the wider environment, including God, rather than in self-obsession. Grenz, *Reason for Hope*, 132, describes it as 'fellowship with God [that] realizes itself concretely in religious trust, in existence *extra se*'.

41 *ST* 2:454.

42 *ST* 3:7–12.

[43] See C. Hodge, *Systematic Theology*, Vol. 2 (New York : Charles Scribner, 1872), pp. 480–527; J.I. Packer, 'What Did the Cross Achieve? The Logic of Penal Substitution' *TynBul* 25 (1974): pp. 3–45; J. Stott, *The Cross of Christ* (Leicester: IVP, 1986); M.J. Erickson, *Christian Theology* (Grand Rapids: Baker, rev. edn, 1998), pp. 779–858; R.L. Reymond, *A New Systematic Theology of the Christian Faith* (Nashville: Nelson, 1998), pp. 631–42.

[44] Packer, 'What Did the Cross Achieve?', p. 5.

[45] Packer, 'What Did the Cross Achieve?', pp. 23–5.

[46] For recent criticisms see J.B. Green and M.D. Baker, *Recovering the Scandal of the Cross: Atonement in New Testament and Contemporary Contexts* (Downers Grove: IVP, 2000); J.D. Weaver, *The Nonviolent Atonement* (Grand Rapids/Cambridge: Eerdmans, 2001), C.D. Marshall, *Beyond Retribution: A New Testament Vision for Justice, Crime and Punishment* (Grand Rapids/Cambridge UK: Eerdmans; Auckland/Sydney: Lime Grove, 2001); A. Bartlett, *Cross Purposes: The Violent Grammar of Christian Atonement* (Valley Forge: Trinity, 2001); S. Chalke and A. Mann, *The Lost Message of Jesus* (Grand Rapids: Zondervan, 2003); S. Finlan, *Problems with the Atonement: The Origins of, and Controversy about, the Atonement Doctrine* (Collegeville: Liturgical, 2005); D.A. Brondos, *Paul on the Cross: Reconstructing the Apostle's Story of Redemption* (Minneapolis: Fortress, 2006); S.M. Heim, *Saved from Sacrifice: A Theology of the Cross* (Grand Rapids: Eerdmans, 2006); R. L. Shelton, *Cross and Covenant: Interpreting the Atonement for 21st Century Mission* (Carlisle: Paternoster, 2006); M. Trelstad, ed., *Cross Examinations: Readings on the Meaning of the Cross Today* (Minneapolis: Fortress, 2006); V. Westhelle, *The Scandalous God: The Use and Abuse of the Cross* (Minneapolis: Fortress, 2006); B. Jersak and M. Hardin, ed., *Stricken by God? Nonviolent Identification and the Victory of Christ* (Grand Rapids: Eerdmans, 2007).

[47] See D. Peterson ed., *Where Wrath and Mercy Meet: Proclaiming the Atonement Today* (Carlisle: Paternoster, 2001); C.E. Hill, R.R. Nicole and F.A. James, *The Glory of the Atonement* (Downers Grove: IVP, 2004); G.J. Williams, 'Penal Substitution: A Response to Recent Criticism', *JETS* 50/1 (March 2007): pp. 71–86; S. Gathercole, 'The Cross and Substitutionary Atonement', *SBJT* 11/2 (Summer 2007): pp. 64–73; J.B. Hood, 'The Cross in the New Testament: Two Theses in Conversation with Recent Literature (2000–2007)', *WTJ* 71 (2009): pp. 281–95; S. Jeffery, A. Sach and M. Ovey, *Pierced for Our Transgressions* (Leicester: IVP,

2007); W. Edgar, 'Justification and Violence: Reflections on Atonement and Contemporary Apologetics' in *Justified In Christ: God's Plan for Us in Justification* (ed. K. Scott Oliphint; Fearn: Mentor, 2007); I.H. Marshall, *Aspects of the Atonement* (Paternoster, 2008), pp. 131–52 and the collected papers in D. Tidball, D. Hilborn and J. Thacker, eds, *The Atonement Debate: Papers from the London Symposium on the Theology of the Atonement* (Grand Rapids: Zondervan, 2008). Note also H. Boersma, *Violence, Hospitality and the Cross* (Grand Rapids: Baker, 2004) and S. McKnight, *A Community Called Atonement* (Nashville, TN: Abingdon Press, 2007).

[48] *ST* 2:422.

[49] *ST* 1:448.

[50] B. Lindars, *The Theology of the Letter to the Hebrews* (Cambridge: CUP, 1991), p. 91.

[51] Lindars, *Hebrews*, pp. 84–5.

[52] H.W. Attridge, *The Epistle to the Hebrews: A Commentary on the Epistle to the Hebrews* (ed. H. Koester; Philadelphia: Fortress Press, 1989), p. 266.

[53] Attridge, *Hebrews*, p. 281.

[54] I. McFarland, 'Christ, Spirit and Atonement', *IJST*, 3/1 (March 2001): p. 89.

[55] *ST* 2:412.

[56] D. Fairbairn, *Grace and Christology in the Early Church* (Oxford: OUP, 2003); cf C.F. Allison, *The Cruelty of Heresy* (SPCK, 1994), pp. 105–51.

[57] Fairbairn, p. 203.

[58] McFarland, 'Christ, Spirit and Atonement', p. 84.

[59] McFarland, 'Christ, Spirit and Atonement', pp. 90–92.

8. The One Who Is All in All: Pannenberg and God

[1] Mostert, 'From Eschatology to Trinity', p. 75, suggests two 'main concerns' in Pannenberg's doctrine of God – the desire to understand God's being eschatologically and problems with the classic doctrine of God. See also Olson, 'Pannenberg's Doctrine of the Trinity', pp. 179–80 and Taylor, *Pannenberg*, pp. 12–13.

[2] *ST* 1:334.

[3] See Taylor, *Pannenberg*, pp. 26–32.

[4] *ST* 1:271–9.

5 *ST* 1:282–9, 295–8.

6 *ST* 1:307–78, 367.

7 See Karl Rahner, *Theological Investigations*, Vol. 4 *More Recent Writings* (London: Darton, Longman & Todd, 1966), p. 94.

8 *ST* 1:332.

9 *ST* 1:331.

10 *ST* 1:360–63.

11 *ST* 1:360, 364.

12 'Anthropology and the Question of God', p. 92. 'Speaking about God', pp. 107–15 and *ST* 2:416 have further discussion of human freedom in reference to the idea of God.

13 'Anthropology and the Question of God', p. 93.

14 *ST* 1:299. Pannenberg is part of a wider stream of modern theology attempting to relate God's triune being to salvation history; see Jenson, 'Jesus in the Trinity' in *TWP*, pp. 197–8 and Taylor, *Pannenberg*, pp. 23–6.

15 *ST* 1:312.

16 *ST* 1:305 notes Aquinas, *Summa*, 1.43.2.

17 *ST* 1:273, 306.

18 *ST* 1:320.

19 Olson, 'Pannenberg's Doctrine of the Trinity', p. 199.

20 See *ST* 1:308–16, 320–23; Taylor, *Pannenberg*, pp. 33–9.

21 *ST* 1:322.

22 *ST* 1:313, 325.

23 So Gregory of Nazianzus, *On Holy Baptism* XL.41, *NPNF* 2 VII, p. 375, states there is 'One God because of the monarchia'; John of Damascus, *On the Orthodox Faith* I.8 *NPNF* 2 IX, p. 9, explains that 'the Father is without cause and unborn . . . the Son is derived from the Father . . . and the Holy Spirit likewise'; Calvin, *Inst* I.xiii.18, pp. 142–3, affirms 'to the Father is attributed the beginning of activity, and the fountain and wellspring of all things'.

24 Jenson, 'Jesus in the Trinity', p. 199.

25 Mostert, 'From Eschatology to Trinity', p. 82.

26 *ST* 1:445ff.; cf. Mostert, 'From Eschatology to Trinity', p. 81.

27 *ST* 1:340.

28 See Olson, 'Pannenberg's Doctrine of the Trinity', p. 189 for a review of Pannenberg's trinitarian doctrine of the Spirit.

29 *ST* 1:314–9, quote is from p. 315.

30 *ST* 1:371ff., quote from p. 377.

31 *ST* 1:383. From modern physics he draws the concept of a field that is 'independent of matter and defined only by [its] relations to space-time'.

32 *ST* 1:373. Pannenberg argues that the Spirit is the biblical *ruach/pneuma* which is associated with force and life, and 'Spirit' embraces the ideas of God's knowledge (his presence to all creation) and power and word. This, he claims, offers a far better conception than the classic view of God as *nous* with reason and intellect based on the Platonic equivalence of *pneuma* and *nous*.

33 *ST* 2:76–84.

34 *ST* 2:84.

35 *ST* 1:321.

36 *ST* 1:322–5. *ST* 2:372–9, states that 'the relation of the Son to the Father is characterized in eternity by the subordination to the Father, by the self-distinction from the majesty of the Father, which took historical form in the human relation of Jesus to God'.

37 *ST* 1:316.

38 Olson, 'Pannenberg's Doctrine of the Trinity', p. 191, explains 'that means that each of the three persons must be understood as related to each other as others and as distinct from themselves. It does not mean . . . that they should be conceived individualistically . . . rather, they are constituted as distinct persons by their inner trinitarian relations, although these cannot be reduced to mere relations or origin'.

39 *ST* 1:389.

40 *ST* 1:387 characterizes God's action as 'a repetition or reiteration of his eternal deity in his relation to the world'.

41 *ST* 1:388.

42 *ST* 1:389. Mostert, *God and the Future*, pp. 80–81, shows how this conception of divine action is an expression of Pannenberg's view that God acts 'from the future'.

43 *ST* 1:391.

44 *ST* 1:385, original emphasis. Grenz, *Reason for Hope*, p. 49, has an apposite summary: 'Pannenberg offers a radical reinterpretation of self-differentiation . . . namely, that the essence of person lies in the act of giving oneself to one's counterpart and thereby gaining one's identity from the other.'

45 *ST* 1:307, and see 328ff. See Taylor, *Pannenberg*, pp. 39–43. Pelikan, *Christian Tradition*, 5:198, traces a reversal of the relationship, so that during the nineteenth century much theology came to see that the

immanent Trinity rested on the economic, where previously the immanent was the 'presupposition' of other doctrines.

[46] K. Rahner, *The Trinity* (trans. J. Donceel; London: Burns & Oates, 1970), p. 48, writes: 'it is a fact of salvation history that we know about the Trinity because the Father's Word has entered our history and has given us his Spirit'.

[47] *ST* 1:329 argues that God 'has made himself dependent upon the course of history'; Bradshaw, *Trinity*, p. 205, comments that Pannenberg has 'boldly sought to integrate Trinity with universal history and creation'.

[48] *ST* 3:642–4.

[49] *ST* 1:331; cf. *TKG*, p. 56, and 'Speaking about God', *BQT* 3:110; and see Bradshaw, *Trinity*, p. 42.

[50] *ST* 1:438 and see pp. 422–8.

[51] *ST* 1:330.

[52] Olson, 'Pannenberg's Doctrine of the Trinity', pp. 198–9.

[53] Bradshaw, *Trinity*, pp. 205ff., offers a fine summary of the way Pannenberg uses his view of God as future to relate God to the world without teaching a 'purely economic trinitarianism which would makes a relation to the world necessary for God'.

[54] *ST* 1:357–8.

[55] *ST* 1:331.

[56] Pannenberg, 'Eternity, Time, and the Trinitarian God', in *Trinity, Time, and Church* (ed. C.E. Gunton; Grand Rapids: Eerdmans, 2000), p. 69, states, 'the Son is the future of the Father, because it is the Son who establishes the kingdom of the Father . . . the Spirit is the future of the Son, since it is the Spirit who raises Jesus . . . the Father is the future of both, the Son and the Spirit, since it is the Father's kingdom they bring about by their joint activities'.

[57] 'Eternity, Time, and the Trinitarian God', p. 69; cf. *ST* 1:410. Mostert, 'From Eschatology to Trinity', pp. 79–80, comments that *ST* represents a development in Pannenberg's thought from an earlier emphasis on God as 'pure futurity' to understanding this in terms of God's eternity. He suggests that this 'represents the replacement of a programmatic (even polemic) line of thought with a more careful working out of the Christian doctrine of God', though this 'represents no substantial change in Pannenberg's thought'. It is a maturing in his thought, and should be viewed as clarification.

[58] J. Cobb, 'Pannenberg and Process Theology', in *TWP*, pp. 54–73, confirms that it is Pannenberg's view of the future which sets him

apart from process theology when he comments that because Pannenberg 'holds that our historical destiny is assured' he cannot fully affirm human freedom (p. 68).

59 *ST* 1:390.

60 *ST* 1:408–9.

61 *ST* 1:405 states, 'the Bible stresses God's transcendence over changing time [and] . . . a real relation of God to time . . . This is only possible if the reality of God is not understood as undifferentiated identity but as intrinsically differentiated unity.'

62 Mostert, 'From Eschatology to Trinity', p. 70, 'if we imagine the simultaneous possession of life as a whole in a solitary subject, all temporal distinction would evaporate, and together with that the quality of life itself . . . it is only in the Trinitarian life of the one God that the Plotinian description of eternity in terms of the wholeness of life is realized'.

63 *ST* 3:644.

64 *ST* 1:407. Mostert, *God and the Future*, p. 88, and Benjamin Myers, 'The Difference Totality Makes: Reconsidering Pannenberg's Eschatological Ontology', *NZSTR* 49/2 (November 2007), pp. 149–51. Both expound the point and argue that Pannenberg provides a successful account of particularity in an 'ontology of the whole'.

65 *ST* 1:397–448.

66 *ST* 1:392, 393–4 explains that the first group of attributes is general (i.e. infinity, omnipresence, omniscience, eternity, omnipotence), the others are revealed (kindness, mercy, faithfulness, righteousness, patience). The general attributes are part of the 'general idea of God' from which philosophical reflection may determine 'minimal conditions' for valid talk about God. It is not till 'the infinite' has been understood in the light of revelation that theology reaches any idea of God's essence: 'the concept of the Infinite . . . will first be linked to a series of closely related attributes. To these we shall add statements about the attributes that are disclosed in God's revelation and that obviously relate structurally to the concept of the Infinite . . . Finally, the statement that God is love will prove to be the concrete form of the divine essence' (p. 396).

67 *ST* 1:396.

68 *ST* 1:412–3.

69 *ST* 1:411.

70 *ST* 1:415.

71 *ST* 1:416. He views abstract omnipotence as that which negates all other power and rules in opposition to what is ruled and so is bound to its own antithesis (p. 415).

72 *ST* 1:418.

73 *ST* 1:420–22 explains that as the Son receives his life and deity in subjection to the Father, so the creation receives independent life only in submission to the power of the Creator.

74 *ST* 1:441.

75 *ST* 1:422.

76 *ST* 1:424. Love not only binds the Trinity in unity, but establishes each person: 'Each of the three persons is ecstatically related to one or both of the others and has its personal distinctiveness or selfhood in this relation' (p. 428). In the treatment of love as an attribute (rather than in his discussion of divine unity), Pannenberg gives the fullest and most carefully nuanced account of the triune relationships, tracing the fellowship between each of the persons, each in their unique self-differentiation (pp. 428–30).

77 *ST* 1:432–44.

78 K.J. Vanhoozer, *Remythologizing Theology: Divine Action, Passion, and Authorship* (Cambridge: CUP, 2010), pp. 274–7.

79 *ST* 1:440 has explicit use of 'anticipation' in the discussion of wisdom, in which wisdom is the historical plan of salvation (1 Cor. 2:7) revealed 'in anticipation of the outcome of history'.

80 *ST* 1:439.

81 *ST* 3:453.

82 *ST* 1:610–11.

83 *ST* 1:620.

84 *ST* 1:444.

85 *ST* 1:445.

86 *ST* 1:442, states that until then 'the world and humanity as they are do not fully correspond to the loving will of the Creator'.

87 *ST* 1:446 insists that the question of God's unity cannot be solved along Hegelian lines, for the unity of the infinite and finite in a single thought must expunge the difference between them.

88 Boersma, *Violence*, p. 49.

89 G.C. Berkouwer, *The Providence of God* (trans. Lewis B. Smedes, Grand Rapids: Eerdmans, 1974), p. 256, observes that many theodicies have a 'common failure to reckon with the real and concrete wrath of God, as it is revealed in Scripture'. He argues that any attempt to 'get rid of

the idea of Divine wrath . . . thrusts inimically at the entire revelation of God', and gives a summary of the importance of the theme of wrath in biblical revelation (pp. 258–61).

90 Boersma, *Violence*, p. 48.
91 *ST* 1:440.
92 *ST* 1:420.
93 M. Mattes, 'Pannenberg's Achievement: An Analysis and Assessment of his 'Systematic Theology', *CurTM* 26 (February 1999): p. 60.
94 Mostert, *God and the Future*, p. 238.
95 T.A. Carlson, 'Postmetaphysical Theology', *The Cambridge Companion to Postmodern Theology* (ed. Kevin J. Vanhoozer; Cambridge: CUP, 2003), p. 62.
96 *ST* 1:432–41.
97 Carlson, 'Postmetaphysical Theology', p. 62.
98 G. Vattimo, 'The Christian Message and the Dissolution of Metaphysics', in *The Blackwell Companion to Postmodern Theology* (ed. G. Ward; Malden: Blackwell, 2001, 2005), pp. 458–66.

Conclusion

1 *ST* 3:xvi.
2 Barth, *CD* II/1: pp. 63–128.
3 *TPS*, p. 273.
4 See C. Schwöbel, 'Last Things First? The Century of Eschatology in Retrospect' in *The Future as God's Gift: Explorations in Christian Eschatology* (ed. D. Fergusson and M. Sarot; Edinburgh: T&T Clark, 2000), pp. 217–41 and D. Fergusson, 'Eschatology' in *The Cambridge Companion to Christian Doctrine* (ed. Colin E. Gunton; Cambridge: CUP, 1997), p. 226–44.
5 Hans Schwarz, *Eschatology* (Grand Rapids: Eerdmans, 2000), pp. 145–6.
6 Shults, *Postfoundationalist*, 206–11.
7 Olthuis, 'God as True Infinite', 322–3. Olthuis comes to this conclusion after an analysis of Pannenberg's treatment of God as the 'true infinite'. On this point, Olthuis' conclusions, though expressed in brief, appear to be the same as those of this thesis, though he arrives at them along slightly different lines.
8 Schwöbel, 'Wolfhart Pannenberg', p. 144.
9 *IST*, 18.

Scripture Index

Luke 22:67 – 23:3, 104
Luke 22:70, 105
Luke 23:3, 105
Luke 12:50, 126
Luke 22:40–44, 126

John 1:11, 4
John 1:14, 132
John 3:12–13, 107
John 3:16, 120, 132
John 5:19, 107
John 5:24, 126
John 8:23, 107
John 8:85, 107
John 10:33ff., 107
John 11:25, 107
John 12:27, 126
John 16:7 , 122

Rom. 1:20, 142
Rom. 3:21 , 58
Rom. 4:25, 117, 120
Rom. 5:10, 120
Rom. 5:17, 126
Rom. 6:5, 126
Rom. 6:8, 126
Rom. 6:23, 126
Rom. 8:3, 116
Rom. 8:3,32, 120
Rom 8:22, 117
Rom. 8:38, 126
Rom. 12:19, 150
Rom. 16:25–6, 58

1 Cor. 2:7–9, 58
1 Cor. 3:10–14, 152
1 Cor. 13:12, 64, 88
1 Cor. 15:3 , 117
1 Cor. 15:24–5, 134
1 Cor. 15:28, 13, 53
1 Cor. 15:55–6, 126

2 Cor. 5:18–19, 120, 124
2 Cor. 5:21, 116, 117

Gal 4:4, 99
Gal. 3:13, 116
Gal. 3:13, 117
Gal 2:20, 117

Eph. 1:10,21–3, 53
Eph. 5:2, 120
Eph. 5:25, 117, 120

Phil. 1:20–23, 126
Phil. 2:9–11, 133–34

Col. 2:20, 126
Col. 3:3–4, 126

1 Tim. 2:6, 117
1 Tim. 3:16, 58
1 Tim. 6:16, 141

Tit. 2:14, 124

Heb. 1:1–2, 58
Heb. 1:3, 124
Heb. 2:10, 98
Heb. 2:14–15, 126
Heb. 5:7, 126
Heb. 5:8–9, 98
Heb. 7:27, 125
Heb. 9:12, 125
Heb. 9:28, 125
Heb. 10:10, 125
Heb. 10:14, 125
Heb. 10:26–36, 150

1 Pet. 3:18, 124

2 Peter 1:16–18, 107

1 John 3:2, 88
1 John 3:14, 126
1 John 4:8,16, 143

Rev. 21:22–5, 53
Rev. 22:5, 53

Index of Persons

Index of Topics

We trust you enjoyed reading this book
from Paternoster. If you want to be informed
of any new titles from this author and other
releases you can sign up to the Paternoster
newsletter by contacting us:

By Post:
Paternoster
52 Presley Way
Crownhill
Milton Keynes
MK8 0ES

E-mail
paternoster@authenticmedia.co.uk

Follow us:

9 781842 277560